W9-CQE-035

"SUPERB . . . The author seems to have gained the complete confidence of the 150 veterans he interviewed for this book . . . some from middle class communities, others from ghettoes . . . some joined out of boredom, others allowed themselves to be drafted . . . we see how callow youths were suddenly turned into bitter and stunned killers . . . a stark and affecting picture!"
—*Publishers Weekly*

"DRAMATIC AND POWERFUL . . . the tellers, given anonymity, hold nothing back!"
—*Newsday*

"CONVINCING . . . and the most horrifying book the war has yet produced!"
—*Newsweek*

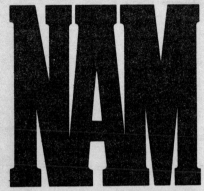

NAM

**The Vietnam War in the Words of
the Men and Women Who Fought There**

MARK BAKER

BERKLEY BOOKS, NEW YORK

*To the men and women who aren't here today to
tell their stories*

This Berkley book contains the complete
text of the original hardcover edition.
It has been completely reset in a typeface
designed for easy reading and was printed
from new film.

NAM

A Berkley Book / published by arrangement with
William Morrow & Company, Inc.

PRINTING HISTORY
William Morrow edition published 1981
Berkley edition / March 1983
Twentieth printing / November 1986

ISBN: 0-425-10144-4

A BERKLEY BOOK ® TM 757,375
Berkley Books are published by The Berkley Publishing Group,
200 Madison Avenue, New York, NY 10016.
The name "BERKLEY" and the stylized "B" with design
are trademarks belonging to Berkley Publishing Corporation.

PRINTED IN THE UNITED STATES OF AMERICA

ACKNOWLEDGMENTS

The people whose words fill these pages had the courage to open their souls to a stranger. A conversation with me was sure to awaken a few personal demons and they knew that. I thank them and hope they find I have justified their trust.

Writers always thank their wives and families in these things. I thought that was just a clichéd formality . . . until now. Although it won't necessarily be apparent to the reader, my mother and father put almost thirty years of hard work into me and this book, and they deserve more than a little credit for that. Veronica, my wife— words seem so empty when I think about all that she has given me. I'll just write, "I love you."

Esther Newberg and Bob Bender had the confidence and foresight to support this project from the start. Frank Fortunato and Gary Smolek read the manuscript. Their criticism and approval were important to me. My old buddy, George Moon, came to town for a fun-filled vacation and ended up typing the manuscript. A person couldn't ask for a better friend.

CONTENTS

INTRODUCTION

"My guy dies, it's no big gig to me. I tag him, book him and bag him," Doc thought to himself. "I see too much of this shit. I can't lose sleep over him. I just can't." Doc wasn't a real doctor. The GIs in Vietnam called every corpsman "Doc," except in combat when they shrieked "Medic!" as they fell.

He looked again at the letter from the parents of a kid who had been in his unit. "Dear Doctor," they wrote. "Our son often mentioned you in his letters home and the wonderful things you did for the guys in his company. If you can, please tell us how our boy died." Their son had been sent home in a closed casket.

"Oh, God," Doc sighed, "how am I going to answer this letter? I'm not going to say he had cold beans and mother-fuckers* for breakfast, took some shots from the other guys about being a cherry* and then went out and got blown into fifty million pieces—which is what happened."

On a routine patrol with his platoon, the boy triggered a land mine rated afterwards at 150 pounds of

---

* Words with an asterisk are defined in the Glossary.

explosives. The resulting crater was the size of the average bedroom in a suburban home. Both of his legs and one arm were torn off. One side of his skull was destroyed.

Six other men were killed with him. It was a common way to die in Vietnam. Thousands of closed caskets were delivered to quiet graves all over America during this country's involvement in the war in Southeast Asia. They remained virtually undisturbed, forgotten, for ten years and more.

Recently, journalists and film makers, generals, diplomats and politicians have decided to tell Americans how and why that boy died. Much of their tale has concentrated on the silence of the closed casket. As the story unfolds, it either ignores the humanity and individuality of the boy inside the box, relegating him to the cold storage of statistics, history and politics, or it capitalizes on the mystery of the coffin's contents, elevating the blood and bones to a mythic realm of heroism or evil or rock 'n' roll madness.

Something is missing from their story, something personal and palpable. They treat the war as though it were a vague event from the distant past, beyond living memory. No one has bothered to talk to the men and women who went to Vietnam and fought the war.

What happened in Vietnam? What did it look like? How did it smell? What happened to you? Vietnam veterans know firsthand the statistics, the heroism, the evil and the madness. They are the ones qualified to look inside the casket and identify the body for what it is—a dead boy killed in a war, who had a name, a personality, a story all his own.

Some of the people who waged the war will tell you through the pages of this book what happened to them.

Until now most of them have been as silent about their experiences and as invisible to society as their dead brothers. They are wary of strangers. Questions make them cautious.

"The bullshit antennae are always out," as one veteran put it. Starting with a handful of contacts, I made my way from interview to interview on a verbal passport of personal recommendations. "Yeah, he's okay. Meet him and see if you want to talk."

They wanted to know what I was doing while they were in Vietnam. I told them I was a college student, involved peripherally with the antiwar protests. I joined the demonstrations when my idealism moved me, if it was convenient. Although my emotions ran high and my convictions were real enough, I had no intention of letting dedication to "The Movement" interfere with my nice, privileged draft deferment. I figure I was typical of the majority of college students at that time. I find it much more gratifying to recall the war stories of the peace movement and the vanished warmth of tribal communion, but I've sorted out the reality of peer pressure and personal motives as well.

When they asked why I wanted to write this book, I first answered practically, honestly: "For the money. I make my living as a writer." But I explained that my interest wasn't entirely mercenary. The project began for me back in 1972. By chance, I became good friends with a Vietnam veteran that year. We shared an apartment and meals and a lot of whiskey. Brian told me about his experience in the war. In the course of those conversations, I discovered things about Brian and about myself that I hadn't known before. His having a chance to talk about his experience and my willingness to listen strengthened our friendship. His stories revealed more about the place, the war and the people involved in it than anything else I had read or seen on television concerning Vietnam. It was apparent that the whole story hadn't really been told. I couldn't tell it myself, but I sure as hell wanted to hear it.

I told the veterans I had no intentions of forging a political document honed on guilt and condemnation. Nor was I interested in glorifying war and the soldier's lot. I just wanted to record what they could remember about the intersection of their lives with the Vietnam war and the consequences of that experience.

Approached with candor and respect, some of them told me nothing, backing out at the last minute from one appointment after another. But most of the men and women I met held the light with a sense of both duty and relief as I examined a dark corner of their lives. They seemed to feel obligated to relate their stories clearly and accurately for the sake of dead friends, dying ideals and a personal sense of worth and honesty. Once I was trusted, the words rushed out like prisoners released from solitary confinement. For a few, there was relief in draining some of the poison that had festered around a wound.

These people are not extraordinary, except in the fact that they survived Vietnam and continue to survive. On more than one occasion, I was specifically asked by the man I was interviewing to mention the fact that he had a good job and was earning a decent living. At night he goes home to his wife and children, sometimes stopping for a few beers at a local bar. In his spare time, he is watching baseball on television or polishing his car—not climbing a bell tower, automatic weapon in hand, to take potshots at innocent citizens.

However, I also talked with individuals who know where the impulse to climb that tower comes from. I met people who can't seem to settle in one place, who have failed at loving others, who are choking on their bitterness, who have attempted to commit suicide. Physically and mentally scarred, their lives have been permanently damaged by their experience in Vietnam. That doesn't make them abnormal, only as fragile as other human beings.

Because of the personal equation, these accounts are commonly called war stories. It must be assumed that included here are generalizations, exaggerations, braggadocio and—very likely—outright lies. But if these stories were told within a religious framework, the telling would be called bearing witness. The human imperfections simply authenticate the sincerity of the whole. The apocryphal aspects have more to do with metaphor than with deceit.

In many ways these stories from Vietnam are as old as war itself. What you will read here has more in common with Homer's classic realism in recounting the graphic details of the carnage at Troy than with Vic Morrow swaggering through an episode of *Combat*. We didn't see it all on television. The Technicolor blotch of napalm flickering on the screen while Walter recited the day's body count like a grim blessing over our suppers had little to do with gagging on the stench of a burning man. We sanitize war with romantic adventure and paranoid propaganda to make it tasteful enough for us to live with it. Because Vietnam veterans lived *through* it, the account they give is as raw and shocking as an open wound.

Death and brutality pervade this book, like the heavy ticking of a clock echoing through the entire house on a sleepless night. But the soul's pain is the nightmare that keeps the household awake. The gory mechanics of death remind us for the ten thousandth time that "war is hell,'' as it has always been. But the blood and guts is only the extraordinary setting within which ordinary men and women played out their very lives.

War poses all the hard philosophical questions about life and death and morality and demands immediate answers. The abstractions of scholarly debate become the very concrete matters of survival. In one short year, Vietnam took the measure of a man and of the culture that put him there. War strips away the thin veneer applied slap-dash by the institutions of society and shows Man for exactly what he is. We must listen closely to the men and women who became both the victims and the perpetrators of the war, if we want to learn something real about this particular conflict, something real about the human spirit, something real about ourselves.

Nam—that piece of a word signifies more than just one of the many wars the United States has fought in its 200-year history. Vietnam was more than ideologies and armies. The war and its cultural ramifications provided the ritual passage to adulthood for a generation of Americans—my generation. It was a time when millions of us made the choices that would set the patterns of our lives. If we are to understand ourselves, it is necessary to know more intimately the event that propelled us onto our present course. Until we deal more honestly and thoroughly with the Vietnam war and the veterans of that war, we can't expect to make much progress as individuals or as a nation.

This book is not the Truth about Vietnam. Everyone holds a piece of that puzzle. But these war stories, filled with emotion and stripped of ambition and romance, may bring us closer to the truth than we have come so far.

You want to hear a gen-u-ine war story? I only understand Vietnam as though it were a story. It's not like it happened to me.

I
INITIATION

ASK NOT . . .

Pious little boys pass much of the time on the hard pews of churches playing war with pencil and paper. First the planes and battleships, soldiers and machine guns, are drawn, slowly with meticulous detail. The killing power of the imaginary weaponry is obvious in the vicious spikes of bayonets and the crude fins of bombs.

As the sermon drones farther and farther away, the final touches are applied: stars on the wings of the jets to mark the good guys, swastikas on the helmets of the stick men to brand the bad guys. The boy's expectant tension is almost sexual.

The battle begins. His pencil traces the deadly trajectory of each bullet and shell. A direct hit. The objective explodes in a burst of scribbles. Inside the boy's head, the flash is fiery red and yellow. Written across the rising clouds of dust and debris in big, black, block letters is the word "KABOOM!"

As the fighting intensifies, the pencil itself becomes a weapon to punch holes in the paper soldiers. In his excitement, the youngster lets the racket of the mental war *slip hissing through his teeth*—"Pssh-pssh. Tchoo, tchoo."

His mother snaps the paper away, grabs his pencil and locks it in her purse. She twists his ear. "Sit still. Keep quiet," she mouths.

The neighborhood war game is an American institution. It's played all summer long with sticks for rifles and forts constructed of scrap lumber and refuse from the alley. The game I played in the 1950s was based on Walt Disney's account of the life of David Crockett, enlivened by our own murderous imaginations. A few years ago, I overheard children playing outside my window, reenacting the shoot-out between the Los Angeles SWAT team and the SLA. But the game was basically unchanged:

"Bang, you're dead."

"You missed me."

"Did not."

"Did too."

This argument led to an arms escalation on my block. The kids broke out their B-B guns and played a suburban version of Lord of the Flies. The bite of a B-B fired at point-blank range raises a swollen red lump like a bee sting and leaves little doubt as to who is dead and who's not.

The role models with the most apparent influence on my peers in Cub Scouts were the Three Stooges. We delighted in making embarrassing sounds with cupped hands under our armpits. We slapped each other repeatedly on the back of the head and tried to poke our fingers in one another's eyes.

Early adolescence brings the joys of torching plastic model airplanes in the backyard and of inventing grisly torture scenes to inflict on the little girl down the street. Insects, toads, and crayfish are clumsily dissected with dirty hands, half in curiosity, half in mischief. I remember one older boy, thirteen or so, who specialized in lighting firecrackers in frogs' mouths. I thought he was pretty weird . . . but I watched, mesmerized by the violence.

Civilization appears in high school. Football provides the opportunity to "get out there and kill 'em" with impunity. In gym class boys bully the kid whose pubic hair hasn't started to grow. They get their hands on cigarettes, one of the few symbols of manhood that can be acquired instead of sprouted. The first amazing scraps of pornography are surreptitiously circulated from locker to locker.

Then they are Men.

What does a man do? A man stands alone against impossible odds, meets the Apache chief in single combat to protect the manifest destiny of the wagon train, plays guitar and gets the girl, leaps tall buildings in a single bound, plants the flag on Iwo Jima, falls on a grenade to save his foxhole buddies and then takes a bow to thundering applause. Death threatens only pets and grandparents.

One thing is certain. Whatever it is that men do, they must leave home to do it. Surprised and frightened by the inevitability of meeting the world head on, for all his bravado, an eighteen-year-old is a child again on the high diving board for the first time. It seems like fun until he sees the water dancing so far beneath his toes. He falters on the brink, wanting to be a big boy, aching to be shoved.

In the 1960s, the long fall from the nest was provided primarily by the Draft. Boys were scooped up by the Selective Service System or enlisted in its shadow. Others felt obliged to serve their country and to learn about life in a way prescribed in books and in movies as well as by law. None of them really knew where they were going. They knew little about where they had come from.

I got into the Marines because the Army wouldn't take me. I was seventeen, hanging out in the neighborhood in Brooklyn with nothing to do. I knew I had to go to court sooner or later for some shit I was into. The Army recruiter didn't even want to look at me since they didn't get involved with court problems or seventeen-year-olds. Forget the Navy and the Air Force. They had intelligence tests and I didn't have any.

One of the big boys who remembered me as a kid on the streets found out I was having a hard time getting into the service. He put his arm around my shoulder and took me down to talk to the Marine recruiter.

This big Marine takes one look at me and says, "This guy's a pussy. We don't want you. Get out of here." So I stand on a chair and get in his face and say, "Tell me about your big, bad Marine Corps."

"How old are you?"

"I'm only seventeen."

"Will your mother sign for you?"

"She ain't around."

The recruiter gave me ten dollars and said, "See that lady standing over there? Go give her the money and I'm sure she'll sign for you." I was in this big courthouse in Queens, huge, with columns and the whole bit. She was standing next to a candy counter where they sold newspapers and stuff. So I go over and say, "Hey, I'm trying to get into the Marines. Will you sign for me?" No problem. She must have been doing this for a living.

That weekend I was in the Marines. I had to leave a note for my mother: "Mom, I went to Parris Island. I'll be back in a couple of months." I had no idea what I was getting into.

* * *

I was in Johns Hopkins Medical School at the time. As a prank, somebody cut one of the fingers off the cadaver I was working on and kept it. When I went to turn in the cadaver, I couldn't account for the finger.

I knew who'd done it. So the next day, while he was doing a dissection on the leg, I took the arm off his cadaver and snuck it out. I put it in an ice chest and drove out to the Beltway around Baltimore. At a tollbooth, I stuck the frozen arm out the window with some money in the hand and left the toll attendant with the arm.

This got back to the president of the school, who was Dwight Eisenhower's brother, Milton, a real fucking hawk. He told me to take a leave of absence to reconsider my commitment to medical school. I thought that was probably a good idea. I said, "Great." A week later I had my draft notice. They turned me right in to the Board.

* * *

I had went down to the Draft Board originally just for the physical to get my classification and a draft card, the regular eighteen-year-old thing. This woman came in and said, "I want you to take this written test." I was late coming in anyways, and they were putting me through a long song and dance. I figured, "Okay, I took the physical, I'm here, I'll take their test, too. It ain't no big thing."

These guys I was taking the test with was just wild. The whole crew was making noise and they was throwing the pencils. Half of them was banged up high as kites. And I'm laughing, because the woman lieutenant who was supposed to be running things couldn't control the group.

"Well, I got something for you," she says, and she walks out of the room. These big Marines come in the door, right? A major with about four sergeants.

They went around and collected all the test papers. The major says, "Seeing as you want to give the lieutenant such a hard way to go, all of y'all just passed the test. You will be leaving in two days . . . *Or* you could leave in thirty days if you come into the Marine Corps."

We get up. "Oh, come on, you jiving."

"No, I'm serious. Everyone of you just passed the test and y'all leaving. If you keep going through all these changes, we have the right to pull y'all out of here right now and put you on the bus to boot camp."

Everybody got kind of quiet. Wait a minute, where they coming from with this? I was talking to this guy next to me and he said, "Yeah, well, I could stand a little extra time before they grab my ass."

About fifteen of us stood up and said we'll go in the Marine Corps, get us a little extra time.

Going through the paper work the guy was talking in terms of three years. Then all of a sudden he says, "You know, when you enlist, you go for four years." That was when they told me that I was enlisting.

I was young, stupid, ignorant, along with all the other clowns. Man, we signed up for four years not thinking, "Hey, if I go in with the Army, I'll be going in for two. Here I am signing up for four years just to get an extra thirty days before they take me.'' Which I didn't get thirty days anyway.

That's not really the whole story. My brother had died that same year and I was ready to get out of the house because we had always shared the same room. All of a sudden, after eighteen years—*whoom*—he's not there no more. My older brothers, they didn't really live with us, so it was all right when they weren't around. But the one who lived close with me, I was missing him too much. I was breaking ties with a lot of friends, because when I saw them coming down the block, I was expecting to see my brother with them, popping up, whistling to let me know he was there.

So it was good for me to leave home when I did. I didn't think in terms of what I did to my mother. She had just lost one son, and here's another one going off to some stupid war. Much later, after I thought about it, I had the chance to apologize. But she said she understood, that it was okay.

* * *

I came from San Jose, California. I grew up in the suburbs and went to public school. I lived on the last block of a new development surrounded on three sides by apricot orchards and vineyards.

The high school was typically middle class. There were very few blacks. We had warm weather and cars. Most of the kids' dads were engineers at Lockheed or they worked at IBM. Most of my friends were preparing for a college degree.

From San Jose, people would go up to San Francisco for concerts. Smoking dope was just coming in at the time and psychedelic music. Some of the kids I knew were involved with that. They weren't pioneers. They were the ones who joined, who wanted to be the first to do this or that—the trendy group.

Then I was conservative. I hadn't experienced any inequality in the social system. Things looked pretty hunky-dory to me. Plus I had read all the war fiction. It never had a particular fascination for me, but it implanted this idea in my mind that war was a place for you to discover things.

I saw older people, World War II age, who weren't in that war. When they were asked about it and what they were doing then, they had to say, "Oh, well, I was in college." It was a major historical event that convulsed the world, and yet they missed it. I was the perfect age to participate in Vietnam and I didn't want to miss it, good or bad. I wanted to be part of it, to understand what it was.

Why should I take the God damn SATs and go off to college? Everybody was going to San Jose State College right there in town. And who wants to do what everybody else does anyway?

I joined the Army at the end of my senior year in high school with delayed induction. I would leave for basic training at the end of the summer when everybody else went away to college. I spent the last summer at home, playing a lot of basketball, riding around with my friends in an old '54 Ford. Nobody's picked up on their adult life. *American Graffiti.*

*   *   *

After I graduated from nursing school, I was looking to go somewhere and do something. Hospitals aren't too gung-ho to hire you if you don't have a master's degree or experience of any kind. I checked into the Army. They were willing to guarantee me my choice of duty stations if I would enlist. Terrific, I'll go to Hawaii.

While I was in basic training, I heard all these people just back from Nam talking about how exciting it was. Professionally, it was the chance of a lifetime. I have two brothers and I grew up in a neighborhood where I was the only girl my age. I used to play guns with the boys all the time. I figured I could manage in Vietnam.

* * *

I came from a town called Wilcox in the heart of one of the richest counties in the United States—at least that's what they told me. Mine was an ideal childhood. Everything around me was "nice." The schools were good. Everybody was responsible. There were no derelicts in town. Everybody lived in a "nice" house with a "nice" yard. I played Little League Baseball and lived the standard American experience. *Happy Days*, only without the Fonz. There was a part of town where there were a few hoody guys, but I always kept my distance. When I went to college, I was really an innocent coming from this background.

In my sophomore year I had had it with school. I didn't know what the hell I wanted to do. School was boring as hell and I was floating along in a state of limbo. About Christmas, I got word from home that Johnny Kane had been killed over in Vietnam. I couldn't believe it.

Johnny was the All-American boy. He held the state record for the high hurdles. He was the quarterback of the Wilcox High School football team who led Wilcox to an undefeated season and the Class C championship. He was about three years older than me. Even though I was just a punk kid, he was always nice to me. I really liked Johnny Kane.

Johnny and I ended up going to state colleges that were rivals, so I got to see him play football in college. After he graduated, he went into the Marine Corps, became a second lieutenant and then went overseas.

For some reason, his death really affected me. I said to hell with it. Instead of going to class one day, I went down to the Army recruiter and talked to him. I was totally unimpressed. The guy was promising me the world and I couldn't believe it. So I went over to the Marine Corps recruiter. This guy was everything you thought a Marine was supposed to be. All creases, squared away, he looked like a rock.

"Well, I'll tell you quite frankly," he said, "you join us, you're going to Vietnam. No bones about it." I figured that was true for the Army, too, but the Army recruiter wouldn't tell me.

I had also been kind of brainwashed since I was a kid. My father had been a Marine in the South Pacific during World War II. Although he never talked about it all that much, when I was in the second grade I had his web belt and his Marine Corps insignia. I always felt the Marines were elite. If you're going to do something, you go with the best—like playing for Wilcox High. We always had a reputation for being smaller than the other teams, but we were faster and our attitudes were better. We beat people on attitude.

What am I going to do? I'd rather be over there with motivated people, people who've got their shit together, as opposed to being in a paddy with a bunch of zeroes who don't even want to be there.

Not that I really wanted to be there. Yet when I found myself right in the prime age and a war was going on, I knew that I had to be part of it. It was my destiny. It had always been meant for me to do this thing. It sounds strange, but once it happened, I knew somehow, somewhere the handwriting was on the wall.

                    *   *   *

I come from a conservative Republican area. I was brought up in a strict, anonymous, nomadic suburban environment, where privilege was part of our legacy. We had our boats. We had our recreation. We had our stability. We had our fifteen-thousand-dollar-a-year jobs guaranteed to us as soon as we got out of college.

I never felt I belonged there, but I never imagined I'd end up in Vietnam. I was in undergraduate school and my deferment ran out. I'd spent some time in Brazil— my junior year abroad. I had thought I was going to get a full year of credits and I didn't get them. During the extra year of college I had to go through, my Draft

Board advised me that they had changed my classification from 2S to 1A.

So I thought, I'll just go back to Brazil or I'll join the Peace Corps. But I really got hung up on finishing school. I had it in my head that if I went off then I'd never come back to school and get my degree. It was a real adolescent attitude. That degree was my working papers, my union card.

ROTC on campus had started a new crash program for guys who had never taken ROTC, but who wanted to go into the service as officers. All I had to do was stick around for one more year and take nothing but ROTC courses, and I'd get a commission. I said to myself, "Fuck it, I don't want to go in and peel potatoes. I don't want to be some private. I'm basically antisocial and I hate authority. If I go in in that position, I'll just get in trouble and end up in jail. I might as well get myself a little autonomy, a little anonymity." I wanted to be left alone and to have my own way. So my last year in college I was an ROTC major.

I was a fuck-up. My hair was always too long, my uniform was always dirty. I wasn't consciously rebellious. I just couldn't take it seriously. I couldn't sit in class and talk about war the way they were talking about it. It wasn't that I was an intellectual or into politics. I had a strong moral upbringing with my Catholic background. I was very influenced by the lives of the saints, and by Christ, his example—more than I'd like to admit probably. I believed it in a way, you know? I'd talk about the Geneva Convention and how absurd it was to try to talk about the legality of war. I thought it was silly to try to reduce what was essentially an immoral experience into a question of legislation.

I remember having to go out to this athletic field and march around in a baggy uniform, feeling like a complete asshole. Older than the other guys, not taking it seriously, I was very aware of my expedient motives in the whole thing. I was afraid of the experience of being just an average grunt.* I was doing what I had pretty

much done all my life, using my wits to get over. I had
this kind of contempt for the other guys going through
all the military paces, who were seeking this power and
leadership, who wanted to move other guys around like
chess pieces on a board.

Out of the corner of my eye, I saw this small delegation of campus SDS outside the gate of the track field. I
felt a tremendous affinity for them. That day, I had a
very strong image of me literally slogging through the
field, dragging my ass, going through the paces, but
having a secret identification with those demonstrators.
But they came from an entirely different world than me.
For better or worse, I was part of the American experience and I thought there was no way I could bridge the
gap. I guess I felt that I wouldn't be accepted, that I was
a different species.

After I graduated, I went to the ROTC summer training camp. Essentially, I tried to be invisible most of the
time. I failed the marksmanship requirement. I hated
guns. I pledged to myself that no matter what position I
was in, I would never use a gun, I would never kill anybody. I didn't try to fail, I was just disinterested.

Everybody else in my company was a junior in college. They had to go back and finish their last year and
then they would get their commission at the graduation
ceremony. I was going to get my commission after
camp. I was able to use the officer's club which was a
special privilege. A buddy of mine from college who was
already a first lieutenant in the signal corps would come
by after the day's training and pick me up in his Olds-
mobile convertible—a big, fat luxury car, a real meat
wagon. I used to feel real cocky. The other guys would
be down there polishing the floors and doing all that
shit. I'd put on my Madras blazer, my jeans, my tassel
loafers and no socks, my buddy the lieutenant would
pull up and there was nobody who would say me nay.

It was fucked in a way, it was really fucked. I was
never aware until recently how lonely I was, disengaged
from my life. How alienated I was from other people,

from society and community. Some kind of weird Jesuit.

* * *

I graduated from college three days after Robert Kennedy was shot, two months and three days after Martin Luther King was assassinated, an incredible double whammy. The war was hanging there like a sword over everybody. I had been reclassified in the middle of my senior year from 2S to 1A and gone through about six solid months of really examining my feelings about the war. Chiefly, I read a lot of pacifist literature to determine whether or not I was a conscientious objector. I finally concluded that I wasn't, for reasons that I'm still not sure of.

The one clear decision I made in 1968 about me and the war was that if I was going to get out of it, I was going to get out in a legal way. I was not going to defraud the system in order to beat the system. I wasn't going to leave the country, because the odds of coming back looked real slim. I was unwilling to give up what I had as a home. Spending two years in jail was as dumb as going to war, even less productive. I wasn't going to shoot off a toe. I had friends who were starving themselves to be underweight for their physicals. I wasn't going to do it—probably because it was "too far to walk." I wasn't just stupidly righteous, there was a part of me that was real lazy at the same time. I wanted to be acted on, and it was real hard for me to make a choice of any kind. Making no choice was a choice.

With all my terror of going into the Army—because I figured that I was the least likely person I knew to survive—there was something seductive about it, too. I was seduced by World War II and John Wayne movies. When I was in high school, I dreamed of going to Annapolis. I was, on some silly level, really disturbed when the last battleship was decommissioned. One of my fantasies as a kid was to be in command of a battleship in a major sea battle, and having somewhere in my sea chest Great-uncle Arthur's Naval dress sword from the eighteenth century.

One way or another in every generation when there was a war, some male in the family on my father's side went to it. I had never had it drilled into me, but there was a lot of attention paid to the past, a lot of not-so-subtle "This is what a man does with his life" stuff when I was growing up. I had been, as we all were, victimized by a romantic, truly uninformed view of war.

I got drafted at the end of the summer. I went into a state of total panic for days. What the fuck am I going to do? I went running off to recruiters to see if I could get into the Coast Guard or the Navy or the Air Force. No way.

There were probably some strings that I could have pulled. One of the things that is curious to me, as I look back on it, is that I had all the information, all the education and all the opportunity that a good, middle-class, college-educated person could have to get out of it . . . and I didn't make a single choice that put it anywhere but breathing down my neck. Even in the midst of the terror after the induction notice came, there was a part of me that would lie in bed at night and fantasize about what it would be like if I went.

The long and the short of the story is that at least half of my emotions were pulled to going. I couldn't get into any other branch of the service, so my final choice was to enlist in the Army. They had a delayed enlistment option. It was August when I got drafted and I figured, "Shit, I don't want to go until October." I took the option. I spent that time at a cottage in Maine, enjoying the wonderful weather, reading books and writing dramatic farewell letters.

*   *   *

I'm from Bakersfield. It's pretty hicky, but a lot of America is pretty hicky. I was born and raised there and that's where I went off to the service from.

When I was in high school, I knew I wasn't going to college. It was really out of the question. Even graduating from high school was a big thing in my family. We were originally from Mexico. My dad was a laborer. He had gone to the third grade, I think. He died when I was five. My mom had to bring us up. I have two brothers and three sisters.

I enlisted a couple of years after high school. At the time I was young and innocent and I was under the impression that enlisting was the All-American thing to do.

*   *   *

It's just a little town where I grew up. I played some football and baseball like everybody else. I was kind of a hard-ass in school. I didn't know how good I had it then. I took little odd jobs and saved up enough money to buy an electric guitar and an amplifier. I started playing in a band.

Near the end of high school, everybody's saying, "What you going to do? What you going to do?" I didn't know. I said, "I'm going to join the service." After I graduated, I went into the Marine Corps. They were supposed to be the best. To me, they were. They helped me grow up. I grew up in Vietnam.

*   *   *

My old man, when the war came, he says, "Oh, go. You'll learn something. You'll grow up to be a man. Go."

Shit, if my folks had to send their little poodle, they would have cried more tears over that than over me. But I'm supposed to go, because I'm a man.

*   *   *

The bus pulls into the receiving area. There's a guy with a Smokey Bear hat out there really looking lean and mean. He gets on the bus and starts reeling this shit off, "All right, you'll grab your bag. You'll get off the bus. You'll fall into the yellow footprints painted on the pavement . . ."

It was really funny, a take-off from *Gomer Pyle*. The guy within arm's reach of the Marine was laughing just like everybody else. Smokey Bear whipped around and smacked him right in the face, knocked him halfway through the window. His head bounced off the luggage rack and he reeled back out in the aisle.

Smiles froze on faces. My heart stopped. We realized, "Hey, this guy isn't fooling around. He's going to come through this bus and kick all our asses." People started flying out of the door.

I came down with a couple of guys who were Puerto Rican street gang material from the big city and they thought they were bad news. They fell down the steps on top of me. We all stumble into the right footprints on the ground and Smokey marches us into some barracks and stands us at attention. He's yelling and screaming, really intimidating. You dumped all of your stuff out on a table and he went by and just threw everything away. We were too scared to say anything to him.

I was next to this big Puerto Rican dude. Smokey catches the dude looking at him out of the corner of his eye. He says, "Are you eye-fucking me, boy? I don't want your scuzzy eyes looking at me. You think this is funny? I hope you fuck up. I hate you Puerto Rican cocksuckers."

Eyes in the back of his head, Smokey sees a guy's eyes flick and he's there to punch him in the chest, five feet to the wall and back again. My knees were shaking. "What the fuck have I gotten myself into?"

Then they march us into some barracks. Bare mattresses and springs. It's like a concentration camp. They turn the lights on and leave us there. My stomach is in a knot. I'm lying there thinking, "What happened to my world?" Reality has suddenly turned to liquid shit before my very eyes. Kids were crying, rolling in their bunks. I'm so depressed, I can't believe this is happening to me.

We're there for a couple of hours. You're in your civilian clothes and you've been in them for a couple of days. You feel like shit. When they march you out, all of a sudden it's by the numbers. All your hair's gone. You don't even know who you are. You get a duffel bag and they're dumping things in it. Everybody hates you and they're fucking with you left and right. You get your shots. You stand at attention. People are passing out on their feet. Going rigid and falling on their faces and the corpsmen are laughing at them. Nobody talks to you, they scream. Nothing they give you fits. You look like shit and you feel like shit. A bunch of drill instructors put you back in receiving and that's when the shit really hits the fan.

*   *   *

They strip you, first your hair. I never saw myself bald before. Not just your goatee, but your hair. Oh shit, no hair. I'd had a mustache, must have been since I was thirteen years old. I *always* had a mustache. All of a sudden, no hair on my lip, no hair on my chin, no hair on my head.

Guys I had been talking to not an hour before—we was laughing and joking—I didn't recognize no more. I'm looking over there at my friend, "Joe? Is that Joe?"

"Yeah, is that you, James?"

"Yeah. Oh shit." It was weird how different people look without their hair. That's the first step.

*   *   *

Very quickly the situation becomes primitive. The leaders are automatically the biggest, the people who can physically enforce their demands. As soon as you get in the Army, they want squad leaders. A sergeant comes by and picks out the biggest guys, because he knows those are the people who can intimidate you into doing something. Everybody understands brute force. Somebody six-foot-two, 275 pounds, is your new squad leader and no matter how dumb he is, he's in charge. The sergeant is the authority figure in the background and this big kid is the bully on the block.

For a long time, I was lost in the shuffle. Everything is relegated to strength and I only weighed 150 pounds. There were very few people smaller than me in the pecking order. It was a shock. I never really got my bearings.

The people in the Army were not intellectuals. Most of them were from working class backgrounds. A lot of them were Southerners. It was my first contact with blacks and they tended to stick together. Certain economic groups like blue-collar kids and city kids adjusted very quickly to the Army. Most of the middle-class kids like me didn't fit into what was going on. We hadn't had to do much on our own before. We grew up in a secure environment where a lot of things were taken for granted.

One of the ways to establish who you were—at least the way that was open for me—was language. I could speak standard English and had a large vocabulary. That made me an outsider because people didn't like it, especially this one older guy with a heavy accent from Georgia.

I don't know exactly why, but I got in several fights with this guy. But I didn't have any peer group pressure. I wasn't well liked. I wasn't actively disliked, but nobody would step in to help me. I was on my own. This kid was quite a bit bigger than me, plus I had really lost my bearings and was sort of helpless. So there were fistfights which were quickly broken up—nothing much really happened. But the feeling of being an outsider was reinforced, because I had this antagonist all the time looking for an opportunity to get at me. I had to be on my toes. It was a whole new education.

* * *

They have you jump. You never get up in the morning like normal folk. You know, turn on the light. Okay, get up out of the racks* now.

Every morning it was garbage cans going down the middle of the barracks, guys' racks being flipped over. You panic. You got two minutes to get dressed, make your rack and fall out.

The first time that happened, you've gone to sleep and forgotten where you're at. When you wake up, the lights are glaring and you hear all this noise like a bomb going off. There's yelling and screaming. You jump in front of your racks. I'm looking, man, and there's all these little puddles. A bunch of guys had peed on theirselves, they were so scared.

After a while I knew every morning we're going to go through this routine, so I figured I'd be partially dressed. I'd get up a half hour ahead of time and get my boots on and my pants. Pretty soon, everybody was doing it. Then they would tell us, "Get undressed, get back in the racks and start all over again."

* * *

"The only way I'm going to get through this," I said to myself, "is to do everything right and not cause any trouble." That's what I tried to do, but you can't help but get into trouble. "What'd you do in college, boy? Learn to push a pencil?"

"Yessir."

"What do you mean by that?"

"Nossir."

"You like me, don't you, boy?"

"Yessir."

"You're queer for me."

"Nossir."

"You don't like me?"

"Yessir. Nossir."

"All right, ladies. You look like shit, so we're going to do a little PT now. Bends and motherfuckers.*
Many, many, many of them. Begin. One, two. One,
two. One, two, one, two, onetwo-onetwo-onetwo-
onetwo.

"Up-downs. Get up, get down. Get up, get down. On
your backs. On your bellies. Get up, get down.

"Knuckle push-ups. Ready, begin. One, two. One,
two. Onetwo-onetwo-onetwo-onetwo. Side straddle
hops. Ready, begin . . ."

Then they'd make you march around the barracks.
When you'd get a couple hundred yards away, they'd
say, "Get back to your rack. Do it!" There'd be a knot
of people at the center of the door, clawing their way
through to get back to their rack and stand at attention.

When you weren't going through that, you had your
recruit regs held up in front of your face memorizing
your eleven general orders. It was a real mind fuck.

We had one guy drank a can of Brasso. After they
pumped his stomach, they sent him away to psychiatric
care. I saw a couple of guys snap. But by the time you
get to the end of that whole process, you feel like you're
the baddest thing that ever walked the earth. When they
call you Marine in the graduation ceremony, there's
tears in your eyes. You are thoroughly indoctrinated.

*   *   *

I foolishly went into the Army thinking, "Hey, with a
few years of college under my belt, they're not going to
put me in the infantry." I didn't see anything wrong
with going to Vietnam. The only part I thought was
wrong was my fear of being killed. I felt that somehow
or other that shouldn't have been part of it. And I
couldn't really picture myself killing people. I had flash
images of John Wayne films with me as the hero, but I
was mature enough even then to realize that wasn't a
very realistic picture.

In boot camp I didn't meet very many patriots. They
were guys that a judge had told, "Either you go in the

Army, or it's two years for grand theft auto." Or they were schmucks like me who managed to lose their deferments. Or they were people who really had decided that the Army would be good for them in the long run.

To discourage us from going AWOL and deserting, all the new draftees were told that only 17 percent of us were going to Vietnam. And of that small percentage, only 11 percent would actually be combat troops. That eased my mind a great deal. Hey, there's still a chance that I won't have to go and get my guts blown out. Terrific.

At the end of our training, with only three exceptions —one fool who had gone Airborne, one guy who kept fainting and another kid who had a perforated eardrum —every single one of us went to Vietnam—200 guys.

*　　*　　*

After we got in boot camp, they ask you to put down on some form why you joined the Marine Corps. I put down, "To Kill." In essence, that's what the fuck I wanted to do. But I didn't want to kill every fucking body. I wanted to kill the bad guy.

You see the baddies and the goodies on television and at the movies. I wanted to get the bad guy. I wasn't a patriot. I didn't join for the country. I mean, I love this country, but I could have given a fuck for the country then. I wanted to kill the bad guy.

They beat the shit out of me for that in boot camp. "Who is this fucking hawg who wants to KIIILLL?" Then they'd get me. They made me go see two head shrinks. The second shrink I talked to asked me all these questions like, "Did you ever kill as a child?" I told him I had a B-B gun and I killed a couple of birds. What the fuck?

It was just harassment. Why does someone join the military but to defend the country which more often than not means to kill?

I wound up in the Philadelphia Naval Yard of all places. I got to watch wet paint get dry. I started putting

in requests to go to Vietnam, but I kept being turned
down. I kept telling them I wanted to go overseas, so
finally they decided to let me go.

I had a couple of accidents before I could leave
though. I got stabbed in the heart at a black cabaret and
ended up in the Philly Naval Hospital. Right through
the cardial sac, nicked my lung. While I was in the
hospital, I saw all these amputees coming back from the
Nam. Even that didn't stop me. I still wanted to go.

*   *   *

I was raised a Roman Catholic. When I was about sixteen I became a follower of Elijah Mohammed as a
Nation of Islam, a Black Muslim. When I was drafted, I
tried to explain to the Army that I did not believe in the
government as a whole. I didn't believe in the system.
Why should I go out and fight for the system when my
people are catching a lot of chaos from being under
it—the slave mentality that our people are in?

They sent me up to see a light colonel. The Muham-
mad Ali decision was sitting in the Supreme Court. The
colonel told me point-blank, "Either you raise your
right hand or you will go to jail. One of the two. On the
spot." I'll never forget his face, he didn't even crack a
smile.

"I don't want to go to jail," I told him. "I never been
to jail in my life."

"Don't worry," he says. "Once you're in the service
and you tell them that you're a Muslim, you shouldn't
have to go overseas. You will stay in the States." So I
raised my right hand.

From there I went down to Ft. Jackson, South
Carolina. That's when the crap started for me. A lot of
the officers as well as the NCOs was from the South, so
they could not understand what a Black Muslim was
doing in the U.S. Army, even if he *was* drafted.

I was harassed, called names. "People like you
shouldn't be in the service." I feared for my life out on
the rifle range. Sergeants told me, "Guys like you

should be dead." So naturally, you got to stop and ask yourself, "Is this guy for real or not?" The pressure was on me.

As a Muslim, we're not supposed to eat pork. We're not even supposed to handle pork, touch it. They would assign me to clean the grease trap on the kitchen grill. In the grease trap you had beef, lamb, fish and all sorts of fried foods—plus pork. I told them I didn't mind pulling KP. I would peel all the potatoes to be peeled in the United States Army, but I didn't want to touch pork. They did it to put me in a spot where I would have to disobey an order for my religious beliefs. I would have been brought up on charges.

Luckily, I found a Protestant chaplain who understood. He intervened and said, "Put the man on KP, but let him not mess with pork. It's his right as an individual." The whole company couldn't understand that.

After basic training I was supposed to stay in the States as a supply clerk or something. My orders came down for the infantry. All of us, we all went to the infantry.

Ft. Polk, Louisiana, is where they sent us for advanced infantry training. I had the same hassles all over again—"Oh, I see you're a Muslim." Deeper in the South I was treated like a Russian spy. They literally stood me in front of a whole company and told everybody what my religion was. "This guy is a Muslim. He cannot be trusted. If you are in training with him, watch your back."

I tried to protest it, but there's nobody to talk to. As soon as I say I'm a Black Muslim, everybody looks at me strange. I was sent to Army intelligence. The officers had to interview me, because they figured I was a traitor. "Are you a Commie? Are you trying to persuade black GIs to turn against the United States of America?"

Naturally, I was preaching Islam to the brothers and sisters that was there. Some of them were very interested and wanted to know a little more about what Islam was. I pulled them together a little bit. That's what the Army didn't like. They considered me a threat because I was always trying to pull the brothers together. I asked them, why should we fight in a war which we don't even understand?

Once everybody finished AIT,* they were sending them directly to Nam after their leave. After my leave, I ended up back in Ft. Polk. I was under investigation by Army intelligence. They had to clear me for going overseas. They pulled me out of my company and put me in a special headquarters company.

I was a duty soldier, assigned to the orderly room, to the supply room, like putting rifles together. I was a security risk but I was putting rifles together. Plus I was doing anything nasty they could think of for me to do. I was picking up butts off the street. They gave me a rifle bore used for cleaning the M-16* and they sent me around to clean out all the little holes in the urinals. I had to take my hand without no glove and clean out the urinal holes for each and every urinal in the company. You know how stinking a urinal is? But I did it with a smile. I said, "It's not pork, is it."

They said, "He's a psycho." They sent me to the doctors. The shrink said, "He's no psycho. The man just believes."

I started agitating the Army. That was my biggest thing. I carried around a book by Karl Marx, just for the hell of it. They brought the MPs in one time to raid my locker, trying to find books from the Soviet Mission or something. The only thing they found was that book by Karl Marx, that you can get in any library. In fact, I got it from the library right there on the post. They returned it with apologies.

They kept me under surveillance. I had to report once a week to Army intelligence. And there was an FBI agent there on base who was like my probation officer. It didn't bother me going to see him. At least I got out of work. I'd tell the guy, "Please don't send me back out there, I'll sit in here all day long and we can talk."

After duty hours I would preach Marxism and Islam. I was a youngblood at the time, nineteen years old. I was serious about picking up a gun and letting the fight be here. Not so much a race fight as a social type of struggle. The system was against my people. If I had to pick up a gun, let me pick it up and turn it on the system, not on somebody in Vietnam who I know nothing about. I was dedicated and serious about dying . . . but I didn't know what death really was.

I had to go up and see the post commander, some two-star jerk. I laid out my beliefs for him and told him I was willing to die for what I believed in.

"Well," he said, "you're going to die all right. But to hell with this fighting and dying in the streets. You're going to die in Vietnam." Intelligence had cleared me and my orders were cut for me to go directly to the Nam.

The assistant to the general told me, "Since you love the Vietnamese people and the Communist way so much, you going to go out there and be with them. Boy, we going to make sure you die in Vietnam." Everybody smiled. I was the biggest joke in Ft. Polk. Send the Commie to Vietnam.

* * *

In the middle of my thirty-day leave before shipping to Vietnam, I was sitting at home in St. Louis watching television. The news flash came on that the Tet Offensive had broken out.

One of the last speeches the Army made to us before we went on leave was, "Listen, it's pretty civilized over there. You'll have swimming pools and snack bars and like that. You won't have to run off the plane and form a defensive perimeter around the air base in Saigon." But that's exactly what the "enemy" was shooting at on the TV. People were being blown away at Ton Son Nhut Air Base.

Friends of mine were saying, "You've got to be crazy. You're going to go there? Michael, think it over." People offered to loan me the money to go to Canada. But I was a little crazy. I was already into it too far.

I spent a few days by myself in San Francisco before I had to report. I must have had a good time. I'd wake up with all my money gone, but without any bruises or gouges on my body. Nobody had hurt me, but the evening would be a real blank. I spent every last dime of several hundred dollars. I had just enough money to catch the bus to Oakland Air Force Base.

*   *   *

When I came home from training, my family couldn't deal with me. My girl friend was saying, "Oh, wow, Jim. You're so patriotic. Where you coming from? They cut your hair and took your brain, too." The Marine Corps had me believing this war was right. She says, "Yeah, but you weren't ever like that before."

I couldn't relate that I had changed. But everybody I knew couldn't figure me out. "Hey, what is this? Patriotic Jim all of a sudden, going to this great war—doesn't know what for."

BAPTISM OF FIRE

Out comes the shoebox of Instamatic snapshots. Un-ceremoniously, the warrior's paper trophies are dumped on the middle cushion of the couch. After ten years on the top shelf of the hall closet, the expanse of sky dominating each photo has yellowed to match the swath of drab browns and greens at the bottom of the frame.

Machinery is a favorite subject. Tanks with muddy treads as tall as a grown man were photographed with the reverence little boys reserve for fire engines. A line of helicopters with their blades still and drooping look like giant, prehistoric flies, special effects created by Ray Harryhausen for some bankrupt sci-fi movie. There is a tent town dusted with dried mud, the streets marked with stones painted white, a Boy Scout camp without papier-mâché totems or beaded belts.

The warrior flips through the stack for pictures of his comrades-in-arms. Boys with plastic guns strike silly poses, caricatures of men. A bunch of rowdy punks, drunk on their first six-pack, try to make poker faces, gambling with government-issued play money. Chubby grins flash from under a wisp of mustache that might have come from gulping milk out of a wide-mouthed glass. One or two sport pipes like college freshmen trying to look "older."

Oddly distinct from all the rest, one picture shows a swollen man, lying in a plastic garbage bag. He has no eyes in the deep sockets beneath his brows—for that matter, he has no brow at all on the right side. His mouth is held open by his tongue. Nothing is red in the photograph, only purple, brown and black. The warrior shuffles it back into the pile.

"Hey, look at this one. This guy here in the middle is my buddy, Geezer," he says as though he were leafing through a high school yearbook. "Boy, he was a pisser." The next instant his face clouds as his memory clears. "He's dead. He got wasted up on some hill."

He reaches for another photo. "That's me on the left. Geezer took it for me right after we got there. I weighed a hundred and forty-five pounds." It is difficult to recognize the thirty-four-year-old man beside me in the baby face smiling from the picture in my hand. There's no beer gut; in fact the boy seems to ripple with hard muscle like a teenage football star. Only the face is soft and unlined, doe eyes twinkling like the eyes of the two little girls who answered the door when I first arrived for this evening's interview.

The children are asleep upstairs now. His wife put out popcorn and beer and left for her Wednesday night ladies' bowling league. He has shown me around the house, pointing out the remodeling work he did himself. He's talked about his job with the public utility, the baseball scores, the company softball team, the television show flashing silently across the screen in the corner of the room. We exhausted the weather report much earlier. Now the warrior has to talk about Vietnam.

He reels off his service number and the designation of his unit in a flurry of digits and military jargon. His story immediately stumbles over half-remembered dates and training camps. Counting back laboriously from the day he first set foot in Vietnam, he figures out when he was inducted.

Once the narrative catches up to his first day in-country, the story wings through the loose details of his war in the mumbled monotone of a jaded tour guide. After ten minutes, he's finished. "I don't know what else to tell you."

But the mental pictures have been brought down from the shelf and he can't resist taking a look. The story begins to trickle out, gaining momentum, a jumble of disconnected anecdotes and incidents. Some are long coherent accounts, like macabre home movies with no real beginning or end. Most pop like a flashbulb, freezing a glance, a gesture, a single moment. All sense of time is forgotten, except for day and night, dry season and monsoon.

Strangely, his tone of voice hasn't changed. Although he is surprised as each distant bit of memory jumps into consciousness, like a snapshot he forgot he had taken, he remains almost too composed. We wander back to where Geezer died as though that was where our conversation was headed all along. Without much warning, his voice squeezes one note higher and stops with a choke. A single tear rolls down his cheek before he has the presence of mind to catch it. He apologizes right away—man to man. Eyes averted, he begins distractedly to put the photos back in the shoebox.

"This is me up at the DMZ after I'd been there about six months," he says, his face and voice returned to normal. It's the same boy as before, squatting in red mud that seeps over the tops of his boots. His pants legs are rolled to the knee, fatigue green barely visible under the coating of clay. The only other piece of clothing he's wearing is a flak jacket—an armored vest with the words "DIE HIGH" printed on it. The grin is gone, replaced by the stony glare of an old man.

The war billed on the marquee as a John Wayne shoot-'em-up test of manhood turns out to be a warped version of Peter Pan. Vietnam was a brutal Never-neverland, outside time and space, where little boys didn't have to grow up. They just grew old before their time.

After boot camp they didn't know what to do with us, so they put all the seventeen-year-olds at this Marine air base in Hawaii. All we did was train for months and months, just doing grunt stuff. Then out of nowhere, they locked up the whole base and told us we were going to Okinawa.

Nobody cared. We all wanted to get off Hawaii anyway. It sucks. Hawaiians think they're God's gift to America. The prices are so high that if you're a short-haired, slimy GI, man, you're just going to be fighting with the military police, the civilian police and the big Kanocks there. To go to Okinawa was a score.

But when we got on the ship, everything was hush-hush. I made friends with a couple of sailors. They told me there was a sub following behind us, armed to the teeth. We didn't know anything was fugazi* until we got to a certain place in the South China Sea. A loud-speaker came over the air, "This is your captain speaking. Be advised that your destination is Da Nang, Republic of Vietnam." Everybody looks around. What the fuck is a Vietnam?

I had just turned eighteen. Oddly enough, there were a lot of guys on the ship that were still seventeen, but they turned eighteen crossing the ocean. Maybe four or five guys didn't, and they made them wait on the ship until their birthday before letting them step on land.

When the ship came in, it was dusk, almost dark. Everybody was on deck for two or three hours watching horror fireworks—fucking artillery, fire fights going on all over the place, flares popping up. Holy shit. Instead of just throwing us in there, they made us wait on the outskirts and watch it. We didn't know what it was. It was all a mystery.

As daybreak came, the firing and fighting subsided. We were going in very slow and tedious, waiting and watching. It was like being sentenced to death. You'd gone to gladiator school and you're in the Class of '68. If you make it, you make it.

It was supposedly a secure area—however secure you want to call South Vietnam. We made a beach landing with amphibious vehicles. We did the whole thing—ya-hoo, boom, boom, boom—with blanks. Thank God, there was nobody there.

I went into a bunker and had a half-hour talk with the Man Above. I told him, "I don't want to die here in this fucking place, ten thousand miles from nowhere. It stinks and nobody gives a shit about anything. I don't want to die at all. If you can, take me later. I know it might be worse in the long run, but this place doesn't do much for me. On the other hand, whatever you want to do is cool with me."

Me being alive now means God had something else planned for me. I don't know if I'm scheduled for saving twenty kids from a burning building or slipping on a bar of soap in the shower. Personally I think he just likes me.

Three nights after I got there, Hanoi Hanna gets up on the bullshit net and welcomes my unit to Vietnam. She dedicated "Tonight's the Night" by the Shirelles to us. "Will you still love me tomorrow?" That's the one. The little cunt face. But I liked listening to her. She put on some good jams.

*   *   *

I arrived in-country at Cam Ranh Bay. It's hot. The kind of hot that Texas is hot. It takes your breath away as you step out of the airplane. We were loaded on an olive-drab school bus for the short ride from the airstrip over to the compound. There was wire mesh over the windows. I said to somebody, "What the hell is the wire for?"

"It's the gooks, man, the gooks," they say. "The gooks will throw grenades through the windows. See those gooks out there?" I look out and I see shriveled, little old men squatting beside the road in the fashion of the Vietnamese, filling sandbags. They looked up at me with real contempt on their faces.

Here we are at one of the largest military installations in the world and we have to cover the windows to protect ourselves from little old men. I didn't put it all together at the time, but intuitively I knew something was wrong.

*   *   *

I arrived in Nam on an Easter Sunday. I flew into Bien Hoa early in the morning and got on an air-conditioned bus and was driven to the 90th Replacement Battalion, somewhere between Bien Hoa and Long Binh. I did whatever processing was necessary. Then in a formation after lunch I received orders to go to Long Binh and process into a transportation unit there. I was greatly relieved.

I thought, "Jesus, Long Binh. That's huge. That's like L.A. That's safe. Long Binh hasn't been hit in who knows how long. There's 25,000 people there. What a great way to go through the war."

At the same time, I was disappointed. I wanted to go to war. It was a test that I wanted to pass. It was a manhood test, no question about it. I did not know then the way I know now how safe my life had been. But some part of me knew that Vietnam was the event of my generation. Some other part also knew that I had led a pretty unchallenged life. I didn't know where I was going, so I might as well detour for a while and come up against something that was really hard.

In Long Binh the roads are paved. The hooches* looked like they were semipermanent. The showers had cement floors, hot and cold running water. The johns had doors on the stalls—you could take a shit in privacy. Nobody was carrying a weapon, because they were all locked up in arms rooms. There were hospitals on the base, but they were out of sight. Convoys went out of there every day but nothing came in. There were mama-sans* and hoochgirls* all over the place. Everything was clean. It was hot, yes, but it was like being in the Army, that's all. It wasn't the war.

I was there for three days when the top sergeant said, "We're sending you forward." I had already written home and said, "You won't believe where I am. They have air conditioning!" He was really evil telling me with a smirk, "You thought you were going to have it easy, but you're not. You're going to one of the least desirable places anybody in this unit can be sent to." I wasn't singled out. It was just the draw. I was new.

I still had no idea what my real work would be. If I stayed in Long Binh, I'd probably sit at a typewriter for twelve hours a day. That was a devastating thought. I mean, this was a nice place to sit out the war, but I'd go crazy.

For a day, I couldn't even remember the name of the place I was going to. I'd heard it once and I couldn't remember it. A few of the guys who had been there told me stories about how often the place was hit. I got very scared. I had not been issued a weapon yet, and I was going to a place called Phuoc Vinh on a convoy.

Phuoc Vinh was a little bit like being at summer camp that first night. People were playing guitars, getting stoned. People were drinking and sitting under the stars. There was a barbecue. Then there was incoming.

It wasn't very close, but it was close enough. I didn't know what it was. Somebody just yelled, "Incoming!"

There had been some quick exchanges of useful information. Give the new guy what he needs to know fast. Part of that was as simple as where the nearest bunker was located. I went to it and somehow managed to get in there in the midst of everybody else.

It was pitch black in the bunker and nobody was saying anything for a while. Out of the silence and the darkness, somebody said, "Where's the new guy?"

"I'm here," I said.

That was that, but there was something about that little exchange in the dark that I will never forget as long as I live. That question in the dark was authentically—I don't know what the word is—generous? Caring is too big a word somehow. Generous is enough. That's a lot. That somebody even bothered to think about me. Who the hell was I? This rather quiet, slightly older FNG* in clean fatigues, whose boots weren't even red yet. I was amazed.

*   *   *

We were flown on Braniff Airlines all the way to Vietnam: stewardesses in uniforms giving us a lot of hot dogs. I figured we'd get at least a roast beef sandwich or something, but hot dogs?

As we landed, the pilot, a real joker, announced over the PA system, "Temperature outside is one hundred and three degrees and ground fire is light to moderate."

The doors opened up and I got my first whiff of Nam. What do you do if you've got 500,000 men and no plumbing facilities? What do you do with all the human shit? The Army's answer to that was to collect it in barrels, then drag them someplace where they soaked all that human waste in fuel oil and set it on fire. Whoever the poor bastard was who had done something wrong yesterday, his job today was to stand there and stir this mess to make sure that it all burned. At midday when these details were going on, the smell of burning shit was incredible. The wind was wrong that day and the whole aircraft was filled with . . . my first smell of Vietnam.

From the time you land, the Army could care less about you—where you slept, if you slept, how you got your food, when you got your gear. They just put us in a big lump and said, "This is where you're staying. Don't go over there. Anywhere else you can go. Three times a day you've got to be available to stand out and wait for your name to be called. Gentlemen, that will be all."

For about four days, we just sort of wandered around in the heat. Three times a day you showed up and waited for your name to be called assigning you to some in-country training outfit. Twenty-five or thirty whose names were called would kind of go off and mill around. The officer in charge would be screaming, "No, no, no! Over here, you idiots, over here!" They'd shuffle over to wherever he was pointing. "All right, you ready to move out?"

"Well, no. All our bags and things are in the barracks."

"Where's your rifles?"

"We haven't been given any yet."

"Oh, son of a bitch, that's right."

Occasionally, if you were unfortunate enough to be standing around, they would come by very unsystematically and grab you to do KP. Real chaos. The level of incompetence really concerned me. These bastards don't know what they're doing.

The only thing to do was to hang out and play the slot machines in the enlisted men's club and drink beer. But a lot of us hadn't been issued military scrip yet, so we didn't have any money to spend.

Finally, my name was called and I was informed that I was going to an infantry division. I was loaned a rifle, so I could sit on the truck with it with my one magazine of ammunition, which I was told not to put into the rifle. That was probably a good choice on their part. A lot of guys were so nervous that they would have blown away the MPs.

They tell all the new guys the same story:

"Two second lieutenants, brand new in-country, were playing poker one night and got drunk. They decided they would have a *Gunsmoke* shoot-out. They stood in the middle of the company street with their .45s and had a fast draw contest and killed each other. That's why we don't give you guys ammo. We don't want you to kill each other until you get out in the field.''

At the division, there was more of the same confusion. For a day or so we were always supposed to be here or there doing this or that, and none of it was what the guy here or there wanted us to be doing.

All of us walked around trying to be real macho. We practiced throwing knives into doors. We were allowed no weapons, until we were issued the rifles that we would have for the entire tour.

They gave us field gear and we went through in-country training. One guy in five got to blow off a Claymore mine. We pulled one night out in the middle of a rubber plantation trying to stay awake looking for the Vietnamese. We didn't know it, but the area was really safe.

I knew I didn't want to be in an infantry company. I looked at the terrain and knew I wouldn't like walking around out there, day in and day out. The ground squished every place you stepped in the Delta. The mud tried to suck you under.

I started volunteering for everything: Lurps,* trackers working with the dogs, the Rat Patrol—those maniacs who ride around in jeeps clearing mines from the roads. I would have taken anything, as long as I didn't have to carry all that shit on my back and walk around living like an animal.

The first sergeant was getting kind of pissed with all my requests. He asked what was wrong with me. I told him that I really wanted to go where the action was. There probably wasn't going to be as much action as I wanted if I were just a straight-up infantryman. The reality of it was that I just wanted to get a decent place to live and spend as little time as possible slogging through the muck. I had no idea what I was volunteering for. I just looked at where the guys with those jobs lived and said, ''That ain't bad. Sure they got to go out occasionally and creep around in the dark, but it's worth the trade-off.''

Eventually I hooked up with my unit which was located at a French fort right out of *Beau Geste* with concrete parapets and big gates, thick stone walls. We went on Search and Destroy patrols. The helicopters would pick us up early in the morning and fly us out someplace, set us down and we'd spend the whole day walking around. Most of the time nothing happened.

We did get into a few fire fights. But what was taking place was so much less terrifying than the pitched battles I had imagined in my head that the level of fear was just not that high.

"Shoot, shoot," people kept saying to me.

"Where are they?"

"They're over there," they would say, pointing in the general direction of some trees about 150 yards away. So I would edge up over the top of a rice paddy dike and I would shoot at the tree line. All right, now I've shot. I'm done with that.

What the hell am I shooting at? Yes, we are getting shot at—there are rounds snapping past your ears, if you stick your head up like an idiot—but I couldn't *see* anything. After a while, I was so bored that I would shoot at the coconuts. Or I'd see how long it would take me to shoot a small bush in half.

Eventually, I was regarded as being "okay." I'd been through some fire fights and I didn't freeze up or shit in my pants. One incident really cinched it for me. In one fire fight there was nothing for me to do. We were crouched behind a dike and weren't in any danger, unless we did something stupid like stand up and charge a machine gun nest, which I wasn't about to do. I fell asleep in the middle of the whole thing. That was considered cool. I became one of the guys—Battle Tested.

* * *

I had a good squad leader. I was lucky with Old Rebel. Rebel was from Kentucky. Big, tall, skinny guy who walked around bowleggedly like. Carried a .45 and a short-timer's stick.* He told me, "The first thing is don't be hollering and screaming. Just stick around. Keep low and keep straight and don't do nothing crazy. You'll be all right. If the shit starts, keep your ass down and keep firing. You don't even have to look, just keep fucking firing. Somebody'll help you out. One of these days, you'll help one of us out."

* * *

I was put on point* at first. Point had to break trail. There's a trick to walking in elephant grass. You don't just walk like you were on the sidewalk. You stick your foot in and twist it to the outside so that the person walking behind you can walk through without doing what you're doing.

Walking point really sucked. I'd spent six months on Okinawa partying. I was in no shape to break trail. This is not just humping one or two hours. This is going from morning till night, twelve or fourteen hours a day. I'd get really exhausted, take ten steps, get this shit tangled around my feet and fall down. "Let's go," the lieutenant says. "This ain't New York City. No paved streets here."

I had no gloves to protect my hands. They got lacerated with grass cuts. That was a pain in the ass, too, because in Nam we didn't get a chance to clean ourselves good and any cut would get infected. The first thing I'd do in the morning was make a fist and squeeze the pus out of my hands. I've still got the scars. I was in pain for the first ten minutes or so.

The first time I got in a fire fight, I got my ass kicked, literally. When the firing first started, I was just standing there. "Wow, shit. They're really busting caps* at us." The lieutenant kicked me in the ass and yelled, "Let's go. Get down and bust some caps out there."

"Oh yeah, right." I wasn't so much scared as I was in awe. "Those motherfuckers are really shooting at us. They're really trying to kill us. Well, fuck them."

I got down and busted some caps from the routine rifleman's position: Get as close to the ground as possible, hold your gun up over your head about a foot and shoot indiscriminately in the direction of the enemy.

I started getting into it after three months. Getting into being a grunt and hunting. I walked my way into shape. I felt good. I was cocky and confident. I was good with my weapons. I was an eighteen-year-old who was proud of what he was doing. At first, I was scared shitless. But when you get right down to it, it's just getting yourself in gear and busting some caps.

*   *   *

About five of us went out on a short recon patrol. We were going to go a mile out and around the perimeter staying one mile out.

We come around the bend and there's two guys in green fatigues throwing hand grenades into the river. So right off we say, "Boy, that's the enemy, man, and we got 'em." We jumped out there and captured them, tied them up with wire and about half killed them. We drug them all the way back to camp. Me and two other guys were going to take them to the POW compound. This was all new to us. We'd only been there two days, but—oh boy—we were in *Combat*.

We dropped them off at the POW camp. The interrogator steps up and says three words to them. Come to find out they're National Guard, Popular Forces. They're on our side. What were they doing throwing hand grenades in the river? They were fishing.

*   *   *

My first God damn patrol in Vietnam, we went out on a night ambush. We set up the ambush in this graveyard and we were sitting in this little pagoda. At night you sit there and look and look and look. Pretty soon you think you see something moving, changing shape, like watching a ghost. I must have thought a million times I saw the gooks moving toward me. Then as the night passes and it gets lighter, you see that it's just some old banana tree.

Anyway, I was all gung-ho, ready to do something. These other guys was every one of them asleep. I thought, "God damn, how can these motherfuckers be sleeping?" Here I am wide awake. I figured there's VC everywhere. They're going to be running all over us. I was scared. I didn't sleep for the first two months I was over there. I always volunteered for watch, because I didn't want to get killed in my sleep.

Three or four VC pass the pagoda. I woke these guys up whispering, "Look, man, it's the VC. Ain't they VC? Don't we shoot them or something?"

"Aw, don't worry about them," they said. "We'll get them later. They'll come back by in the morning. You'll get your chance." They didn't even want to mess with them VC. They'd been over there a long time and had that give-a-shit attitude: If I get it, I get it. If I don't, I don't. Try my best. Laugh it off. Fuck it anyway.

* * *

I saw where the fire was coming from that first time I got shot at. It was like a barn. I ran in there, knocking over shit, looking for the guy, but I couldn't find him. I seen fresh tracks leading to another hooch which was like a little barber-shop. There were four gooks standing there. I throw them all up against the wall. I got my M-16 out.

My sergeant comes up. "What are you doing?" he screams. "You can't do that."

"What do you mean? One of these God damn bastards was shooting at me and I'm going to find out which one did it."

"No, you can't do that."

"What, are we playing games?" He made me leave.

"Get out of here, Sonny. You can't do that shit. You ask them. If they talk to you, they talk to you. You can't push them around."

"But, Sarge, they're *shooting* at me!"

"I don't care. You just can't do it."

"What a place this is going to be."

* * *

"Going down South" they called it in Okinawa. Braniff Airlines comes down all painted in their designer colors, puce and canary yellow. There were stewardesses on the plane, air conditioning. You would think we were going to Phoenix or something. But you know that you're going to Vietnam with a plane full of Marines.

It's about a two-and-a-half-hour flight down there. I was looking out the window as we were landing in Da Nang and there ain't nothing. It's just sticks, hovels with tin roofs. It's Dogpatch. That's what they called the area where we were.

The door opens and there's a blast of hot air that drops you to your knees. The head stewardess gets up and says, "Well, we're here in Da Nang. We hope you boys have a good tour. We'll see you one year from now." Those words kicked in an echo chamber in my mind—One Year From Now. Oh shit.

You grab your seabag which seems to have doubled in weight and you walk down the stairway. All the Marines waiting by the runway in jungle utilities* start laughing at you. I felt like a total jerk. Everything is barbed wire and guns and I got nothing.

We were thrown in the back of a six-by* and led through processing. You don't know what the fuck is going on. Back on Okinawa they had told us, "Okay, some of you will go to the Third Marine Division which is up at the DMZ. The rest of you will be going down to the First Marine Division which is at Da Nang. First Division is operating in the most heavily booby-trapped area in Vietnam." So I got assigned to the First Marines.

I get to headquarters and they said, "Okay, of our battalions, Second Battalion is in the most heavily booby-trapped area. You're going to Second Battalion." That's great, just don't let me get blown up on the way out there.

So we ride out to some little ville,* check into battalion. I meet the colonel, a very impressive man. He says, "You take care of your troops and I'll take care of the officers." Gave me a little pep talk and everything. "This is what's happening with our companies. Echo Company is working in the worst booby-trapped area and that's where I'm assigning you." I hit it all the way down the line, perfect. "Your company is operating in the field someplace and the battalion is moving tomorrow, so go to bed."

I go to supply and get a helmet and a flak jacket. They give me a .45, but they don't have any magazines for it. Now I've got a gun but I got no way to load bullets into it.

I spent the night in some officers' hooch. They came in and were talking about this and that, the worst things they could come up with. Half their conversation is aimed at me, although I'm not included. I sat in the corner and didn't make any noise.

"Yeah, he just came in. They hit some resistance down in Dodge City and one of his platoons caught some shit. But they kicked the hell out of a platoon of VC. Called in artillery and really greased the fuckers."

There was an aura about the people who were over there. These guys were kids, but they weren't kids. There was something in their eyes that made them absolutely different. I was fascinated, mesmerized by these guys. I couldn't take my eyes off them. There was something very old about them, but I still felt like a kid.

What was I doing over here? I'm twenty-one. I can't believe they're going to give me a platoon. I've forgotten everything I ever learned. I'm supposed to know how to call in artillery, I can't remember nothing. Oh my God, this is bigger than anything I ever imagined.

I'm a boot* lieutenant and that's the lowest thing in the Marine Corps. There's nothing as dangerous as a second lieutenant with a map and a compass. The first sergeant used to get pissed at some of the PFCs and threaten to bust them to second lieutenants if they didn't quit fucking up. I went to bed since nobody really wanted to talk to me much. I take all my clothes off and I'm in my skivvies. Everyone else goes to bed with their clothes on, but I'm not picking up on nothing.

About 2:30 in the morning, out of nowhere, the shit hits the fan. There's explosions all over the place. I go, "What the fuck is going on?" This guy Larry, who was a first lieutenant, gets up and says, "Head for the bunkers. We're getting hit. We're being overrun."

So I jump up and just then I feel something—like getting hit in the back with hot gravel. *Boom*. I was knocked forward a few steps and I actually saw stars like in a cartoon. I feel something inside me.

Your brain detaches itself and goes outside. It says, "You're hit. You're hit." I can't believe it. I just got there.

I go down. I don't know if I'm dead, paralyzed or what. This guy Larry, the last one out of the hooch, looks at me and says, "You're okay." And he runs. He was scared shit. Just left me there. Thanks, Larry. Never said a word to him about it when I came back.

Lying there, I suddenly wanted to be home in my bed with my parents in the next room. I was really frightened. In the Marine Corps, they have what they call the Pucker Factor. They joke about it. You get so scared that your asshole puckers. But it's true. Your asshole literally puckers up inside your body. It's an involuntary reaction.

I was afraid to move. I said to myself, "Let's see if you can move your fingers." They worked. "Now, can you move your toes?" I could feel my toes, but then I realized, "Wait a second, guys who lose their legs—I seen it in the movies—they think they got toes. Then they wake up and they don't." So I looked and I could see my toes moving.

When I looked down, there was a pool of blood, growing about a foot in diameter, draining off between the cracks in the floor of the hooch. There's a couple of pools, so I'm losing a lot of blood. Suddenly, I hear gunfire real close by. I prayed to God, "Don't let me get hit again. Please, don't let me get hit again. I'll devote my life to the cloth, anything you want, Lord. Just don't let me die."

The door swung open and everything got blown away around me. The VC had come in and sprayed the hooch, thought they got me again and left. I just laid there, playing dead.

They had hit the tear gas in a bunker and it was all over the place. I grabbed a sock and put it under my nose. In the meantime, I heard somebody come in the hooch. I looked up and it was a sergeant, standing at the window and firing out. He looks back and sees me breathing through the sock. He had thought I was dead. He runs back to me and says, "Does anybody know that you're here?"

"Yeah, there's one guy," thoughts of first louie Larry flying out the door.

"I'll get help." He runs out and gets a jeep from the battalion aide station. A bunch of guys throw me on a stretcher and run me out to the jeep.

I look around and everything is on fire, bathed in red. I can see tracers* going out, tracers coming in. People are yelling and screaming. Pop, pop, pop, small arms fire. Fast pops, automatic weapons fire. Total chaos. Above it all, somebody had left a radio on in a hooch and it was Mary Hopkins singing that song, "Goodbye."

We go flying across battalion around all this shit to the aide station. It's full of people, holding their stomachs, with IV bottles dripping down into them. The third medevac chopper was mine. You can see the helicopters way up in the sky. The lights go off and they just spiral down—boom, boom, boom. They throw me into the back and I just sail out of there.

I'm near a window looking back. It's like watching it on TV. You're in the middle of it one minute and the next you're a million miles away. It's all below you.

They had Spooky* standing on a column of tracers, just circling around battalion, tilling the earth. I pity anything that's out there. For every tracer you see, there's four rounds you don't see. That's throwing some heavy lead.

They took me to an Army hospital south of Monkey Mountain by Da Nang. They hump me out of the chopper and run me into a quonset hut. There are all these doctors and nurses inside, scrubbed up with the masks on, waiting. Bare light bulbs hang down the center of the quonset hut. The floors all slope toward the middle to drains. There's sawhorses lined up.

The three guys in front of me, their stretchers are placed on a pair of sawhorses and I'm balanced on some sawhorses. They start operating. They shoot me up with things because I got hit in my back. They give me a tongue depressor to bite on and just start cutting away.

I could feel them pull some stuff out of my neck and I felt a geyser of blood shooting out. They were operating on the knee of the guy next to me and I could see white bone glistening. There must have been ten operations going on in this place at one time.

I don't remember a whole hell of a lot after that. Just that I was glad when they stopped cutting on me, because it felt weird. It doesn't hurt, but you can feel the pressure. I've got a hole in my back, but it missed my spine by about a quarter of an inch. It looks like a keyhole, about four inches long.

I went to the hospital on Guam for a month. We watched two movies a day. A lot of pilots were out there, guys being wheeled in with no arms or legs. Or if they did have limbs, they were like burnt-out twigs. I kept picking pieces of shrapnel out of my head. They come to the surface between the bone and the skin. I still got a few pieces in me, but after a month was up, I went back to the field.

*　　*　　*

I went to Nam in September of 1970. There were only a few other people on the plane going for the first time. The rest of the guys were returning from emergency leave, their mother died or something. I had to be dressed in my Class A uniform, which meant nylons, high heels and a skirt. The flight was twenty-six hours long. You got a girdle holding your nylons up and your ankles are swelling. You can't imagine the pain. Plus, all those guys on the plane—there were only three or four women. No way was I going to get up and walk that whole aisle to go to the bathroom. It seems silly now, but it didn't at the time.

There was this big black MP that sat across from me. He was about six feet tall and real skinny. His name was Midge. He kept my spirits up all the way over. He said, "You just a baby. You don't know what you in for." Midge knew what I was in for and he tried to keep me laughing. He had this big rubber snake and he would throw it in my lap every time I got ready to take a nap or anything. I don't think I slept the whole way. I must have finally gone to the bathroom. I don't remember it, but I'm sure I must have.

As we were landing at Bien Hoa, the pilot comes over the PA system and says, "They're taking some fire at Bien Hoa. When we touch down, as soon as the doors are opened, everybody down low and run." We took some fire as we came in because you could feel it underneath.

We landed and they shut off the air conditioning so there wasn't any fresh air. It got hotter and hotter. My anxiety got higher and higher. I didn't know whether I couldn't breathe because there was something wrong with my lungs or whether there really was no air.

All of a sudden the door opened and Midge yelled, "Come on. Come on. Move it. Move it." I've got high heels on and I've got great big fat ankles. I'm wearing a tight skirt and I'm trying to run across the airfield.

The place smelled like an old urinal. Sweaty, stale and dank. All the nasty smells you can imagine.

We ran into a dimly lit room. On one side were empty chairs for all us turkeys who just landed. On the other side were all the guys going home. This horrendous roar came up from these guys because they were going to take our places on the plane. I looked at those guys and how glad they were to be getting out and it started to dawn on me what I was getting myself into.

We sat there for I don't know how long. It takes hours for a briefing. Then you get your name read off a list and you're checked into this and checked out of that. I got my orders.

I spent my first night in a little shack. The next day I woke up real early, but it was already hot outside and the sun was bright. I'm here. Man! I got to go out and see what's going on. I'd seen my dad's slides of Korea a hundred times and I was fascinated. I ran outside and, God, there's all these little people with their coolie hats running around on the other side of the fence. It smelled different and it looked different, so I was pretty excited. You're stupid at first and you really don't know.

Then I went down to what was the latrine. After I got in there and realized that I couldn't knock all the bugs off the toilet paper, I decided that I didn't need toilet paper. I didn't want to take a shower because I'm not really into bugs. I'm not what might be called typically squeamish, but I wasn't used to so many all at once. A roomful was too much.

There wasn't much to do except hang around and play a little pool, waiting for our assignment. The enlisted men had to have some kind of formation every morning. They'd have all these guys lined up for roll call, I guess, and every morning Charlie dropped mortars on them. These guys got killed before they even got their orders to go wherever they were going. They just put them in a bag and sent them back home.

They had told us we could take 200 pounds of stuff to Nam. I'm sure I'm the only nurse who only brought 99 pounds of luggage. I splurged at the PX though and bought about $40 worth of underwear and bras when I got there. I carried everything in two brown suitcases that my parents had taken with them on their honeymoon. They were held together with rope. I had been told not to bring anything good because it would rot away. In the pouring rain at the airfield, the wind was blowing hard. The guys were always willing to help the little nurses, so this guy picked up my suitcase and threw it onto a truck.

The rope was rotten, the suitcase busted open and my underwear went flying all over the airfield. The guys lined up nearby broke rank. They were over the fence and tearing onto the tarmac, all this brand-new underwear and bras everywhere. Guys were running for souvenirs.

I wasn't going to admit that it was mine. No way, Jose. There were quite a few nurses standing around, but I was just as busy looking to see whose suitcase it was as everybody else. Jees, who's the poor kid that this happened to?

The suitcase finally got on the truck, went out to the plane and ended up in the hospital where I would be stationed. We were at the base of a mountain that never looked real to me. It was strange. If you had a railroad track for electric trains, this would be one of the plastic mountains. They always looked like they were just put there, like they didn't belong. They were furry and green, but then it was still raining so everything was furry and green. It must have rained for the first two weeks I was there.

Everybody was very nice. They were glad to see me and they got me settled. My first roommate was a Red Cross director. She was always drinking and dropping a drug that you take if you've got a cardiac condition. If you have irregular beats, it's supposed to put you in a sinus rhythm. She was always sneaking a shot and dropping one of those. I was sort of concerned. I thought it was a little weird.

I walked on the ward the first time and was afraid to take a deep breath, it smelled so bad. I worked on the Intensive Care Unit. It held about twenty–twenty-five patients. They said, "Well, we might as well start you in, Lieutenant. You can do the dressing changes."

This involved taking the cart around that had all kinds of bandages on it and putting fresh gauze and cloth on the wounds. Everybody over there had pseudomonas.* When you saw guys with a pussy-green drainage on their dressing, you know they had pseudomonas.

The first dressing I changed was a guy who had lain in a water-filled ditch for two days waiting for somebody to get to him. Not only did he have pneumonia, so that he was full of fluid, but I took the dressing off his arm and he didn't have an arm. All he had was bone. It had gotten full of maggots in the ditch. The maggots are what probably saved him, because they had eaten all the dead tissue. I'm trying to talk to this guy and trying not to gag and throw up. He really didn't care because he was out of his head with a high temperature. I didn't have the slightest idea what sort of dressing to put on. Then I figured out what was on there before and put on some more of the same. There was bone and there was muscle. The maggots were all gone, thank God, because I would have just left. Okay, I quit. I'm ready to go home. Somebody else can do this shit. Not me.

I had to go into the little utility room with the mops and brooms to regroup, get my shit together to go do the rest of them.

* * *

I really wouldn't have had any problems in Vietnam, but I made the mistake one night of opening up my mouth. I said, "If I saw a Viet Cong and he didn't see me, I would know that he had a wife and children, and I wouldn't kill him." The next morning I was on the airstrip with everything I owned, going to a combat unit in front of the front.

I went to a small base camp, a star-shaped perimeter in III Corps of Vietnam, Central Highlands, about one kilometer from the Cambodian border. It was so close to Cambodia we could see the North Vietnamese troops being indoctrinated. They were close enough to fire mortars and rockets at us, but we couldn't shoot back because that would violate the border agreements.

The airstrip was considered enemy territory. When a plane would come in, it would kind of corkscrew down to avoid enemy fire. You had ten seconds to get off the plane and roll into a bunker or you were gone.

The day I flew in, we stayed up in the air watching the whole place get hit. I couldn't believe *that* was the place I was going. After the mortar attack, I got to my unit and asked to see the captain. They told me he was away from the main area of the camp.

"Well, can I get to him?"

"Sure, he's right out there under those trees somewhere."

I walked out to meet him and take over command. He was dead with his head blown off and his dick in the air. He had been out there masturbating when the mortars hit and got his head blown right off. Stiff as a board with his cock in his hands.

*   *   *

In Okinawa you hear a whole lot of shit. "They're going to give you your weapons on the plane and your flak jackets. When you land, you get off the plane running like hell. Run, because you're probably going to get blown away." It scares you to death. These guys just did their thirteen months and they're going home. So they're juggling with the youngbloods headed over. We're saying, "Oh shit, man. What are these guys talking about? I don't want to go over there."

"It's too late now. You're on your way."

It was similar to what they were saying. When we got there, the plane went over and an officer was standing up saying, "Look out your window. There's Vietnam. I hope we don't get no flak up here on the way in."

I thought, "What is he talking about? Ain't this safe right here?" He was saying it ain't safe anywhere.

Luckily, we didn't get no incoming when we first landed. So the only thing that got us was the heat. When we came off the plane it must have been a hundred and change. There's no air or nothing. I stepped to the door and was drenched. The sweat just popped.

As soon as we came off the plane—we didn't walk— they ran us into this big quonset hut, a piece of metal bullshit that keeps in the heat. They started handing out salt tablets. They said, "Take two tablets a day. Don't fail, because you'll get heatstroke and you need it to sweat." Some of the guys was shucking and jiving. I didn't have time for that. Hey, they said take the salt tablets, I'll take them. They gave us flak jackets and helmets, lined us up and started calling off names.

When they called me I got on the side and they issued me an M-16. I thought, "Man, they sure give us a lot of stuff right away. What is this?" Then they told me I was going to join the Second Marine Division. "You will be transported by plane from here in Da Nang to Quang Tri," they said.

So this is Da Nang. I wasn't too happy with Da Nang. I didn't know it was the best I'd see over there. The women in the streets was breast-feeding they kids, which blew my head. "Holy shit, that baby's sucking a titty." We were cracking up.

The guys there, they boots is spit-shined, they had creases in they jungles. They was talking and shit. They was smoking and they was laughing. They were all Strak.* They had all they ribbons, too.

I said, "Well, it ain't great, but if it's like this, I am over. I got it." We knew that some of them even had cots to sleep on, mattresses. I said, "Hey, light stuff."

When we got to Quang Tri, it started to look a little bit worse—not much, but a little bit worse than it had been down at Da Nang. We got off there and they started to split us up again. They stuck some of us into trucks heading up Highway 1 to Phu Bai.

Phu Bai was a little like Quang Tri. People didn't seem quite so clean-cut. But although things was dirtier the living quarters and such were about the same. I said, "Well, I'll be stationed here. That ain't so bad."

At the battalion they said they were splitting us up into companies and I was given to Fox Trot. I said, "That's a bet. I like that name." By now it was beginning to get a little dark so they told us we would get to our outfits the next day. "All right," I said, "damn, tonight I'll get me some sleep."

"But all you guys got guard duty."

"Guard duty? But we just got here. I didn't really *get* here yet. Me, I'm still in the air."

They put five of us in each bunker with one guy that's been there for a while. Those guys got no sleep, no sleep whatsoever.

He told us, "Don't shoot. If you see something, wake me up." I'm standing there on duty and I thought I saw something black go by at a real slow pace. I looked again, "Oh shit." Now the other four guys are wide awake looking up at me, because their turn is coming next to guard. Our main man, he was sound asleep. He didn't care, I could tell. "Wake that guy up. Wake him up."

"What?"

"Something is out there."

"That's a water buffalo, you stupid motherfucker."

"I don't know, man. Hell, you told me to wake you up if I saw anything moving."

"How much more time you got?"

"Another ten minutes."

"Next man on watch."

The word had spread on down the line, so all the new guys in the bunkers is going, "Wake up, wake up, wake up." We're 100 percent alert. The commander calls, "What the fuck is going on down there?"

"Aw, this kid is seeing things." I tried to get some sleep which I didn't.

We had breakfast at six the next morning, got on some more trucks and they carted us over to LZ Stud. That's the last real outpost before you hit the shit. LZ Stud is where I really started noticing that things are beginning to look bad. Now, there is nothing but bunkers. You got a couple of regular hooches but they're not quonset huts and they're not constructed of wood really. These are just pieces of two-by-four with some hunks of canvas hung over them however they can hang them. They do got cots to sleep on, but there are no more mattresses to go around and there are no pillows. Guys got their pack bundled up for a pillow. You could still get a hot meal there, but I was only there long enough to get lunch. Then they told me I was going up to Khe Sanh.

"You're going up to Khe Sanh. They need you."

"When we going? It'll be a couple of days, right?"

"Nope, you're leaving now."

"But we just got here. We just got off guard duty down there at fucking Phu Bai. Then we bumped up here and we got to go to Khe Sanh? Don't the new guys get broken in or something?"

"Yeah, OJT."

"Whoa, back up. What's that OJT?"

"On the job training. That's how you will be broken in." That was not too good at all.

Everything was starting to look really bleak. I was scared shitless. I was scared from the first, but I was worse the farther north I got. Damn, things are looking bad. I'm seeing more and more woods. I'm hearing more and more about people getting hurt. I'm seeing these guys laying around in the LZ Stud area with rat bites and wounds. Shrapnel messed up they legs and they're limping around until they get better or waiting until they get medevacked home.

We got in helicopters. Coming over Khe Sanh, I looked down and it was one big round mountain with a jagged line around the top of it. That line was the trench line. The choppers could only go out there when they said there was no incoming, but they had incoming five times a day.

For the first time the reality of where I was and where I was going slapped me back worse than a bad nightmare. Now, I'm in a war. Oh, God, I could really die out here. Up until that point I never took it seriously. It was happening, but it wasn't real. It was TV—hey, heroes and shit. No, I could really die in this fucking place. I wasn't ready for that. It grabbed me and shook me every way but loose. We landed and they ran us off the choppers.

"Company. What company?" somebody yells at me.

"Fox Trot."

"Fox Trot that way, Fox Trot that way." Pointing

and waving. "Delta Bravo, that way over there. This way, this way. Shut the hell up and keep going. Move it."

Who the hell are these guys? I didn't see no rank on nobody's shoulders or helmets. Everybody looked like privates to me. They're all yelling and screaming at me like I don't got no sense, but I'm running anyway. Everybody is running all over the place.

I was supposed to be a machine gunner. I didn't really want to be a gunner, but that's the MOS* they gave me. I knew according to training that I'd be an ammo humper for a while and then work my way up to assistant gunner, then I'd make full-fledged gunner. It would take me a couple of months. I figured, okay, I got time to build up.

When I got to my unit, they said, "I hear we got a gunner here."

"Yeah, I'm a gunner."

"Okay, there's your gun."

"Oh no, I got my M-16 right here."

"No-no, that M-60* machine gun is yours."

"Wait a minute. Ain't I supposed to be an ammo humper first?"

"Yeah. You will carry two hundred rounds . . . and your gun." I didn't even have jungles fatigues yet. They had give us jungle boots* back at LZ Stud but they didn't give us time to change socks and put them on. Then I met my squad leader. He walked up and said, "Put on your jungle boots and hurry up. We're going out."

I'm scared and I'm hurrying, because they tell me to. But I'm looking at these bunkers and that long trench line and that barbed wire and cans and holes all over the damn place. My mouth fell open. All us new guys had that look of fear on our faces, like where the hell am I at. It did look like Hell to me.

Then I saw these piles of clothes. There were piles of shirts and piles of pants. Now, I just changed into my brand-new jungle boots, and I'm scuffing them so I don't look too green. This lieutenant comes along and tells me, "Get your shirt from over there and your pants from the other pile." I'm looking at his boots and his didn't look a whole lot older than mine. Everybody else's boots looked terrible. They were red like the dirt. But I figured a lieutenant can have however many pairs of boots he wants.

I got me a shirt and I looked through the pile and found me a pair of pants that looked halfway like they would fit me. I put the shit on. I take my Stateside fatigues and roll them up thinking I'll put them in my hooch. "Where's our hooch?"

"What hooch? There's a bunker. You climb down in the trench and you walk around into that hole. That's where the gun squad sleeps." I wasn't too happy climbing down into that dark place and trying to find someplace to stow my gear.

When I jumped back out, my squad leader looked at me and he kept looking at me. Why is this man looking at me so hard? He looks me over again and screams, "Where did you get that shit from? Where did you get it?"

"What? What are you talking about?"

"Them jungles you're wearing."

"I got the shirt from that pile there and the pants from this one here."

"Get them off, take them off!" The same time that he's yelling for me to take them off, he's pulling them off me with both hands like a crazy man. I'm trying to get away from him, calm him down.

"Okay, okay, give me a chance. Wait a minute here. I'll take them off. You don't got to rip my clothes off."

"Get that shit off. Don't you know what piles those are?"

"How do I know? The lieutenant told me to get jungles out of there."

"That damn boot's only been here two weeks. Them clothes is from the KIA."

"What the hell is KIA?"

"Killed in action. That's where he told you to take clothes from? We don't touch that shit. We send that stuff to the rear, let them boys down there wear that crap. We'll find you some jungles. You're not going to jinx yourself and our squad."

Somebody gave me a pair of pants. This Indian dude gave me a shirt. He was a big dude and the shirt he gave me came down to my knees. The sleeves were four inches past the ends of my fingers. I looked like a clown. The Indian said, "Don't worry about that. I'll cut the sleeves and then roll them up."

I had been there about an hour at this point, when they said, "Okay, chow down. You got a patrol in fifteen minutes."

"Wait a minute. I haven't even been up here a good hour yet."

"You're lucky. We *waited* for you."

"You didn't do me no favors. I'm supposed to be happy you waited for me? Hey, go on patrol without me."

"We need a gun team on this patrol. Since you are the boot, you're going and the other gun teams are staying here. Tomorrow *they* got the patrol. We rotate. It's simple. You'll fall into the routine."

What blew my head was what they did to calm me down. The whole team got together and they're sitting around, laughing and bullshitting. My squad leader lit up a joint. He said, "Here, puff. You smoke, right? Well, go ahead. Light up. Relax. You got plenty of time to be scared later. Just relax."

My hand was still shaking, but I'm smoking. They was laughing and telling these weird stories. Their jokes is about this kill and that kill and what this one clown does when there is incoming. He gets his chair, sits in front of his bunker and writes his letter. The only time he writes home is during incoming—"Oh, that's light shit." I wasn't too enthused about their jokes, but I didn't care. After a while I started relaxing. About that time, fifteen minutes had come up on me.

"Saddle up!" I know what that is—get my gear together to move out. Oh shit.

That first patrol we went to where some Marines had

ambushed a bunch of Viet Cong. They had me moving
dead bodies, VC and NVA. Push this body here out of
the way. Flip a body over. See people's guts and heads
half blown off. I was throwing up all over the place.

"Keep doing it. Drag this body over there."

"For what?"

"You're going to get used to death before you get in
a fire fight and get us all killed. You're a gunner and
gunners can't panic on us."

That first time everything just kept coming up. Scared
to begin with, then all of a sudden I'm looking at this
shit. I moved some more bodies and after a while I
stopped throwing up. But I wasn't too happy about the
whole situation.

They noticed that I wasn't throwing up no more and
they gave me about a ten-minute rest. They're laughing
and joking. They found a lot of funny shit to talk
about.

Next, I had to kick one dead body in the side of the
head until part of his brain started coming out of the
other side. I said, "I just moved a dead body. What are
y'all telling me?" The logic, I didn't see it then. I understood it later. At the time I thought, "These fuckers
been up here too long. They are all insane." I'm going
through my changes and the rest of these guys are
laughing.

"Kick it," they said. "You are starting to feel what it
is like to kill. That man is dead, but in your mind you're
killing him again. Man, it ain't no big thing. Look-a-
here." And they threw some bodies off the cliff and
shit.

"Go ahead. Pick one up and throw it off. But when
you can kick his brains out, you'll know what it is when
they say to kick out someone's brains. And you can say,
in your life that you have personally kicked somebody's
brains out. So . . . Kick." They meant it. The chant
started, "Kick . . . Kick . . . Kick."

Here I am just barely touching this clown's head with
the toe of my boot. "Kick. Kick. Kick." Then all of a
sudden all I'm hearing is, "Kick, kick, kick!" Louder

and louder. If you don't kick, they'll get you and they'll kill you. So kick.'' I'm looking down and ''Kick, kick, kick,'' is drumming in my head.

I'm kicking now. I'm kicking and I'm kicking and all of a sudden, the brains start coming out the other side. Oh shit. I thought I was going to die when I saw what I was actually doing. I thought I was going to die. I started throwing up again, but there was nothing left to bring up. I'm dry heaving. God, it was killing me. I kept trying to drink some water so I could bring that back up. Didn't do me no good.

They were serious men, dedicated to what they were doing. At that time the dedication was to teaching me, to preparing me for when death do strike—and it could strike any one of them or myself—not to fall apart if a friend dies. I saw it happen. I saw guys get themselves killed and almost get an entire platoon wiped out, because they panicked or because they gave up or because they got wounded and couldn't deal with their own blood. They had this thing about teaching a boot exactly what he's got to deal with and how to accept the fact of where he really is.

BOOM. BOOM. BOOM. There's about ten or fifteen loud thumps. I'm jumping behind rocks with my machine gun. I'm ready. They were laughing at me again. ''Hey, that's going past us,'' somebody said. Then I heard them whistle overhead. This is incoming going on to Khe Sanh proper from the big guns that the NVA had in Laos. I could see a flash of light back in Khe Sanh. Then the sound of the explosion reached us.

''Be thankful you're out on patrol,'' they said. ''Because they're catching hell back there. Tomorrow, we'll be back in there when the incoming hits and they'll be out here in the boonies. They'll be watching.''

''Is there incoming every day?''

''Yeah, five times a day. We wake up to incoming. We have incoming for lunch. It hits again about seven in the evening and again about ten-thirty or eleven. It depends on how the NVA feels. If they want to go to bed early, they give it to us about ten P.M. If they don't

mind sitting up and bullshitting for a while, they give it
to us at eleven. Then there's some nut over there that
gets up in the middle of the night sometimes and shoots
off a few. After a while you just run inside."

I'm saying to myself, these guys are professionals, but
they're crazy. How could you remember these things
that they did? It became a way of life. I didn't know
where the hell those shells were going. I didn't even
know what they was. But every death sound there is,
you start to detect it—you know it. You start to know if
death is going over you or if it's coming right at you.

*   *   *

My platoon was pulled to do sentry duty at a place
called Anu Tan, a rice mill surrounded by huts. Things
weren't so safe at Anu Tan. People got killed. I was
living in a bunker but couldn't go in there at night
because the rats were so bad you'd get bitten. If a rat
bites you, you're sure not going to catch the rat and turn
him over to find out if it has rabies. It was just assumed
that all rats had rabies. You would undergo the shots.

We were living very primitively. Meals were flown in
to us. We could buy one can of warm beer a night.
There was nothing to do. The boredom was incredible.
There was nothing to buy. The place was small enough
that the officers were able to keep track of you: "No,
don't go in there to the whores." There were only three
or four whores, so they kept track of them, too.

We would draw fire from the tree line about every
third night or so. One of the places the fire came from
was a graveyard about eighty meters in front of my
bunker. It was harassment more than anything else.
They would sneak in and shoot at us a few times.

Once early in the evening, before it was really dark
yet, I was by myself on top of the bunker when they
started shooting at us. I didn't panic by this point in
time. Calmly and methodically, but disconnected, like
you're watching yourself do it—Clint Eastwood would
have been proud of me—I moved my M-16 so that even-

tually the muzzle flashes from the graveyard lined up through my sights. The guy fired and I fired back on top of him, emptied eight or nine rounds right back at him.

I heard this scream, high in volume but like the stuff you use to scream with had been disconnected. I knew that I had really blasted somebody for the first time. The gurgling went on for thirty or forty seconds, a retching scream for a long time. I felt strange. The consequences of pulling the trigger came home to me the next day when I found blood, hair and tissue all over this one tombstone. I probably killed the guy.

*   *   *

I looked out the window and all I could see was jungle on both sides. This is Nam and it was beautiful. I'd never seen jungle in my life.

Coming out of the South China Sea we begin to climb up so the rockets don't get us. We're all trying to laugh that off. But as we're descending again in-country, we had an escort of a couple of Air Force fighters. I saw them strafing along as we were coming in. They were under fire. Below us on the left and right they were dropping napalm. Trees was going up in the air.

As we set down at Bien Hoa, the Viet Cong were dropping rockets on the field. But still, I wasn't frightened. I said to myself, "I know that I'm going to die. But I'm going to die in the bush. Not here."

As soon as we hit the airfield they open the doors and tell us to get out. The thing that I can't forget about the Nam was the smell of it. The smell. You smelled the napalm and you smelled the human flesh burning. That will live with me to the end of my days. Nothing smells like Vietnam smells. We ran out through that smell into the bunkers and waited for the rockets to stop.

After it was all over, they brought us out and lined us up for an orientation. In front of us is this lieutenant, a guy from the field. His uniform is filthy, all raggedy with the grenades hanging off of it, the bandolier, the M-16 strapped on him. You look into the guy's eyes and

you saw that there was no joy there. Everybody I saw at
the air base was in a zombie type of world.

"You're in the Republic of Vietnam," he said. "This
is the program for the day: You're going to get killed in
Vietnam. We're in our own world here. If you don't do
what I tell you, you're going to be taken out of our
world." It hit on people, "Hey, I'm really in the Nam
now."

We stayed there until evening. That whole day I saw
gooks but they were dead gooks that were all blown up
on the wire there.

We went from there at Bien Hoa to Long Binh, a
couple of miles down the road. They told us what to do
and what not to do. They issued us rifles. That night we
didn't sleep. We had to go out on perimeter, because
they were under attack. It was the Tet Offensive.

It was automatic. I didn't think. It was spontaneous.
All of a sudden I wasn't the Black Muslim revolutionary
any more. I became one of the guys. The VC were
coming in the wire and I was shooting them. I was
shooting the M-16. I was shooting the M-60. Whatever
was available to shoot, I shot it.

There were gooks on the wire that night. It was regular gooks, VC, local people. They your friend during the
day, but at night they Viet Cong. We shot a few of
them. I killed a couple myself. I thought in the back
of my mind that I was going to break down and cry
because I killed one, but to me it was nothing. I seen
them get shot up. So many people were shooting from
different bunkers, it didn't bother me.

After the fire fight was over they shot up a white flare
to say that it's clear. We stayed there all night. The next
morning, we had to go out and pick up the bodies. It
didn't dawn on me at that time, but this was the body
count. A couple of GIs was killed. We took them and
laid them on the ground, stripped them of the things
they had on them. Then they call the Quartermaster
Corps who handled the bodies. They brought in these
green bags. They throw you in the green bag and they
snap it over you. They didn't have no doctor pronounce

you dead. I believe a lot of guys died in that green bag.

"Medic, check this guy out."

"Yeah, he's dead." They throw them in the green bag and that was it.

We took the gooks' weapons off them and stacked the bodies next to each other. You ever see them safari pictures, when they go to Africa and they kill an elephant? The hunter steps on the elephant and he puts his rifle on it, like a picture of Teddy Roosevelt with a water buffalo. This is what it was like in the Nam. They shot up the bodies, then they would pile the bodies up. Then they would call over the news people, like NBC news or CBS. They wasn't out there when we was shooting, but they was out there when it was over for the body count. They took pictures of the bodies strowed out there and the Americans standing around. It was like a trophy. Hey, this is trophy day. What is the hunter's kill?

They count the bodies. Then they take them out in the bush and just burned them. They didn't bother to bury them. They just pour diesel fuel on the gooks and set them on fire. I'm really in the Nam. Seemed like I just fell into it.

We had to go down to Saigon which was under attack during the Tet Offensive. We had to fight in the Cho Lon area. They needed bodies to liberate Saigon.

We fought from house to house and street to street. When we had to go inside a house we'd just shoot inside with our rifles and then the M-60. Then we had to go up into the house and make sure that they were dead. We didn't have no flame-throwers. I didn't see no tanks in Saigon. They didn't have things like you see in the movies on TV about World War II. It surprised me. I was expecting for the tank to come up there and do the John Wayne type of things. We just had to shoot down the door, walk in and shoot the person down.

Those people were funny. They would shoot at us. Then when we come into the house, they would hide their weapon—they had special double walls where they would keep them—and they would say, "Me no VC. Me no VC. I no know VC." We had to search the house and find the weapon. Once we found the weapon or the little Chinese-made rocket, we would shoot them. Everybody seemed to know that this was the customary thing. I had just been in-country for a day or so. I figured that's the way things are done around here.

I don't understand when they talk about taking prisoners and stuff. We didn't go through that nonsense. I used to shoot them. We'd stand them up against the wall, put a gun to his head and say, "Talk. If you don't talk, we're going to pull the trigger." Or they take the man's wife or daughter and screw his daughter in front of him. And made him talk. If he didn't talk, they would shoot the woman. Then shoot him. Taking a life was nothing. It was customary.

After a week or two we more or less controlled Saigon. It was back in the hands of the American forces. They still had action. You'd walk by an area and they would throw a grenade at you. That was common practice. You got used to it. They would snipe at you. You expected that. It was like a fly coming in and landing on your ear—you flick it off.

We gathered up a hundred bodies that day, shot. Not only my unit, but the various units there. It looked to be about a hundred bodies. We had a thing in the Nam. We used to cut their ears off. We had a trophy. If a guy would have a necklace of ears, he was a good killer, a good trooper. It was encouraged to cut ears off, to cut the nose off, to cut the guy's penis off. A female, you cut her breast off. It was encouraged to do these things. The officers expected you to do it or something was wrong with you.

I was in another environment where I had to act according to them. Two or three days being in-country, I was a little leery about shooting them right up close, point-blank. But it didn't bother me. Then after being in there two weeks, I started cutting ears off. I used to fight with a couple of guys just to get to an ear. I had a necklace around my neck, made out of a green string, nylon string. Ears can only stay on your neck for about three days and they turn brown and they start rotting and the flies get to them. I wore a necklace of ears. That showed that I was an effective soldier.

We threw those hundred bodies in the Saigon River that flows through Cho Lon. It was such a problem. So many VCs was killed that it clogged up the river so that the Navy complained to the Army about throwing bodies in the river. They didn't say, "Why didn't you bury them?" The Navy was complaining because the patrol boats would get tangled up with the bodies. Somehow the propeller would get caught on an arm or a leg. You got three or four bodies fall into a propeller, it can really mess up a boat.

All this came down and the Army command unit told us to go pull the bodies out. So we had to go back down to the Saigon River and pull the bodies out. This is a body that's been sitting in there for a while. It's swelled up, it turned color, the fish are biting on it. We got the bodies out on an embankment and we poured diesel fuel on them and had like a big bonfire.

It was like that lieutenant had told us back at the airstrip, "This is our world. You went to Hell and you're still alive." I understood it.

In fact, I started to enjoy it. I enjoyed the shooting and the killing. I was literally turned on when I saw a gook get shot. When a GI got shot, even if I didn't know him—he could be in a different unit than me—that would bother me. A GI was real. American get killed, it was a real loss. But if a gook got killed, it was like me going out here and stepping on a roach.

This was the whole thing about the Nam that people fail to understand. You kill a gook, there was nothing to it. American gets killed and he's laying in the bush or the streets of Saigon, he's sitting there with his head blown off and you felt sympathy. You said, "Hey, look, where's the medics? Why don't they come and get this guy out of here? Don't let the guy lay in the streets of Saigon, and just blow open and let the flies and maggots get to him." The guys would get pissed and demand the company commander to get the man out. We would call in on the radio to the slicks* to remove our wounded regardless of where we were at or what color that man was. Because we knew that he was a real person. A gook laid out there in the Saigon River for two weeks, but it was nothing for me to pull those corpses out of there.

* * *

I remember the first guys I saw killed. We were providing security for Army engineers on an island formed where two rivers split apart. The island was an R&R resort for the VC. The engineers were bulldozing it flat, making the whole place into a big parking lot to deny the VC that area. We'd go on sweeps and they would follow us in with the bulldozers. I was weapons platoon commander which meant I just sort of tagged along with the CO. It was all horseshit.

We were walking along and there was an explosion, we got popped. Then just dead silence.

"Corpsman up!" I was right next to the corpsman, so I went running with him. There was a guy up the trail who had been hit and a guy right next to us. The man closer to us was writhing on the ground, his back arching up. He was gasping, hoarse, dragging air into his lungs. There was a perfect round hole about the size of a pencil, right in the middle of his sternum.

Then he just stopped moving. The corpsman started giving him mouth-to-mouth resuscitation and I was giving him heart massage. No response. So the doc gave him a tracheotomy, opened his throat and stuck in a black tube. I started breathing through that and the corpsman gave him heart massage and we switched off.

We did it for about five minutes to no avail. The kid was gone, dead. Except for that little hole, there was no blood—just that little hole in his chest.

I looked at him—blond, All-American, crewcut with these pale ice-blue eyes. I stood up and looked back into those eyes. Those eyes looked right through me, right through my skull and out the back of my head. I turned around and looked at the sky in the direction that his eyes were looking to see what he was staring at. I thought I was going to see something.

It ran through my mind for a moment, "Did his mother feel something, did his father feel something, did anybody? Was she reaching for a can of peas in the supermarket and feel a tug or a jolt and not know what it was? Does anybody close to him know that he just died?"

We're out in the middle of the boondocks. There isn't shit out here. We are in Nowhere's land. Some green-brown, oblivious place that looks like shit and feels like shit. And this guy is gone.

Just sticking out of the pocket of his flak jacket was a box of Hav-a-Tampa cigars. You know, they got those wooden tips on them. To this day, I cannot go near Hav-a-Tampa, don't want to be around a cigar. It gives me the willies.

I ran up the trail to the other casualty. It was weird. The front of his head must have been six inches extended in front of the natural line of the forehead. Everything that the other guy was, this one was the opposite—a bloody mess. I couldn't believe a human being could bleed that much. Just shallow breathing. He took a round right in the skull. He was gone and you knew it. The corpsman was covered with blood. There weren't enough bandages in the world to catch all the blood that was coming out of this guy. He died in the chopper on his way out.

*   *   *

In my first fire fight, a woman walked by us and she was nodding. Normally that far up north, nobody walked past. We know all of them are Viet Cong. That day the guys just wanted a fire fight, because they let her go by. I pipe up, "I thought we weren't supposed to do that. Ain't we supposed to take them prisoner or shoot them or something?"

"Don't worry about it," they said. "But take your

weapons off safety. We're going into that tree line shaped like a horseshoe." Everybody flipped off his safety.

"That's an ambush area," I said. "Even I know that. They show you that in the books. What the hell are you guys doing?"

"Just don't worry about it," was the answer. I just knew they were going to get me killed. They were walking right into it. They hadn't had a fire fight in a while and they wanted the excitement.

The shit broke. I'm jumping behind a dike in a rice paddy. I'm firing. All of a sudden this broad peeks her head up with a big smile on it. Something told me that she had to pay. I capped her. That was my first confirmed kill.

Now, I was blaming her. It took me a long time to realize that the "blame" laid on the guys I was with. They made a conscious decision to get into that fight. The ambush had been telegraphed. If we didn't hit these gooks now, they could attack somebody else later when our guys weren't prepared for it. We got a chance to get our weapons off safety. Mentally and physically we were up. The adrenaline had already started pumping.

When it hit, I was firing, rolling with the machine gun going off. I had learned to fire in bursts of only three. I had to learn to fire only three shots at a time so the enemy at a little distance couldn't tell who had the M-60. They would gear their fire on me otherwise. They wanted the machine gun out of the way.

We were moving steady. My assistant gunner said, "Left eleven o'clock." He made me practice to respond to his voice commands. All he had to do was find my targets. I would gear on them. We were running it and hitting it. He says, "Run it!" and we would run. "Okay, down!" I'm down and then I'm up again. He was just hollering commands. "Ammo up!" The first squad had to do *whatever* they had to do to get a couple of hundred rounds to me, whatever amount I needed. It's up to my a-gunner* to keep up with the situation. He would actually clip the ammo belts on to the gun.

When I got down to between fifty and seventy-five rounds, he's supposed to clip another 100 rounds on to me. Plus he kept the ammo out of the mud. We moved all the way in like that, hitting and running.

I made my very first mistake, which almost cost me my life. A couple of them had run into this little straw hooch. I hit the ground and was tearing them up—rat-ta-tat-tat, chopping them to pieces. I hear, "Get up, get up!" My a-gunner has got up and moved behind one of their little grave mounds. The snipers were setting for me once they found out where the M-60 was. The dirt was popping up.

I'm thinking, "I ain't ever going to make it out of here." All of a sudden my gun got heavy. Before that, my machine gun hadn't weighed a thing. My ammo was heavy. I was out of breath. I got so close to dying, it just drained me. Everything was gone. I can't hold this shit up. But I jumped and I ran behind the mound.

The M-79* man came over and said, "Well, I think I spotted them." We called in the 80 Mike-Mikes*— mortars—because we wanted to walk the tree line with them. We planned on pulling out. They called in the position on the radio. The M-79 man sent in one Willie Peter—white phosphorus—with his grenade launcher. Then the mortars sent in one White. When their Willie P. went off in the right place, the sergeant said, "Okay, fire for effect." They walked it in. Each time they walked it, they were going to bring it closer to our position. It was up to us to get out of that closing circle. The mortars would keep the gooks on the run and we would sneak out behind it.

So we ran and we ran and we ran. Then all of a sudden, we heard capping by us—Cap-cap. Cap-cap. We turned around. That whole squad almost got killed by me. As I spun around, I saw a little spark coming out of the trees. I opened that M-60 up and just ran it back and forth, spraying. Everybody behind me had to hit the ground, lying flat. I was firing thinking, "Damn these fools. These suckers ain't getting me." I would have shot all of them, even my own men, if they had stood up

in front of me. I didn't care, and they knew it. I was just
damned scared.

"Okay, come on." And we started running some
more.

We got back. We was all out of breath. The first thing
they did was, they started laughing. I'm looking at these
nuts and then I'm laughing with them. That's when you
find out that laughing at death is laughing that you
made it alive. You faced it, dealt with it and survived.
All of a sudden, it's a joke.

"Well, ol' Jim is pretty good."

"Yeah? How'd he do in his first fire fight?"

"Well, the sucker likes to stand up and run around."

*   *   *

My first encounter with death was a booby trap. I was
the point man and had passed through the area. A bomb
was in the ground with wires leading to two VC, sitting
in a hole about a hundred yards away, just waiting until
the main part of the column got there. Then they stuck
two wires to an eight-volt battery and eleven men were
blown up. We were walking along and suddenly there
was instant death.

That first time was not horrible. It was shocking in
that there were these men, that I knew and really cared
about, dead—blown up. I was angry. Angered because
we didn't have a chance to fight back. We just got
blown up.

Our colonel flew out and he jumped from the helicopter. I was standing by the wounded when he walked
over to us. He had this angry look on his face. He had
looked out for us and was good about taking care of his
men. The medic was putting a patch over a GI's eye.
The colonel said, "How are you, son?" And the kid
looked up at him and said, "I'm all right, sir. I think I
just lost my eye."

"We're proud of you and your country is proud of
you," the colonel told him. He was as helpless as we
were.

We went into the jungle totally different from that moment on. We walked in there looking to kill, looking to get back for what had been done to us.

We could not fire during those first years. We had to get permission. Being on point coming out of a jungle area, I saw five guys running in a rice paddy with guns. The initial reaction is to shoot. But then our orders say you can't shoot unless you get permission. I'm yelling at the lieutenant who's on the radio. He calls headquarters. They tell him to wait because they had to call S2*—their intelligence. S2 has to call G3* at the command. Meanwhile, we have to watch them run without being able to do anything about it. We knew that they were the ones that had done it—blown the booby trap.

We changed a lot. The change was individual. It was silence. It was reserve. The anger came from within, for seeing the guys blown up. The unspoken words behind the anger were, "You fucking bastards, you're going to get it now. Let me find one of you and you're going to die just like they died. I'm going to blow your fucking brains out." We went into the jungle angry and silent and very determined to do what we were trained to do—which was to kill.

About three days later, we stopped asking permission to fire. On an operation, if we saw and killed VC without authorization, we would shoot up our radio before we got back to camp. We'd say that we got into a confrontation and we couldn't ask for permission. We were beginning to see what the war was all about.

*　　*　　*

I didn't know shit about Vietnam or war. I thought, "Nah, they must send grown-up guys to do that. They don't send asshole kids like me." But there I was with the rest of the asshole kids, having a ball. Making do with a bad situation is what it was all about. Making do with nothing, on our own. You get young kids, throw them into general chaos, they make do with it. You get stable right away, or you don't make it at all.

It was like the fantasy life of a kid. I'd played cops and robbers as a kid, so when I saw what was happening in Nam, I really wanted to cash in on it. Why not? It was like being invited to play with the big kids.

They always called us men, Marines or troopers. Never boys. But during my first fire fight in Nam, I was giggling. We got pinned down by some VC with an automatic weapon. Our machine gunner opens up. The next thing I hear is, "Oh boy, I got 'em. Man, did you see his fucking head fly off?" A kid'll do that. Nobody in the unit was over twenty-one.

You try to have fun with things. Ambush was fun. It's supposed to be professional, but it's not.

"Oh boy, here he comes. I got that one."

"This one is mine."

"Nah, I got this one. You got the last one."

"Man, this one's for me. Get your own."

"He's mine."

"Is not."

"Is too."

"Is not."

I loved flying in helicopters because you went fast. It's power, like having a Corvette. I got to do something I'd wanted to do since I was a kid, which was touch clouds. When we went up high and there were clouds around, I'd dangle out the door and try to grab them, just to say I did it. Plus I seen the end of a rainbow and found out why you can't get the pot of gold at the end of it. 'Cause as you move toward it, the rainbow jumps away. For a while I thought seeing that was what kept me alive. But the guy I was with got killed and he seen the end of the rainbow, too.

I was one of those jokers who would stick a helmet up on a rifle when we had a sniper homing in on people. Anything to break up the monotony. I would run through a barrage of fire and clam up next to another Marine who was hiding behind a pagoda, right? I'm chewing bubble gum and blowing bubbles. I look him in the eye and I say, "This your first time, kid?" There's this six-foot monster staring at a little city kid with all this shit on his back. "This your first time? You get used to it." Of course, it was my first time, too. But I had a sense of humor.

I had a yo-yo. I'd be hanging out, or even if we were on a long walk and I felt good, I'd take it out and start doing Walk the Dog, Over the Falls, 'Round the World, just yo-yoing. One day I was playing with it and the captain says, "Give me that fucking thing. What the fuck do you think you're doing?" He grabbed it out of my hand and threw it into the jungle. "This ain't no time to play here. You're a fucking Marine. Act like one."

I'm chewing gum, looking at everybody else, just scratching my head. Well, what the fuck is *he* talking about? So I just mosey on down the line.

It was one of the few times I seen this guy off his rockers. What it did was throw him off. He don't like to believe that he's out there with kids. He's been told he's got men. He treats us like men. We're Marines. But when it comes down to the nitty-gritty, he realized that he was dealing with kids. It helped them to win the war, but it flipped out a lot of officers.

We had one officer—a good one—who just leaped up in the middle of a fire fight and said, "It's just kids and they're all fucking dying. Just kids, kids, kids." They had to take him away.

Use kids to fight a war—if you're going to use anybody. They're the best. They're still learning. They can hump the hills. They can take it. And they don't take it personal.

Thank God for your eighteen-year-old. Politics is not why he's there, the whole right and wrong thing. For us, it was like on the streets back home in Brooklyn: I know you for a long time, and me and you are walking down the avenue, right? You run into somebody, I don't know him. You come out in his face and you say something stupid to him. He smacks you and you deserve it. I still got to jump on him though, because you're my friend. I don't care if you deserved it or not. That's the type of predicament it was.

I was a grunt radioman. So I used to hang back with

the CO and keep squads together. I got to watch the whole war with my eyes. I loved to just sit in the ditch and watch people die. As bad as that sounds, I just liked to *watch* no matter what happened, sitting back with my homemade cup of hot chocolate. It was like a big movie.

Seeing guys get blown away, it didn't freak me out. You feel bad—"Aw, they got Zamallo" or "They wasted Baird." But what mostly goes through your mind is, "Jesus, I hope I don't have a big chunk of metal rip my head like that."

Watching guys die is a drag, but there's a weird educational side to war, too. Like the first time I seen a guy's guts laying on top of him, as disgusting as it was, I said to myself, "Oh, wow. So that's what they look like." If you want, you can go in there and help yourself to a handful, you can wash them off and keep them. You can perform major surgery, right there.

The whole world gets absurd after a while. You do things that seem not right now, but which seemed right at the time. I used to love to go over to guys who would catch rounds in the chest or the guts and pretend I was a doctor. You had the license to do whatever you wanted. I'd go over there and I'd take my hand and I'd stick it inside their guts, pick it up, wash it off or do the old chest routine. I would sort of experiment. You know, I couldn't do nothing to hurt these guys, they were dead. But there was something about sticking my hands in warm blood that I used to love especially during the monsoon seasons.

Here you are with bodies going up all around you, so if you're going to do something absurd, do it and don't worry about it. That's something that I think everybody was doing there. I can actually say I never felt bad about anything I did in Nam, except for doing something like that once in a while. Or getting the pleasure out of it.

If someone you're close to dies, you feel the pain in your heart, naturally. But the attitude you pick up quick is, "Oh, shit. Dime a dozen. Travel light and carry a heavy bag." A heavy bag was a bag of dope.

It's hard to believe, but I didn't have a care in the

world while I was in Nam. I'd get up in the morning all covered with mud, look up in the sky with the rain splashing in my face and just smile. "I'm alive." The only worry you had was dying, and if that happened you wouldn't know it anyway. So what the fuck.

You know what scared me in Nam? We had a guy die from an act of God. He was swimming on vacation and he drowned. I had forgotten that you still had to contend with God, too. I didn't have it figured in the plot. That scared the shit out of me.

II

OPERATIONS

GRUNTS

It was a job. Most of the work was boring menial labor. GIs were ditchdiggers, pack animals and file clerks, slogging through a swamp of their own cold sweat. What little enthusiasm they brought to the task quickly oozed away, with nothing to replace it but the instinct to survive. The only diversion was the possibility of getting killed. "I'd pray for a fire fight, just so we could stop walking for a little while."

Adrenaline junkies, zombied out on fear, working the assembly line on the nod, they shuffled about the business of the war factory. Anxiety, even death, gets to be routine. They made a life of trying to endure.

"War is not killing. Killing is the easiest part of the whole thing. Sweating twenty-four hours a day, seeing guys drop all around you of heatstroke, not having food, not having water, sleeping only three hours a night for weeks at a time, that's what war is. Survival."

Home was very far away, even farther in mind than in miles. The longer they labored for the American Dream, the more they resented the management. Broken ideals, unattended, began to knit together in a hard cynicism.

"I remember July 20, 1969. I sat in my hooch and watched satellite relay after-the-fact footage of the astronauts landing on the moon and Neil Armstrong's first step on the surface. When I heard that fucking-bullshit nonsense phrase, 'One small step for man, a giant leap for mankind,' I was so angry. I thought to myself, 'Come here and step with me for a day, mother-fucker.'"

It'd get daylight. You get water out of a shell hole and throw your halazone tablets in there so you could brush your teeth. We were pretty ragged. but you sweat yourself clean every day. Then you pull out a piece of C4*—plastic explosive—and light it up to heat your food.

I get out the map. Okay, we've got to go up the blue line, which would be a river. We'd walk down the side of the mountain into the valley. It was harder walking down mountains than walking up.

There were scout snipers with us, so I would use the scope on one of their rifles to check out where we were going. You could see the veins on leaves with those things. I'd send out the flanks for protection of the main body, so we couldn't be ambushed from the sides. It was tough on the flanks, because they had to hack through the bush. The rest of us would be walking down by the river bank, so we had to wait up for the guys out there on either side from time to time.

You'd hump your God damn brains out, up hills, over rocks, through water. Sometimes it was hand over hand through the roots of trees. You sweat your balls off with the sun beating down on your head.

Ninety percent of the time, nothing happened, just boring, a walk in the sun, like sight-seeing. But you're always aware that you could get blown away. You always protect yourself tactically to make sure your ass is covered. Just the dispersion of your people insures that you can put down suppressing fire.

You're hunting the smartest animal there is and that's a human being. You can't believe how fucking smart a man is. If you get one, it's blind luck. In the entire time I was over there, we got one confirmed kill on a day patrol out of battalion. It's their show, you're in their backyard.

Hump through the paddies and into the villes. A ville would just be a few bamboo hooches with dirt floors in a little clearing. Each one had a little shrine inside. There would always be cooking. Their diet was very hot, fish heads and peppers, that type of thing. You never saw any men or even teen-agers, just small children, women and old men.

They pray to their Buddha, go out to work the paddy. Come home, go to sleep. A very simple life. A water buffalo was the family car.

"Honcho, hey honcho," the kids come running out of the ville. "Cigmo, you got cigmo, Joe? Chop-chop, you got chop-chop?"

You tell them, "*Didi, didi mao*." Get the fuck away. They'd swear up and down at you. The war had been going on so long there that these kids never had a childhood. You'd be in a fire fight in the middle of a paddy someplace and they would just go right on about their business—a woman and her son with a bucket tied to a rope whipping water over a dike from one paddy to another, old women humping what looked like 150 pounds of brush across their backs.

Westmoreland used to make me crazy with all that bullshit about winning the hearts and minds of the people. Sometimes you felt like trash walking through these villes. Some of the people were beautiful, aristocratic, more civilized than you ever thought of being. They'd come up to you and say, "America and Americans are No. 1. Vietnam is No. 10.* You got girl friend? You should be with her. We don't want you here." Who was it that wanted us there?

Sometimes it was beautiful. We were in a bamboo forest and came upon an old Buddhist temple with vines climbing all over it, big Buddhas, brightly colored with reverse swastikas and leaf designs. It felt like being the first explorer to walk into the ruins of Angkor Wat. The monks came out to meet me. I set out some security and made everybody entering the compound take off their weapons. I knew we weren't going to get any trouble from them. They were very educated men, very holy men.

I was constantly fatigued. The killing part is easy but you're just so fucking tired all the fucking time. Your strength is zapped out of your body by the heat. Waiting in a column going down a hill, you go to sleep leaning against a tree. Every day you're out on patrol. Intelligence says they're out there, so here you go walking around in little geometric triangles. Go to this checkpoint, go to that checkpoint, go here, go there. Day in, day out, day in, day out. You get into a mind-numbing routine and before long you're a fucking zombie.

Humans are out there watching you. They know where you're going before you even get there. You see them running very far away in their straw hats and black outfits.

We had a constant attrition from booby traps, seven out of ten casualties a month were traumatic amputees. On a sweep you all get in a long line and walk in. You're watching every place you step wondering who's going to hit it. You know someone is going to. Sweep and sweep and sweep, halfway through the day and nothing's happened. Are we going to hit a booby trap today? Who will it be? It was mentally draining.

Boom! Just like that and a guy is missing a leg, somebody is missing a foot. Everything stops for a second and there's a lot of action on the radio. A chopper comes down to pick him up. *Zoom*, he's gone. I thought, "Boy, there's going to be a lot of people walking around after this war with no feet." But I still haven't seen them. Where are they?

Then you're back at it again, hunting humans. I hope one shows up, man. I'm going to blow that motherfucker to kingdom come. If the world could only see me now. This is bad news out here and I am bad. We are armed to the teeth. If I could get back to the States with my platoon intact, I could take over the world. Somebody fuck with me, just somebody fuck with me. Come and get me.

When they came to get you—holy shit. I can't even talk on the radio to call in the fire mission. I'm warbling like a kid going through puberty. You swallow slowly and force yourself to say the coordinates. Everything hits slow motion, like you're in your own movie. You try to be cool, calm and collected, and you are . . . kind of. You certainly ain't John Wayne.

Where's it coming from? Who's getting hit? I don't want to die. You can see everything that's happening in immediate terms—life-and-death terms.

When something went right in a fire fight—you call in a fire mission real good, you get your fields of fire right, deploy your men so that you outflank them and you stand up and walk right through them—it's thrilling. There's nothing like it. It's so real. Talk about getting high, this is beyond drugs—ultrareality.

There's nothing like a confirmed kill either. They make you crazy. You want more. You know everybody back at battalion will look at you with envy when you get back in. You scored a touchdown in front of the hometown fans. You get a lot of respect from your peers who are all doing the same thing. When somebody else got one, you'd go, "Son of a bitch, the lucky bastards. Why couldn't we have been there?"

All of a sudden that's over with. It's something everybody talks about to mark the days. A point of reference. You tell the new guys about it. "Hey, remember the day that motherfucker, Jay-Jay, jumped up in the middle of that fire fight, man?" Then you go back to the mind-numbing routine. You're a zombie again. Take a walk in the boonies.

It starts getting dark, you occupy the high ground. You set up the perimeter, send out the LPs—guys on watch called listening posts. No big deal. I was always near the radio, nothing much happened anyway.

But then the sun would go down and I could feel my stomach sinking. There goes the light. There goes one of your senses, the most important one. Life stops. There's no electricity. There's no technology. It's just hovels made out of corrugated tin and Coke boxes, cardboard, sticks, thatch. There's nothing else over there. The only technology you have is death: M-16s—black plastic rifles—grenades, pocket bombs, Claymores, M-79s, M-60s, mortars, jungle utilities, flak jackets, jungle boots, C4, radios and jet planes to drop the napalm. That was the only technology happening.

You think about people back in the world walking around downtown, going out to get a beer. You'd be staring into the dark so hard, you'd have to reach up and touch your eyes to make sure they were still open.

You try to sleep out there on operations. I'd take off my helmet and my flak jacket and arrange the plates in the jacket just right to fit my back. Then I'd tip my helmet and get my head just right in the webbing. I never went anywhere without my lucky green towel. I'd wrap it around my face with just a little hole for my nose. Put on my long sleeve utilities, tuck my hands up under my armpits and just listen to the mosquitoes whine all night long. You know one is going to fly right up your nose and suck the blood out of your brain. It was miserable.

You know it's going to be the same tomorrow as it was today . . . only maybe it might be worse. It won't be any better. We had a saying about how bad a thing could be: As bad as a day in the Nam.

* * *

The Central Highlands is called the Highlands because there's nothing but fucking mountains everywhere. All we did was hump the mountains. My ass was kicked. We're walking up and down these hills. It must be 103 degrees and I'm dying. The heat beats you. The jungle is humid. Although I had a hard time keeping up,

I kept up. But every time they took a break, I'd collapse. I didn't drink a whole lot of my water. I threw it over myself to cool off. I was in bad shape from humping.

Every day we'd hump rucksacks that weighed over a hundred pounds. There were only two people in my company who could put on a rucksack standing up. You took them off when you were facing a tree. That way when you put them back on, you were sitting on the ground, you put your arms in and you could grab the tree to get yourself off the ground. We humped these things every day, four, five, six, seven klicks.*

In the late afternoon, we'd always pull a night logger position on the highest hill within the area—for security reasons. You hump all day—which is killing you—then at three or four in the afternoon, you get to hill 600 or 604 or 723 and you hump the biggest hill when you're already exhausted. The hills were steep. Many times the person in front of me going up the hill, his feet would be where my face was.

When you made it to the top of the hill, the company was moving into a perimeter, a circle. Areas of responsibility are marked off for different platoons. All the units hook up to complete the circle with no break. Then we move in and we stomp all the jungle down in the center so they can bring choppers in for resupply—water, food, ammo.

By then it's two or three hours till dark. We had to dig in. The hole had to be big enough for three or four people in width and what we call titty deep. The soil in the Highlands is so resistant to agriculture that we also had to hump axes, picks, shovels, regular carpentry tools. A pick swing would sink into the soil maybe three inches. So the first person up on the top would start the shape on the ground for the hole, just start picking and pick out a couple inches of dirt. Then you clear it with a D-handle shovel, put it in a pile. Each man carried twenty-five empty sandbags. You fill them with the dirt from the hole.

While one person is picking, other people go down the hill and cut overhead. The trees we cut down were four or five inches thick. We chopped them down with a machete. It was an absolute bitch with a machete. It was just as efficient as digging a hole three inches at a time. The handles break off the machetes all the time and you have to wrap towels around them or tear up your hands.

What's eventually done is you dig a hole that is titty deep. You fill up 100 sandbags. You build up the sides around the hole with the sandbags. Cut overhead, put the overhead on top of the rim of sandbags, then put more sandbags on top of that, in case of mortar attack.

It didn't change day to day. You get up. The first thing you do is pull down your overhead. Kick the overhead into the hole. Empty your sandbags to fill up the hole. Then you leave and you hump all day long.

What's really strange is that I got credits for humping my own rucksack every day, because a lot of people couldn't even manage that. They would break down at the last hill, they'd be so beat. The new guys would always fall out at the bottom.

I was an FNG, but I never fell out. I'd keep up. They'd always be saying, "Step it up. Keep up, keep up." I'd see people who dropped out from other platoons. Out of it, lying by the side of the trail, sweating, rucksack off. What the procedure was normally, the lieutenants and sergeants would try to physically coerce the stragglers into humping their rucksacks. "You pussy, you fucking son of a bitch." Sometimes they would slap them or kick them. It wasn't strong physical abuse. It was mostly calling them names. "You piece of shit, you can't hump that little rucksack up this hill? Look at the rest of these guys. They're making it." They kicked them when they were down.

Whether it was happening to you or not, you could see it happening to these other people and it was very ugly. No one particularly liked to do it, but for some reason there seemed to be a certain sense of responsibility, almost like team spirit, of making someone conform and hump their rucksack.

Nonetheless, I found it frightening, because I knew that I was a marginal case. That could be me on the ground. It never was, but I was barely hanging on by my fingertips.

You see them abused, cursed at and kicked. Then they take away their weapons and leave them. Before dark, they would come up, half an hour, sometimes a couple of hours later. You knew that you got no break. If you couldn't cut something, nobody took anything into consideration. A dog-eat-dog environment. They didn't give a fuck.

The people that humped well looked like they were ready to have a heart attack when they were done humping. You look at a guy who has humped up a hill and he looks like he just jumped into a swimming pool and jumped back out. He was that salty and wet from the sweat. You could hardly pick up your feet at the end of the day. It doesn't get any better.

*   *   *

I had jungle rot so bad on my hands that the only way I could carry my rifle was to cradle it in the bend in my elbows with my hands up in front of my face. I couldn't hold on to it my hands were so sore and burning. My feet were like that, too.

*   *   *

You were sitting on the side of some nasty red hill, loaded down with mud. You're practically nude and you got your hair filthy with dirt and grease and sweat and twigs. You ain't washed it in months. Here's some guy combing your hair and trimming it, because he wants to practice being a barber for when he gets out of Vietnam.

*   *   *

It became a ritual that I did the exact same way every time. When I'm getting dressed, I always started with my left foot. Put a sock on my left foot, put a sock on my right foot. Then I'd put my left boot on, then I'd put

my right boot on. I couldn't tie the laces on my left boot
before I got my right boot on. I don't know where I
picked up that green towel. It was a useful thing. You
used that towel all the time. I'd hang it around my neck
and tuck it down into my flak jacket. It became lucky.
My lucky green towel. If I didn't have it, I wasn't comfortable. I felt naked. I felt vulnerable. But when it was
around my neck, it was like an invisible protective
shield. Everything was complete and I was ready to go
and meet whatever I had to meet. It was good to touch,
too. Maybe it was that if I died I'd make a good-looking
corpse with the lucky green towel around my neck.

I carried a plastic white spoon in the big pocket on the
right side of my jungle utilities. In there I had my map
and I also had a picture of Raquel Welch from the neck
to the thigh, wearing a suede bikini. I'd take it out and
look at it. I liked looking at her body. It was something
to take out and touch home base. There was a woman's
body that I could look at. It felt good. She was cut off at
the neck, but there were those curves. I used to carry a
frag* in the lefthand pocket of my flak jacket. I never
used it, but it was always there.

*   *   *

You know how you stop the shits? You eat the peanut
butter in the C-rations. You wouldn't shit again until
you had the grape juice. Drink the grape juice, you shit
your brains out. Between the grape juice and the peanut
butter, you were regular.

*   *   *

In the mornings in the Nam, when you wake up, you
always see the sun coming up. It's really beautiful, but
it's cool then and that's when you really want to sleep.

You come down off the hill and there's big rice paddies all around the bottom of the hill. Maybe 10 percent
of the company gets across them to the far tree line and
somebody opens up on us.

I'm running and running and running. I'm getting

dinged at over and over again. Guys are falling, not from getting hit so much as sliding in the mud. It must last at least five minutes. That's a long time to be running with all that shit strapped to you.

I turn around and say, "Jesus Christ, man, cut it the fuck out."

Crack, crack, crack. And you're helpless. A guy gets wounded and you don't hardly want to pick the poor fucker up, because you can't make it across the field yourself. But you do pick him up.

You got a base fire set on the sniper, artillery goes on the son of a bitch and he's still dinging at you, the cocksucker. You're so tired that you just want to lay down in the rice paddy. The only reason you didn't was because most of the guys got off their fucking ass and kept moving. If they had laid down, I probably would have too.

*   *   *

There was no reveille. Everybody kind of got up around sunrise. You get cleaned up, wash your face, maybe shave. Then drift on over to the mess hall. Sit around there and wait to go in. Have some coffee and whatever you could stand to eat that come out of a can.

We'd come back to the area. The first thing that I would do is take care of my weapons—go clean the guns up. In the morning it was always pretty slack.

The Vietnamese would start coming in about 10 A.M. to the corpsman's tent. Guys would goof around with the young girls. Kid around with them and sell them Cokes. We'd buy vegetables from them or dress their wound or give them Band-Aids or aspirin or sell them a soda pop. Some ARVNs would come around with their jeep and sell us what was supposed to be a twenty-five-pound block of ice for a dollar a pound. It always had a hole in the middle of it.

A guy comes up from the village and says, "I'm the barber from the village and I'd like to come up here and set up a little stand and cut everybody's hair." The gunny and the cap think that's great. "Oh boy, we're going to get haircuts, so everybody's going to be disciplined again." So the barber comes up with a little straight chair and everybody lines up for haircuts. It's twenty piasters or something like that.

None of the guys went that much to noon chow because it started getting real hot. About 1 P.M., we'd send out a recon patrol. You get your troops up, you inspect the weapons, get everybody dressed. You get your squad leaders together and look at your maps. You make sure everybody's got ammo. You grab the corpsman; you got him going. You got your radio operator. You run your radio check. Out through the wire and away you go.

"Let's go check the whorehouse and see if we catch anybody over there." We'd go over there and we'd check that out.

"Oh God, Sarge, I really got to have some of that."

"Aw, go on. We're going to camp over here and eat anyway. Bring us back a couple of cold beers." That was your day.

Then you come back and everybody is sitting around playing pinochle. You post your security watches. You got your duty roster all set up. Everybody knows who's going to relieve who. "Keep the Beer out of the Bunkers," like the sign says. Guy sits out there drinking beer at night, he passes out and somebody come through your wire and people will get killed.

You didn't fight them. You had to wait for them to want to fight you. Then you had to just protect your butt. They could get you, but you couldn't move on them conventionally. You had to say, "Well, I'm stationed here. It's like a duty assignment back in the States. Can't sweat it. Stay calm."

Every time you got a full moon, you got a big order down, "Expect to be hit tonight, because the VC have the light of the full moon." They wouldn't hit us. If there was not any moon, a big order comes down, "They're going to hit you." And we wouldn't be hit. "There's no clouds tonight, you're going to be hit." No hit. "It's raining tonight, you won't be hit." And we'd be hit. Every night you're going to be hit and they always got a reason for it.

The first month or two, everybody is trigger-happy at night. Everybody. The guy looks in the wire and sees an old C-ration box. The breeze hits it just right and it flaps. He pops three rounds at it. Another guy across the compound, he pops three rounds out of his bunker. All of a sudden, the machine gunner down there, he decides, "Hell, I been sitting here for two weeks and ain't even pulled the trigger." So he pulls the trigger. Then you got fire direction control calling for illumination from the One-Oh-Five * battery. Man, you got a full-scale fire fight going and there ain't nothing out there. All you did was shoot a bunch of old Vietnamese houses and scare the hell out of the population.

Or you sit there at night with the infrared scope from a scout sniper's rifle and watch a Charlie come through four rolls of concertina wire. He started just about ten o'clock and he didn't get through the last strand of concertina wire until almost four o'clock in the morning. It took him six hours and we had every kind of possible trip wire you could think of inside there, along with mines, finger charges* and Claymores. He come through and then we shot him.

You go out there to take him off the wire next morning, and it turns out to be the barber who's been shaving you with a straight razor for the last two months.

We might go out two weeks straight and never fire a shot, never even see anything. Then, that night, we have some sappers* try to come through the wire. Or there might be a village of ten or fifteen families that you walk through for weeks. All of a sudden, "It's a known VC village. Go in and burn it." Our artillery went two and a half months one time without firing a round except for H&I. *

The combat stories are common to any war. In a fire fight you got twenty guys over there shooting at you and you got twenty or thirty guys over here, shooting back at them. We'll call in artillery fire. They're calling in mortar fire. Somebody decides, "Okay, I've had enough." Then that's over. But there was no ground taken. Nobody won anything or moved their lines.

For a while there, all the action was with the South Vietnamese troops. I sat there on a hill watching the South Vietnamese Air Force swooping the South Vietnamese Army, because two generals got mad at each other. How would you like to read in an American newspaper that the United States Air Force bombed Ft. Bragg, North Carolina, because General Jones and General Smith had words. President Carter is intervening, but the present government is weak. The generals are strong, they have airplanes and guns. That's the way it went.

I came back on emergency leave. I'm sitting there at the funeral in my dress blues. Some woman looks up at me and she says, "I understand you're back from Vietnam."

"Yes, ma'am, I am."

"Oh, but you're not where the fighting is."

"Yes, ma'am, I am." She was shocked that I was in the fighting. But you're not up there all the time. You don't get up in the morning and say, "Okay, let's get the fire fight going. Okay, it's five o'clock. Let's stop the fire fight now and go get some sleep."

It comes and it goes. You got your standard duties to attend to in the meantime. It's just a bunch of guys trying to make the best of things.

*   *   *

Most of the patrolling we did was on the other side of what was called Booby Trap Alley. We had to go through it all the time. It was about four or five miles long. You knew that considering the time it took you to get through there, you would have to stop somewhere to rest. We had lessons on how you stop and rest in Booby Trap Alley. Or anywhere else for that matter.

Before you sit down you take out your K-bar,* or your bayonet. Where you know that you are going to sit down, you go real slow and dig into the ground, probing all the way around as big as your butt, or bigger if you intend to lean back. Most of the time you would find something. You didn't tamper with it. You just find another spot to sit down. Once you did that you felt fairly safe, but there was no guarantee. Some guys just said to hell with it and flopped down and leaned back—went for broke.

There was a lot of tedious nonsense you had to put up with around there. There was a knack to doing everything at a slow pace. You had to learn patience. You wind up learning.

Bouncing Betty was bad. A Bouncing Betty is a land mine. You step on a spring here and Bouncing Betty come up somewhere else over there. She would jump up about four or five feet and then she blows, spraying down and out. When she goes off, about the only thing you can do is try to get under it. Dive, hit the ground and lie flat as tight as you can. If you're close enough, it will miss you or you may just get a little piece of shrapnel here or there, something you could live with. Problem is, it's always someone else who sets Betty off on you. You can be as careful as you want, but if some asshole goes skipping down the trail, he may pop Bouncing Betty on you.

There were a lot of those punji sticks, swing limbs and little spring-detonated bombs in old C-ration cans. That's why I didn't like that area. I could deal with a man. That meant my talent against his for survival, but how do you deal with him when he ain't even there. Some guys wound up being better with the booby traps than they were with one on one.

*　　*　　*

There was such a scary thing about going out to the bush, like jumping into a cold ocean. You hit the LZ and it's hot. That door opens up and you run out screaming. There's little rocket ships whizzing through the air. You feel you can stick out your hand and catch a round. I could have beat Bob Hayes in a foot race with all my gear. I could have hidden behind a pack of

Camels, with no part of me protruding. That's got to be the hairiest thing in the world. Adrenaline for days.

*   *   *

My friends over there gave me a medal for digging a hole with my bare hands and walking across water. I was known as a definite survivor. I didn't chase Charlie that far after I left the helicopter. I didn't. I'm sorry, but I have to tell the truth. One of the first things you realized when you got to Nam was that you weren't going to win this war. There was no way we could win doing what we were doing. After the first month, me and everybody else over there said, "I'm going to put in my twelve months and then I'm getting the fuck out of here. It's not worth it."

*   *   *

Going out the gate. Locking and loading the weapons. Making the Sign of the Cross. It gives you goose bumps. Trip wire and bamboo are set up so no one can come running straight in at you. Only one man can go out at a time. The rest keep down. He gets to where you can barely see him, then the next guy goes out. You use rudimentary hand signals to maintain contact.

It was Hutchinson's first action. Just as we're going out he says, "Oh, I think I'm sick." Splat! He spit up. We didn't think too much of that shit. It was more like butterflies before a big football game. I knew he wasn't sick. He knew he wasn't sick. The whole fucking world knew he wasn't sick. But he got out of going that time. I told him, "Okay, go check yourself in. Go see the corpsman and get yourself squared away."

*   *   *

I had this real close friend, name of Bobby. He was over there for eighteen months. He had extended because he had MP duty in Phu Bai and was getting all the pussy he wanted and everything like that there. They promised him that he would have had an easy job, so he went ahead and signed up again. Then they stuck him back with the grunts. That's how we got to know one another.

We wore old camouflage helmets with a piece of rubber tube hanging around the bottom of it for you to stick your matches and your bug juice in there. Bobby had a scalp hanging off his helmet. So when you saw him from the back, it looked like he had real long hair. He'd always have a frown on his face, and he was always talking about riding motorcycles, riding motorcycles. "When I get back home, I'm going to buy me a big ol' Harley and I'm going to *ride*."

That fucking day he got blowed away, Bobby and I had been arguing about who was walking point. We was going out on a night ambush just 'fore dark and we was both up front. I said, "I'll walk fucking point."

"Naw," he said, "I'm walking point." He had a brand-new pair of utilities on. He had his rifle all cleaned up and his boots were all nice-looking.

"Where the fuck you get them utilities at?"

"I saved them," he said. "I saved them for a special occasion."

"Special occasion, my ass."

"Yeah, the occasion is I'm going to walk point tonight."

"No, man, it's my turn. You walked it yesterday. I'm walking it now."

"Naw, I got it."

"Okay, you can have it." He pissed me off, you know? I said, "I'm going to be right behind you though, motherfucker. I'm going to be *right* behind you." I was, too.

Bobby had always told me from when I first met him, "Don't go through an open gate, don't do it." I was hopping over the fence just getting ready to say, "Don't go over the open gate, Bob." Man, he hit that fucking gate and a shaped charge* blew his ass all over the place. He was just laying there screaming, "I'm going home! I'm going home! I'm going home!"

I got hit with a little piece of shrapnel and his skin and blood and shit was all over me. I went up to him and I didn't know whether to cry or scream or go nuts. Here he is being carried off and he's got all these bandages all over him—the corpsman used every bandage he had. His fucking foot was gone and one of his legs. His face is all black and he's screaming, "What about my motorcycle? What about my motorcycle? I'm going home. I'm finally fucking going home."

The corpsman says, "You're God damn right you're going home."

He stayed awake like that in the hospital until the next afternoon. Then he died. I'd have just wanted to die.

We had to pick up his stuff. His canteens, you could shake them and hear the shrapnel rattling around inside. You pour it out and there's blood and water all in it. Couldn't find his helmet and his rifle. Just blown to shit. His cartridge belt was ripped in half.

But his canteen, you could shake it and hear the shrapnel sounds. Blood come out of it when you poured it out.

Of course we went on that night patrol anyway. Coming back the next day, we kicked ass all the way through the fucking village. Just getting even, we beat up a few people. We had just been operating around there a day or so, asking them had they seen any VC. They said, "No VC, no VC." So we thought it was cool and we trusted the people.

And Bobby walked through the open gate. He shouldn't have done it. He knew better. He was always telling me, "Don't walk through no open gate." He screamed at me more than a few times, "Don't walk through that gate. You're going to get your ass blowed away, you fucker."

Yeah, look who's talking now. Poor fucker. He was supposed to leave out of there in a fucking week or so.

* * *

I never had such a sense of solitude as during the monsoon. Walking along with my poncho over my helmet. You can look out and see everything. The rain is really coming down. But I had my helmet with my little poncho around me and I was safe. I had shelter. I was all by myself in line with all the other guys.

*   *   *

When the monsoons came everything went under water. You go in the shitter and you're floating, sitting on half a fifty-five–gallon drum and you're rocking on the waves.

Going out to an ambush one night, it rained so hard, I started to choke. I couldn't breathe. I bent over to create an airpocket under my chest. In that moment, it was filled with mosquitoes.

*   *   *

Whenever you went through a stream and got on the other side, people used to check themselves—oooh, oooh, leech—and burn it off. But you got so hardcore, you would just go through a stream and, if you get leeches, you wouldn't even bother with them. You say to yourself, "Fuck it, they'll fall off after they drink enough blood."

*   *   *

The first day I saw him, he stuck out like a sore thumb because he had no rifle. Everybody seemed to treat this guy like shit. The commanding officer would make him go on all the shit details. If they send squads out on patrols around villes, they make him stay in and burn the shit and walk the perimeter. If he did go out with the squads, everybody cursed him. He would be loaded down with all their stuff, twice as much as most people carried.

I turned to one of the squad leaders and said, "What's the matter with him?"

"He's a conscientious objector."

"What does that mean?"

"It's against the guy's religion to kill." That struck me as odd, because I thought it was that way for everybody.

I still remember his face. A very sad expression that never changed. Wire-rimmed glasses and really burning kind of eyes that caught you off guard. When we would go through villes and burn them down on Search and Destroy, all he would do is carry everything. Nobody bothered about him. He spoke to no one and just did what he had to do. This guy must have had something on the dome, because he took all the shit. Everybody hated him.

I never said nothing to the guy, I just thought, "Wow, he's got a lot of balls." I liked him even more, because although he objected to killing people, he had no objection to going and serving his country. Most people in Nam weren't there serving their country. They were just there for their own personal reasons.

*　　*　　*

Miss America came to the hospital. I was on my way to work on the ward when she pulled up in a car. She had all these sweet young things with her in little red, white, and blue miniskirts. I'm not *too* jealous. Granted I haven't had my nails done and I haven't had an honest-to-God bath in eleven months, and these young things roll in. They looked good, they smelled good and they didn't have rings around their collars.

They were pissing and moaning about not having any decent food. Plus they were tired of the guys talking to them all the time. I thought, "Then what the hell did you come here for?"

We had a lot of patients just then in really bad shape. A couple of guys had died but we had run out of body bags so they were just covered with a sheet. We were trying to stuff this one dead guy into the last of our bags.

We got a lot of support from the patients, because

they knew it was bad for us, too. Like, if they didn't want to eat, they would eat for us anyway, because they knew we'd had a bad day. They'd say, "Okay, Lieutenant. For you, I'll eat this crap." The guys knew what was what. They had seen us. We had blood and piss and shit all over us. Not to toot our own horn, that was just the way it was. We looked like shit and we smelled even worse.

In walks Miss America. She bumps and grinds over to a patient and says, all breathy, "I bet you just never thought you'd see anything looking so pretty and smelling so sweet." If he could have hit her, he would have. Instead, he just started crying and turned his face away.

The other nurse working with me was from Texas. She was short and fat. Her nickname was Meatball. Meatball was very angry about the whole scene. We were so angry in fact that we threw the woman off the ward. Well, well, Miss America thrown off the ward. She had alienated everybody. We weren't going to take it and we weren't going to let her bum out the guys in those beds.

Word travels fast. The whole hospital heard about us giving the boot to Miss America. At night as it got dark, we used to show a movie outside. All the patients who could walk would be sitting outside. The docs would be sitting on the roof and the nurses would be scattered around. Meatball and I got through on the ward about 7:30 and we were walking back to our hooch. As we passed the movie crowd—like the last act of a bad play—everybody stands up and starts clapping for us. Then they sing, "There they go, Miss Americas. There they go, our ideals."

*   *   *

Sometimes, we'd get near the South China Sea and I'd set up a squad to provide security and the rest of us would take off all our clothes and our gear. Then we'd jump in the ocean nude and swim for a while. Stark-ass naked, running down the hard-packed sand on the South China Sea.

I was jumping around in the waves one time, and I saw a speck way off shore. All of a sudden I was eye to eye with a Phantom jet pilot. He gave me a nod and I'm looking at tail pipes, a black speck and he's gone. Came and went in the wink of an eye, about five feet over the water.

I said, "Wow, that guy must be coming in his pants. What a fucking rush that's got to be. Kicking with some heavy horsepower. Give me one of those and I'll own the world."

*   *   *

You get an attitude: They can kill you, but they can't eat you. Don't sweat the small stuff. My men used to say, "There it is. There it fucking is, Lieutenant." Like, what are you going to tell me, what are you going to show me? What is it in the scheme of things that is going to give me any more insight on this whole situation? You ain't showing me shit. Dead is dead. That's it. That transcends day-to-day living.

*   *   *

It's always the boots, just big boots sticking out from under a poncho. They always made us be with the bodies. If they threw thirty bodies inside of an APC,* five or six guys would get in there, too. Bodies were a common sight after a while. It got so common that you would actually sit in a bunker with two bodies waiting to go out. Even if they started to stink after two or three days, you wouldn't even move them.

I had to report all the names of the guys that got killed over the radio. I knew every guy that got shot. I never cried for them. I feel bad about that now. But the truth of the matter is, you were always told, "Well, you'll get your turn to die tomorrow."

*   *   *

This one guy I knew, he was crazy. At night, he lit a cigarette—flash—right there in front of me, right by our position where we could just be blown away. I panicked and yelled, "What are you doing?" I blew out the match.

"When it's time, it's time," he said. "God only knows." I believed him, too. I seen so many guys who took precautions and still got blown away.

I remember distinctly about one lieutenant. He was in the field for about three months. He kind of froze one day in battle, so they sent him to the rear with extreme exhaustion. When he got back to the base camp, he more or less snapped out of it. But when he walked around back there, he always wore his helmet. People didn't usually do that since it was fairly safe. He had his little hut two or three sandbags thick all the way around—on top, too. He slept on the floor instead of on a cot, with his flak jacket on.

One night we got rocketed. He was asleep on the floor of his hooch. After the rocket attack was over, I was the medic in charge of checking around all the hooches and buildings to see how everybody was. The lieutenant, he was killed. A piece of shrapnel had entered the side of his hooch somehow through the sandbags or between them. It had hit his chest. It went in on the left side and struck his heart. It was a nice sharp piece.

If someone was protected, it was the lieutenant. After that I decided that there was nothing you could do about it. Once you were there, you're there and who knows who's going to get it next?

*   *   *

We had One Shot Charlie. Every time we would fly into our base, this little gook would haul a huge weapon out. It must have been a hundred-year-old blunderbuss. It was so big he couldn't lift it, so he propped it up between two stakes. He would aim at the helicopter, fire one shot, take the whole thing down and drag it back inside his hooch. We used to wave to him while he was shooting at us with this ancient muzzleloaded flintlock.

He did his bit for Ho Chi Minh—he shot at the Americans as they came in every day. He wasn't hiding. He set it up right in his own backyard.

Besides One Shot Charlie, when we would have an NVA sniper who was a fucking bad shot, we would leave him alone. If we killed him, they might replace him with a man who really could shoot. Better to have this dude who can't hit a barn. We loved the bad ones. He'd fire and all of a sudden you'd see a cow fall down a few yards away. The schmuck.

We did have one sniper who was a phenomenal shot. He was accurate from 500–600 yards. It's hard to believe that a guy could judge the rise and fall of the bullet over that distance, but this guy was one of them. He used to snipe us like mad. It was his bread and butter.

*   *   *

We had a sniper up at Khe Sanh that we called Zorro. He was a headache. He rarely hit anything, but sometimes he'd really piss me off.

The choppers were coming in one day with hot food and Zorro is puffing up smoke on the hill, taking potshots at us. They'd just started to unload some chow and the choppers took off because of Zorro and snatched the rest of the food away. In the door of the helicopter was this five-gallon carton of ice cream. It fell about fifty feet and we had mud and ice cream all over the place. We just went crazy. We didn't give a shit. We started eating it anyway, scooping up handfuls off the ground, mud and all.

*   *   *

Every time you came back to battalion from being on an operation, you get the day off, all the steaks, hot dogs and hamburgers you can eat, all the beer and soda you can drink. You just eat and get fucked up. You're relieved of all responsibility.

You hang out, bullshit, talk about women. Look for something cold, which was nonexistent. Go by the PX.

Watch AFVN television. They used to show *Star Trek*. I loved that shit. Beam me aboard, Spock. Take me away.

I'd see if I could commandeer a jeep and go up on Freedom Hill where they had a huge PX and a beer hall. You could talk to the Red Cross nurses, who were totally out of it.

"Here, GI, have a cookie."

"Fuck the cookie. I want your pussy." You couldn't get them. They were all with colonels and didn't want to know no brown bar * out of the bush.

I'd been in the bush on an operation for fifty-four days straight one time. After all the beer and steaks, I went back to my hooch to have a conversation with my platoon sergeant. Just hanging out was incredible, the feeling of life. You were so aware of time over there you could taste it.

We were talking and I happen to look over my shoulder. There's another person in the room. I was really surprised, because I hadn't heard anybody come in. Then I realized I was looking in a mirror and hadn't recognized my own reflection. Was that me? I had to smile to make sure. I was looking at a stranger. I'd changed. I'd never seen myself before. I'd become one of those guys that I'd seen when I first arrived in-country. Now I had that look in my eyes.

* * *

I hit country and I made PFC automatically. In three months I made E-4. "You keep this up," the sergeant tells me, "and you'll be E-6 before you leave the country."

"Probably. Boy, I hope so." I was real gung-ho, you know. If I'm going to do a job, I'm going to do it all the way. But within two weeks that sergeant leaves.

I was in the bunker when we got our new first sergeant. We had just come in off a fifteen mile Search and Destroy. Freaking tired. We got in early at about three o'clock and chow wasn't until six, so we throw all our shit on top of the bunker and we go inside to go to sleep.

I hear somebody tapping on the engineer stake that we used to hold up the canvas over the sleeping position. "Who's in charge of this position?"

"Who wants to know?" I says.

"Me."

"Who's me?" We got a new first sergeant, a black one. He's about five feet, four inches, 210 pounds. He didn't want to come out in the field. He was an artillery guy. But they were short first sergeants, so he got orders. This is the monsoon season and we're getting mortared at this place.

"You see this behind here," he says. We had a rack made out of crossed stakes to hang the picks, shovels and axes on when we didn't need them. He looks at me and says, "You see anything wrong here?"

"No. Why, Top?* You the new first sergeant?"

"Those tools have got rust on them."

"Yeah, so what? It ain't going to hurt them."

"I want that rust off."

"Uh, okay. We'll get it."

"You see anything else wrong here?"

"No. Wattaya mean?"

"You see that puddle over there and that one over there?"

"Yeah, I see them. Those are mortar holes."

"I don't care what they are," he says. "I want them drained because they breed mosquitoes."

"You got to be out of your mind," I tell him. "They breed mosquitoes? It rains three times a day. That stuff ain't staying stagnant."

"I want them drained."

"Do you know what it takes to drain a hole like that on a hill? A two-foot-deep hole? You got to dig down two or three feet to the bottom of this thing and you got to keep going all the way down the hill with it. But . . . we'll get it. We'll get it."

He leaves. We want back to sleep. He comes back about a half hour later. "Specialist, get out here," he yells. He forgot my name, right?

"Look, Top. We just came off a fifteen-klick S&D. We'll get it tonight after chow."

"I don't care where you've been. I want it done now." He leaves. We go back to sleep.

This time he comes back with my platoon sergeant who was a real crazy-ass type. He was an E-6 waiting to go E-7 and hoping to go higher. The platoon sergeant says, "Roma, come on. Do what Top tells you to do."

"All right," I says. "Don't worry. We'll do it now." They leave. We go back to sleep.

Then the Top comes back with my lieutenant. This lieutenant was a nut, a weirdo. Not a bad guy, just goofy. He was the type of guy who wanted to make a career out of the Army, but the only way to do that was to go through the infantry first. He says, "Roma, you better clean this up."

"Lieutenant, you're supposed to be on our side. We just came in. We'll clean it up after chow. It's still hot out. The sun's still burning bright. Wait till it cools down and we'll do all this shit—which I think is bullshit anyway."

"I don't want to hear that," the lieutenant says. "I want you to do it and do it now."

"Okay, we'll do it, for Chrissakes." We get up and we start doing it. We did the rust shit, but we didn't drain the holes. Top comes back again. He comes up to me and stands face to face. I wanted to punch him.

"What did I tell you?" he says.

"What are you talking about?"

"What about those God damn holes?"

"Wait till after chow. We did one thing and we'll do the other one later."

"Troop, what's your name and when are you going home?"

"I'm going home in June and my name is Roma," I yell right back in his teeth.

"Well, I'm going home in June, too, and we'll probably be on the same God damn plane together," he says.

"Do you mean to tell me that I got to put up the rest of my year with a fanatic like you?"

"If this shit ain't cleaned up," he says getting real mad, "I'm going to get you."

"Okay, Top." It took us two hours to drain those freaking holes. There were about fifteen of them. So we drain the holes and I call him over. I says, "Now are you happy?"

"I'll never forget you," he says.

We were limited on water. I'd see him shave every morning. Pat it nice and easy, then wash it again. Shave it and wash again. It took him an hour to shave. I says, "That's all you got to do, you son of a bitch. We got all this God damn work and you got an hour to shave."

When we went on patrol he hardly ever went with us. He used to get an excuse, he got sick. He was a real bastard. He was no God damn good.

But he went with us one night. I'm out there with a radio on my back. With the radio, you also carry sandbags, smoke grenades, hand grenades, as well as your weapon, three canteens, twenty magazines of ammunition—I got maybe seventy-five pounds on my back in this iron frame all tied up. He comes up with a rucksack on that's almost empty. I picked the thing up and it might have weighed ten pounds. It probably had his shaving equipment in it.

You had to know how to walk in the paddies. Some of them were just water waist-deep. But some of them were like a marsh with floating grass over the water. If you didn't know how to walk on it you'd sink in up to your neck.

It's night. When it got dark, it got pitch black and you couldn't see nothing. Top's walking a couple of guys ahead of me and he falls in. I'm walking past him and he says, "Help me out of here."

"You got in there, you bastard," I whispered, "you get yourself out of there." Everybody started laughing, because they know me and him had a battle going. They start ribbing him, "Hey, Top, we can't lose contact. You ain't got shit to carry and we're all loaded down. And be quiet, you ain't supposed to be making so much noise splashing around in the water."

He wanted to kill me. He says, "Roma, you ain't never going to get a promotion."

"I don't give a shit, not with you around here."

* * *

Sometimes, right before you'd get hit, mama-san would sell you spiked grass. You smoke a joint and nod right out. Probably, it was heavily opiated.

We were up 100–125 feet in a tower guarding an air base. We smoked this dope and passed out. The next thing I knew it was 6:30 in the morning. I woke up when I heard a jeep running across the middle of the airstrip. I thought, "Oh God, we're in trouble. We didn't call in, we didn't answer the radio." So I cut the radio and telephone wires, and said we had some problems.

Of course, they didn't buy it. They made us pull duty another whole day and night afterward. Everybody was really pissed because during the day, this fucking tower was really hot. And it's like sitting in the bull's-eye of a target.

There was a woman bent over about 500 yards away in the fields. She was just harvesting something. We're talking to each other and somebody says, "I'll tell you what. I betcha I can hit her." I said, "Don't be silly. Don't even bother." She was obviously not an enemy agent or anything and she was way out of range.

Everybody started taking potshots at this woman, just to see if they can hit her. I was the only one that didn't . . . at first. But something came over me. I was pissed off. I was fucking hot. It was the second day in that fucking tower, you know. I said, "Fuck you guys. Here, watch this." I shot at her and she keeled over dead.

I was so aware of my lack of regard for life at that point. Before, I couldn't relate pulling the trigger and seeing somebody fall, because I'd been doing mostly night ambush. You never see who the hell you're shooting at in the dark and then you run like hell. The next day you look for blood on the floor of the jungle and try to estimate how many you killed. But you really can't tell. I just couldn't believe that I had done it.

* * *

Up at Khe Sanh, a guy told us how we had to sleep.
I'm sitting up on a bunker watching. There were about
six boots, most of who thought he was bullshitting us.

"All right, when you go to bed, you are going to sleep
this way. Take your quilt and tuck about six inches under your feet. You pull it tight up along your legs and
start tucking—tight—all the way up to the middle of
your chest. Then lay your weapon across your chest.
Take the top of the quilt and flip it over your head.
Bring your elbows in. Reach over your shoulders with
your hands, grab the top corners of the quilt behind
your neck and pull them down so that the quilt is tight
behind your head—like you're in a cocoon. When the
shit hits the fan, you can get out fast enough. But
nothing can get in."

You were on this little narrow cot like you were in a
coffin, your hands resting on your weapon. I said,
"Why?"

"I knew you was going to say that. Everybody does.
Well, I'll tell you. We have rats and the rats we have
would eat any cat and give most dogs a hell of a way to
go back in the States. You haven't seen rats until you've
seen these rats."

This one guy from Chicago says, "Hell, man, I seen
rats, man. We got rats in Chicago that *kills* dogs." All
of a sudden everybody is bragging about the rats they
got back home. "We got rats in New York. We seen
rats."

"Yeah," my man says, "but you haven't seen rats
this big or this mean." He was not lying.

I said to myself, "Okay, if this is what they want me
to do, I'll do it." I get all wrapped up in the quilt about
like he told us to. I'm sleeping, or what passed for
sleeping—half asleep, half awake. I couldn't be comfortable. Something jumped on me and was walking. It
landed on my legs and started up to my chest. I'm
scared shitless. "What is this on me now?" It felt huge.
I couldn't move. I couldn't raise my weapon to shoot
because it was tucked too tightly under the covers. It got
off me. I didn't even know how long it was there.

Suddenly this guy is yelling at the top of his lungs.

Everybody broke and jumped up with their weapons. It's pitch black and we're running down to where we hear this guy screaming. Flares are shooting up. We thought some VC had snuck into the perimeter and was killing somebody or cutting them up.

This dude is running down the trench line, and a couple of guys grab him, shook him and said, "What's wrong, what's wrong?" They struck a light and looked at him.

He had a hunk of meat out of his face. He had slept with his head out. He don't like to sleep with his head covered up, was his remark. He looked up and the rat was above him in the bunker rafters. The rat looked at him and he looked at the rat. He realized too late that the rat was going to get him. When he tried to move, the rat just jumped. When it jumped, it just bit and took that meat out of his face.

He had to stay the rest of the night. They wouldn't send a chopper up there in the dark to get him. He was all bandaged and crying. He was so mad and confused. Most of the guys went on back to bed, but I sat up with him a good while. I knew I wouldn't get to sleep no more that night anyway.

He was on his way home, no doubt about it. He says, "Damn, I didn't get a chance to kill nobody. I ain't seen no enemy. I ain't did nothing."

I said, "You're a jerk-ass. You got bit in the face and all you're worried about is you didn't kill nobody? Now that you've already got it done, why don't you tell them to send me home in your place? I *do* know I don't want to be here. I *do* know that you could die in this place. If you want to stay here, you can stay for me."

"Well, maybe it will be all right for me to go home. I got a million-dollar wound."

"Yeah, a rat kicked your ass." They started teasing him about that right away next morning. They called him Rat on his way out. He's whining, "Yeah, I won't forget you guys."

"Well, we forgot you, man. Go on home." He was in-country one day.

* * *

For where I slept, I used to just take a cardboard box from C-rations and lay it out flat to sleep on. You and your buddy'd get together, take off your ponchos and made a little cubby hooch that two guys could sleep under rolled up together in one ball. You go out on night patrol, you're not going to knock down the hooch. You just leave your poncho over the other guy and go out and get soaking wet. You sleep with the enemy right there like your hand in front of your face. Right there, saying good night to you.

In Nam at night in a full moon, guys would play poker on watch. You could see everything for fucking miles. You could write letters. But without a moon in monsoon, it got too dark.

These are guys who aren't supposed to fear nothing. You know how they go on patrol in the dark? You're holding on to people's hands and the back of the shirt of the guy in front of you like little kids, like baby elephants in a row. Everybody's really asshole to belly button, 'cause you don't want to get lost.

After the ground in the jungle gets really rotten, the phosphorus does something to the wood and it glows. So we would tag this stuff on the back of our helmets to keep track of each other at night. It would be this little psychedelic train with green lights bobbing along in front of you.

We were working out around the Elephant Valley the first time I went on night patrol. The grass was head high so you couldn't see much more than fifteen feet even in the daytime. There's NVA and guerrillas hiding in the elephant grass. We're supposed to be sweeping through and sneak up on them in the dark.

Marines are the noisiest motherfuckers at night. People tripping and cursing. We were getting scared and getting lost. We were yelling out for one another. "Hey, Joe, where are you?" "Hey, over here, man, over here." Thank God, the Vietnamese out there that night didn't speak English. They figured we were just crazy, running around in the dark shooting and hollering. Some of them started jumping out in front of us, throwing down their rifles, screaming *Chu Hoi*.* Naturally, we were so scared, we were blowing them away anyway.

*   *   *

You had a lot of time to yourself while you were standing watch at night, three or four hours in the dark all to yourself. What else are you going to think about, man? Your fucking friend got blown off. He died on you. You try to make some kind of sense out of it, to come to terms with it at a new level. Not at the old level where you exist with him. Now you have to exist without him. Why? Wherefores? What does it mean?

My analysis then of what was going on was pretty unsophisticated. I was ignorant about life in general at eighteen. At the time I was trying to put it in a mystical-theological evaluation. Although I was starting to reject God, I was still thinking, "Well, there is a God and he must want it to be this way." It was simplistic and naive, but it was still painful.

The hardest thing to accept is that it's for real and forever. It was permanent. I'd been to funerals in my time. I'd been an altar boy and served at funerals. I had family friends and relatives that had died and I'd been to funeral parlors and seen dead people. But these guys were really young and peers of mine. When they died it was so shocking, so rude. The concept of permanency just isn't about somebody eighteen years old. Ask someone that age about death and they'll say, "I'm never going to die. I won't get old." You don't think about death. I was a young healthy man. I felt like I could kick the whole world's ass. Then you see it happen and it's hard to come to grips with.

Put it out of your mind. You can't dwell on it, yet you do think about it. It comes and goes. I'd say to myself, "I won't think about it tonight. I don't want to think about that. It's too fucking spooky." But you're so tired, your mind is weak. When death comes into your head, you don't have the strength to push it aside.

You're just so fucking tired. Nineteen-year-old bodies with thirty-five-year-old minds. That was twice our age. Here I am now fast approaching it and I see what a young motherfucker I really was. I felt so much older and tired than I had a right to be within my physical frame.

How to keep awake on watch was always a source of contention. You'd play with your weapons. You'd do anything. You're bored. You can't read a book—it's dark out there. So we used to beat off, masturbate. I did it sometimes as many as four times a night, in a four-hour period—which I wish I could do now. We didn't like to talk about it. I guess we were a little puritanical. But we all knew that everybody else beat off, too. We didn't bring it up in conversation. But say some guy blew away a tree stump in the middle of the night. They'd say, "Hey, what the fuck you firing at, your fantasy?" And pretend that he'd been beating off and saw his dream girl coming through the wire.

* * *

At night it would scare me. I couldn't see anything. I would sneak out and set up trip flares every night. They would all go off and I would never see a God damn thing.

Then there were the lungfish. There was water all around us and these fish would swim up. Then when the tide would go out, the fish would get caught in puddles in front of my bunker. Lungfish have lungs and they sound like human beings breathing. You'd be laying there trying to sleep, hearing horror-show-monster breathing right in front of you.

One night while it was my turn to be awake, somebody, very clearly and distinctly and right in my ear, said, "Fuck you." I knew that I was dead. I'm grabbing my rifle like one of the Three Stooges in a comedy routine. The only thing I could see was this little lizard six inches long. There was a frozen moment when the lizard blew out its little gills and went, "Fuck you," again.

I was waking up the other guys. "Hey, man, this lizard just told me to go get fucked." The three of us— relatively grown men, three old kids, at least—had a standoff with an ounce-and-a-half lizard. Finally, the little sucker said "fuck you" for them, too.

* * *

Sometimes at night you'd just be drifting off to sleep and all of a sudden they'd fire the artillery and you would literally be an inch off the deck, like a cat with its fur in all directions. The back muscles are so spasmatic that they actually lift you up. If you could grab on to the ceiling, you would sink your fingers into it and stick there spreadeagle. *Bam-ramaramadamdamdam*. Your heart would be going and you'd get pissed, so mad you wanted to kill. The noise drove you crazy and you wanted to rip somebody's throat out. To this day, I hear loud noises I get pissed. I want to hit something.

* * *

I was out on LP one night up on some hill, I don't remember which one. I hear a thump. I look and I see somebody's throwing rocks. I think, "Oh, shit, they're probing the lines to see who's asleep." I got really scared and I took it personal, too. I says, "Man, why are they probing this side." You don't want to open up if nothing is there, because then you're so embarrassed. Not only that, but they're going to take all your ammo. Then still make you sit there. They don't fool around. I was really starting to get nervous. It happened again, a pebble hit me. I thought, "Fuck, man, I'll just make like I'm sleeping and I'll blow away whoever comes up."

This thing rushes up to me in the dark. It had a leather face. I didn't have time to be scared. I just opened up on it. As I opened up on that, they were jumping out of trees, coming from everywhere. Guys were opening up all over. It was panic time, USA, and we're being overrun. The next thing I know I'm out of rounds. I didn't even change my magazine, it was so quick. I slapped another one in and *bbbrrrroooom*.

We stood up all night, panicked, everybody trembling. After everybody let loose, it got quiet. We went over all the lines, nobody was hit. We started calling all sorts of people to back us up. They told us they can't do nothing till daylight.

As the sun comes up there's maybe six or seven monkeys laying around. We had been attacked by rock apes. I didn't know, I thought they were NVA guerrillas or something. So to speak, they were gorillas.

*   *   *

You're sitting out there in the dark. You been out there every God damn night for a month and you ain't seen the first VC. Where in the hell are they? We'd about decided to go buy a few and import them. You sit and sit and sit. You're supposed to be real quiet and serious, because you really don't know when it's going to happen. But it's been a long time, so you figure, what the hell—*brrrippp*. Somebody'd let out a fart that would blow your God damn socks off. Everybody'd start laughing.

*   *   *

We spotted three figures making their way up the side of the hill. First of all we weren't sure, because of the intermittent light from the moon. We weren't supposed to see people in that area. There was something about the way they were moving that didn't seem to be realistic. So we called up. Is there anybody in this area, here? No. So they told us to fire and move back.

The next morning a patrol was sent out and they found three people and one was still alive. One woman had been killed. One man was dead. They were Montagnards* who didn't pay much attention to a free-fire zone. I don't know if the kid ended up dying or not.

*   *   *

Any time anybody went to the rear they had to bring back liquor for the officers and hot beer, but for the rest of us they brought back smoke. They'd have a bag full of smoke or we used to get Party Packs which was ten rolled joints to a pack. We paid $5 to the pack. Like cigarettes. Fantastic. They was wrapped in plastic, so if you got wet you didn't have to worry about them getting all messed.

Then they came up with another one they used to call 100s, which was longer than a cigarette. But they cost you a dollar for a joint. Those were soaked in opium so you paid ten for ten. A half of one of those joints—and those guys were smoking two or three joints by themselves and just getting mellow—half a joint got six guys high. We saved it for when we could go to the rear, because you couldn't function on that smoke.

When I got short—when you're under seventy-five days or so, you're starting to be a short-timer—my platoon commander gave me a jive job sending me to the rear with my shotgun to get the mail, make sure the company got beer and the officers got their liquor. I used to take the order on smoke. Each guy would come to me. I had a little booklet and next to their names I had a number. The number was how many Party Packs they wanted this trip. I would come back to the bush with a little overnight bag full of smoke. When I stepped off the helicopter, they would start yelling, "You, come here! Come here!"

"Wait, don't be snatching at me. I got to give the officers their liquor first." They get their liquor and they were just as happy.

*   *   *

There were a couple of real assholes smoking dope and riding around in some jeep. They came up to me and said, "You want to toke up with us?" I was one of the biggest pot freaks that you've ever seen. But for some reason, I said, "Nah, go ahead."

They drove into this parking lot where there's only one way to go in and out. A couple of high ranking officers were in there and they saw these guys laughing and screaming. To make a long story short, about six people got busted for smoking dope. A guy named Ortega was with them and he had a broken arm in a cast.

What happened was, Ortega took the joints and put them inside his cast when he saw the Straks coming over. Then during the interrogation, the joints all fell out. They were ready to break open his cast anyway. To try and reduce his legal obligations, he turned in everybody's name—including the battalion chaplain—as dope smokers. He included some of the locations of mama-sans who were dealing dope.

The Straks were going to use this as an excuse to harass the hell out of us. They would run up to me at night, shining flashlights in my eyes to see if they were red. Periodically, they would strip all my possessions to see if I was holding. They were really on my case.

I was pissed and I wasn't the only one. By this time, there were about 500 people that hated Ortega's guts. The Straks kept putting him in different camps. Wherever he went, the guys wanted to beat the shit out of him. They had to keep him under guard in the sergeant's shack.

At the height of this, Ortega was bit by a rabid rat. Now, when you're undergoing rabies treatment, you should never drink. For some reason, it reacts and really fucks you up. Ortega, being the Chicano juicer that he was, really boozed it up. He went into a frenzy. They had to tie him down to a bed in the shack.

I heard that he was tied to a bed and couldn't believe my good fortune. We got some gasoline and went running over there. Somebody hit the first sergeant over the head—he was taken away with a concussion. I didn't pour the gasoline over Ortega. He was twisting on the bed, ranting and raving. The other guys soaked him down with it. I threw a match.

They took him out with burns on 85 percent of his body. I don't know if he was dead or not. At that point, I didn't really care.

*   *   *

I noticed that guys who took their R&R early came back and always got killed. You look for little signals. Get everything on your side. Guys would come back and tell you stories about the girls they were with, and then they'd get blown away, because they had nothing else to look forward to. I knew if I took it early, I would have nothing to look forward to. The only thing that kept me going was the thought, "I can leave whenever I want." Which wasn't true, but it comes in handy late at night.

Helicopters were coming in with supplies and the VC were pounding the shit out of us. The gunny yelled, "Anyone who has R&R coming and wants it, jump on that bird." I was the closest to the helicopter and I leaped on. I says, "Where am I going?" When they told me Hong Kong, I tried to jump off. I wanted Australia. Hong Kong? That's one of the most expensive places, plus you're dealing with slant eyes. I wanted to see something with round eyes.

I went to the rear at Da Nang and they gave me a new set of duds, except for the boots. I cleaned up a little and got used to flushing toilets. The first thing you do is go over and play with the toilet like you're a kid. You flush it three or four times and you call your friend over to watch it. It's a big thrill.

Then we went to Hong Kong. I hadn't seen civilized life for ten months and I'd never been alone in a strange city in my whole life. I was totally shocked to the point of fright. They said, "Okay, you're a big boy. You don't need anybody to hold your hand." But I did. Nine or ten hours earlier, I'd been in a fire fight. I walked out of a war zone with $500 in my pocket. It was time for me to live like a king, but I didn't know how.

I finally went and got a room in a hotel. The Hong Kong tailors would come up, knock on the door and say in a soft voice, "Hello, my name is Lou Chow from Kowloon, Hong Kong. We wish to give you suit now." They give you the suit just for the night so you'd come by the shop and buy one. Everybody bought suits. I got a couple or three of them for $30 apiece.

Me and this other Marine, we had beautiful three-piece suits, but we're still wearing jungle boots with mud on them from Nam. We walked around the city the first night, stepping on the concrete with jungle boots and beautiful suits. You do the usual thing: We went in and bought ourselves some women. They were very expensive, $50 for the day and night, where in Taipai you could have bought a girl for the whole week for that. I was a little pissed off, but I got used to it. The shock was going back to Vietnam.

Three days and four nights in Hong Kong, living like a human being, like a king. Beautiful clothes, I had a beautiful broad, nineteen-year-old girl—she was older than I was—fucking and sucking all night long. I was having bacon and eggs and pussy for breakfast. Then that same night I'm back in the fucking rain and mud with leeches and people trying to kill me. That was a twist on the head. No wonder a lot of these guys would die. It was like a hand coming out of space, picking you up and putting you on another planet for three days.

I was sorry I took R&R. Before I left for Hong Kong, I'd forgotten about napkins. I forgot about beds and sheets. I'd forgotten that when you wanted light on a dark night, you could just turn it on. You could put 15¢ in a machine and get a candy bar whenever you wanted. I'd almost forgotten about broads.

* * *

The routine was bone-numbing dumb. Every day was really a matter of going to the gate and waiting for the convoy to come in. Sitting there in the dust, we'd check off trailer numbers, how many loads of what. How many trailers of ammo, how many trailers of gas, how much diesel fuel, how many trailers for the PX. Just supply categories. Then we'd call it in on the crazy Army phone system, filled with high piping Vietnamese female voices which you couldn't understand. But you'd finally get through.

My day was usually spent going from one point to another on the base, seeing who got what. Doing things like talking the warrant officer at the ammo supply point into letting us borrow his forklift and driver for an afternoon to piggy-back broken-down trailers on the backs of other trailers so they could go back on the next convoy.

The job took three or four hours a day at most. The rest of the time was ours to do what we wanted with it. Mostly the time was spent dodging rockets and mortars. When I first arrived, they were coming in three or four times a day. Fairly predictably. There was a certain regularity. Quon Loi was reasonably hot at the time. We were very close to a major outlet off the Ho Chi Minh trail. There were a lot of NVA* active in the area with a lot of LZ out there that we were in support of. We also had two or three artillery batteries. Basically, it was a supply point for units operating in the field.

In addition to the cavalry brigade, there was a Special Forces unit. There were some Lurps around. There were the usual unknowns who flew in and out in unmarked planes. Every once in a while, a band of Montagnard mercenaries would get on a plane with some guy in civilian clothes and disappear toward Cambodia. It was no secret to us that the U.S. was in there.

The hooches were constructed in a row. Between each hooch was a bunker that was mostly underground and dug in. People slept down there. There were also people who slept above ground, but I made an early decision that I would sleep below ground. I saw no reason to tempt fate. There was space available in the bunker so I took it. Seven people slept in each bunker.

The bunkers and hooches were interconnected. You could get into the bunkers without going outdoors. But you couldn't get into a bunker from the outside, without first running in through the hooch.

The location of the hooch I was living in was one of the worst possible places to be under normal circumstances. Behind us was the airstrip where the cav kept their wonderful helicopters. On the other side was the jet and helicopter fuel point. Right across the road was the chief gasoline and diesel point on base. Not too far away in the third quadrant was the ammo dump. The fourth quadrant was where the big guns were. Ammo dump, fuel supply, airstrip and big guns were prime targets. We were in line for any shell that overshot or fell short of any of those particular targets.

One had to program taking a shit or taking a shower in and around prime rocket time. I got very used to organizing my life that way. I didn't want to be occupied when the rockets came in.

I quickly came to realize that I would rather be where I was than in the relative safety of Long Binh. That piece of information was a bit of a surprise to me. For mild-mannered me it was opting for danger. It was a trade-off: more danger for less bullshit. There was no bullshit. There was no officer in charge of the little transportation unit. There was an officer with the quartermaster platoon with which I was billetted. He had some day-to-day authority over me. I was called for various details. I was on the guard-duty roster, for instance. But not all the time.

There were after all only three of us and we had to do our job every day. We couldn't pull twenty-four-hour guard duty and still do our job. So mostly we were exempted from guard duty. I must confess that was a real relief to me. I knew that the perimeter was not remotely safe. I looked at the fucking guard bunkers around the perimeter and realized that they weren't even positioned in support of each other. They were just in a line around the base. They weren't staggered so that fields of fire would cross. I hadn't learned that in training, I just knew it. I'm sure that Alexander the Great's bowmen knew that.

But of course, that was part of the daily insanity of it all. I mean, who was going to attack this place on foot anyway? There was so much firepower in each of those bunkers whether they provided real good cover for each other or not. How those little people ever did it, I don't know. But they did it very effectively and often.

Some of the post was very beautiful. Gorgeous French plantation homes ringed the airstrip. They were mostly empty, but they had caretakers. A few Vietnamese were there in the daytime. The windows were still clean. Every once in a while you'd see a little laundry hanging out on the line. With all the incoming we had, not one of those buildings was ever hit.

The mythical Frenchy who owned it all, or managed it, was also in control of our water supply. We paid him for our water as well as for every rubber tree we cut down. We rented the land that the base was on from the plantation owners. They in turn paid off the local VC or the NVA or both to protect their interest. The plantation was still operating in the middle of all this bullshit. At maybe one-third capacity from before the war, but it wasn't shut down.

Within our perimeter—which was another insane thing—there was a little Vietnamese village. All those people worked for the plantation, but I think at least half of them were VC. There were tunnels in and out of the village. Everybody knew that. But they were behind barbed wire.

That's where I took my laundry. I'd throw my dirty clothes over the barbed-wire fence to Linn, my laundry girl, at her house near the MP headquarters. Then I'd go back a day later and she'd throw it back over the wire to me. I'd wad up some money and toss it to her. It was all illegal, but our business transactions went on right under the noses of the MPs.

I've spent a lot of time thinking about the degrees of the Vietnam experience. The degrees of being close to the center of the real craziness and the real horror of the thing. I realized that I was several degrees removed from the center almost the entire time I was there. I'm several degrees removed from the intensity of the experience of somebody out in the field, humping those hills every day. But I also know that where I was is several degrees closer to the center of things than the guys in Long Binh pounding their typewriters. I was in a strange kind of middle ground where the environment was not healthy at all, but where I was relatively safe.

I was in daily contact with the people who were at the very heart of the war. It was part of my job to be dealing with these people or I would be drinking beer with them. There are things that they know that I don't know. Things that they felt that I will never feel, I hope. There are places that they've been that I never want to go. It's odd though. Sometimes when I think about them, I experience a guilt that is akin to the guy who didn't go at all.

Maybe because I was in the middle or maybe because I was twenty-five years old, I was a little more detached from what was happening, at least emotionally. Or I created a detachment as one of my defenses that was different than most of the people I was with, who were much younger than I was.

My emotions were less on the surface than everybody else's. Guys who were nineteen years old were reacting more off the tops of their heads than I was. I was more analytical. I didn't blow off steam, I buried it. I didn't get wildly drunk or rambunctious or aggressive or in a fighting mood as easily as other people did. That's not to say that was a common pattern, but when the occasion called for it, the reaction was apparent.

I spent a lot of time watching what was happening around me. That was part of me before I went. It's the faculty in me that I call The Watcher. Everybody watched. There was a kind of implied voyeurism without the nasty connotations. Everybody was to a certain extent a voyeur, except the guys who really shot it out. Experiences are sorted out between the ones you had and the ones you saw. I saw a lot.

I didn't know what the war was doing to me, but I could see what it was doing to other people around me. It wasn't that I was disillusioned, because I knew too much before I went over there for that. But after I had been in Quon Loi for a week or two, I was very angry. I stayed angry almost all the time I was there. I brought that anger home with me like a lot of other men. What I saw *angered* me.

I watched what happened to Lawrence, a nineteen-year-old kid from Brooklyn with love beads and wire-rimmed glasses. We had a very heavy ground attack. Lawrence and a guy named Whip were on guard duty that night and they happened to be on the same bunker.

We were hit a little after midnight. That was prime time. It usually happened between midnight and one o'clock in the morning. It always went on until just

before dawn. You knew it was going to be serious, when
you had a kind of nonstop barrage of incoming. You'd
hear the first few and think, "Ah, here they come
again." Then it would just keep coming. The choppers
would be in the air. Tracers all over the place. Rockets
being fired all around the perimeter. The Cobras*
diving. If the shit was really heavy, a Spooky gunship
would come in and destroy the greenery.

There were people who could sleep through a ground
attack. I couldn't do it. Ostensibly, every time we had a
real ground attack, none of us were supposed to be
asleep, because we had our own inner defensive positions. I always got dressed and I always made sure I had
ammo sitting around and my weapon was intact and
clean enough. Little did I know—because I never used it
that much—how easy it was to fuck up an M-16 with a
little bit of dirt. Had I known, my weapon would have
been cleaner.

After the horrendous, almost hour-long barrage of
incoming stopped, the rockets and mortars, everything
else that was going on was down on the perimeter—
which wasn't very far away, but it was far enough.

I would put my helmet on and sometimes my flak
jacket and I would sit on the sandbags outside my hooch
and watch the war. Flare light everywhere, the smoke
trails making patterns all over the place and strange
shadows in the sky. Tracer bullets coming down. All the
catalogue of noises. Picking out an RPG* sound. Our
mortars or their mortars. AKs* as opposed to M-16s.
All those noises that I know that at ninety I would be
able to recognize and differentiate. I still look up every
time I hear a Huey.

That particular night the lieutenant in charge of the
quartermaster platoon was up and around and being
very efficient. He was an incompetent fool, but it was a
heavy attack and word from brigade was that we were to
be ready to assume our inner defensive positions. Somebody had a field radio down in one of the bunkers and
we were listening to the chatter from the guys on the
perimeter. Guys were calling for more ammunition and
for flares. Southern drawls, Puerto Rican accents and

Midwestern twangs, the gamut of American voices all in a supercharged state.

At one point a phone call came from the TOC.* Our lieutenant came running around to tell us all that the enemy had broken through the wire down near the laundry and they would probably be heading for the airstrip. We were between the laundry and the airstrip. I went through the most incredible, quick scenario in my head. I kept thinking, "What am I going to do if I see a little person running across the yard?" I was pretty fucking scared and very wide awake. I don't remember how it came to me, but for the first time I knew beyond a shadow of a doubt that I was perfectly capable of shooting somebody. I hadn't really confronted that until then. It was just suddenly there as a fact. It was a fact that disturbed the shit out of me, but, I must say, from that moment on things were easier all the way around. It was the ultimate choice, at least intellectually. Had been for me all along. Was I capable of shooting somebody who I had no reason to shoot other than to save my own life, maybe? Was I capable of shooting somebody who had no more reason to be there than I did? Suddenly, I knew that I was. I wasn't any less afraid. I was stunned.

The night finally ended and the dawn came. The firing stopped as it always did before the dawn. Shortly after that the guys started coming back from being on guard. They had been under heavy fire for five and a half hours, nonstop.

Lawrence and Whip came back in. For some reason, I was down near where they lived as they walked into the yard. It was David Douglas Duncan photograph time, "Smoky dawn"—gun smoke in the air, strange smells and fading fire, a few grenades popping off still. The day was misty the way it often was in that place early in the morning.

These two guys were coming out of the vagueness, all blackened, dirty, crazy. It was the first time I had dealt with guys coming out of a version of that. I was dealing with it as The Watcher in a real way.

Lawrence was first. His eyes were what I saw first. Eyes are what you always see first. It's hard to talk about it without being clichéd. It's hard to avoid using "1,000-yard stare." What I saw in Lawrence's eyes was the horror, The Horror. What spooked me as much as anything else was that I could tell immediately that he knew that everything was different now.

They were both wiped out, but not ready to go to bed. There was a story to tell first. Whip did all the talking. Lawrence didn't do any.

They had burned out their M-60 in the middle of it all—just melted the barrel down. They had run out of ammunition about three quarters of the way into all this shit. There was at the time a squadron of Armored Cavalry on the post, so there were lots of APCs and Sheridan tanks around. It was such a heavy night that the Armored Cav had been ordered in between bunkers.

These poor little people who wore black pajamas and shorts were not only facing bunkers that had at least three GIs on them—which meant at least one M-60 and three M-16s and a bunch of grenades and Claymores and in some places around the perimeter command detonated barrels of napalm set into the side of the hill—but also in between bunkers there would be an APC with a .50 calibre machine gun and ten guys with M-16s or a Sheridan tank firing beehive rounds.* I still don't know how they ever could do that.

Usually the pattern was locally recruited kids were the ones that were first thrown into it. Highly experienced sapper teams would cut through the wire, blow up a bunker or two and open up a hole in the line. Then these kids—literally kids, they couldn't have been more than fourteen or fifteen—who had been snatched out of the nearest hamlet were sent in. Then the hardcore NVA unit, if indeed we were up against NVA, would come in after them.

Whip was reasonably certain that they had accounted for eleven killed, some of them very close to their bunker. They had gone through who knows how many moments of terror when they ran out of ammo and there were people coming through the wire in front of them. They were saved only by the arrival of a tank to fill the slot which had been made by sappers blowing up the bunker next to them with a satchel charge or two.

I don't even begin to know what those two guys went through that night. All I know is what I saw the next morning, and all the ways that Lawrence was never the same person again.

Lawrence hadn't been there very long. He was happy-go-lucky and naive, everybody's teddy bear. He sounded like he was from Brooklyn, but he wasn't a rough street kid. He was coming from some tough places, but somehow he was too gentle for that. In spite of all the beads and the peace medals and the longish hair, Lawrence wasn't even into dope. He had already passed through his dope stage and he was just very mellowed out. Very nice.

I guess he was trying to get through with the best time that he could have. So at the little enlisted men's club, Lawrence was often the guy who was changing the half dozen records that we played endlessly, tending bar and being cooperative and helpful and funny. A very loose hanger.

The guy who came back that morning was not the guy who went out twenty-four hours earlier. And he was never that person again. He probably still isn't and never will be.

Lawrence didn't talk much at all for over a week. When he did start talking again, he never spoke with the enthusiasm he had had before. His eyes were masked and dull like an old man's. They seemed to sit deeper inside his skull. If he had been wrinkled and lined, he would have been a cynical seventy-year-old man.

That first ground attack that we had was severe. There were 200 plus of "Them" left lying around outside the base and in the wire the morning after. Who knows how many others were wounded or killed and had been dragged off? We had taken twenty-two KIA. I don't know what the wounded total was. But twenty-two KIA for an evening's engagement on a small post was fairly remarkable at that time.

Thirty-five feet away from my hooch was the GR Point* for the base. I lived with the men who worked there. I watched those twenty-two bodies come from the

medics to the GR Point. There was only room in there
for maybe eight at the most in the reefers—Conex con-
tainers with little generators on them to refrigerate the
bodies. The bodies started piling up in the yard. The of-
ficial report of American deaths was only eight. It's
horrible to think about that. That's just statistics, that's
not even people.

I got angry when I realized that our casualty reports
in the *Stars & Stripes* were being falsified. In every case,
I *knew* what the total was—I knew it—but the numbers
were always reported as less. We falsified the enemy
casualties. Why not falsify our own? I began to realize
the extent of the lie, all the kinds of lies. I don't believe
for a moment that there were only 53,000 people killed
in Vietnam. I don't know how it's possible to disguise
thousands of deaths, but I believe that there were
thousands more Americans who died than were reported. I saw it with my own eyes constantly.

MARTIAL ARTS

Physical prowess and special skills were coveted for the prestige they imparted, which raised a young man above the mulish mass of GIs. Lurps—those night-crawling members of long range reconnaissance patrols—could buy and use hand made, mail-order hunting knives. They carried freeze-dried spaghetti and meatballs into the field. A Green Beret was guaranteed a barstool anywhere in South Vietnam, Cambodia or Laos, as long as he wore his hat and camouflage fatigues.

Specialty work held out the promise of movie star glamor, something with a taste of The Guns of Navarone *or* The Dirty Dozen. *The elite were accorded respect and privilege. A man might even become a legend.*

"The rumor around battalion was that there was a guy on Rat Patrol called The Prince of Darkness. The Prince of Darkness never came out in the daytime, never saw sunlight, would sit in a dark bunker all day long totally blacked out. His visual purple was built up over months, so he had the ultimate night vision for driving his machine gun jeep. Wouldn't even light a match. I'm

sure he got stoned. He'd just close his eyes when he took a puff.

"According to legend, I never saw him because of his nocturnal habits. I don't know if he existed or not. But people believed he existed."

One man told me that after he moved from the infantry into Lurps he "developed the ability to smell gooks, just sense where they were." But the image was difficult to live up to. Most men settled for writing some appropriate graffiti on the backs of their flak jackets. "Yeah, though I walk through the Valley of Death, I will fear no evil, because I'm the meanest motherfucker in the Valley."

They were specialists. They chose to lock themselves tighter in the war's embrace. Willing to inhabit the center of the insanity, some of them truly were madmen hooked on walking the razor's edge. But the flash was Hollywood cosmetic. The helicopter door gunners, intelligence officers, Green Berets and Lurps were just skilled laborers on the same demolition site. Under the fancy costumes and the make-up, behind the swaggering act was another work crew of scared, sweaty grunts.

"Since ya'll were so far up north, ya'll could shoot any and all people that ya'll found. They were enemy or they had no business being up there. You don't do that down here." We said all right. We were laughing and joking because we didn't figure there was going to be that much shit anyway. Hey, Rat Patrol. We would run up and down the highways supposedly keeping them gooks from putting mines on the road. But they were still doing it. The jeeps kept being blown up.

There were four of us on a jeep. The driver carried a shotgun. His shotgun driver carried an M-79. The gunner on the back had his M-60 and the a-gunner had his M-16. There was a nice little piece of firepower on this little jeep.

The first day on Rat Patrol, we go out and get sniped at: Pow! I spin the gun around and look. It's a village. So I'm saying, "What are we supposed to do? Do we open up, or don't we open up?" The driver, who was a corporal, he said, "To hell with it. Open up." We were all brand new in that area. We opened up and raised some hell. Two other Rat Patrol jeeps heard the fire fight going on and they pulled up. Now you got three jeeps, all with the same type of weapons, shooting the hell out of this village. We ain't got no business doing it, but we don't know that. Hell, a guy sniped at us.

We got back to the base and all hell broke loose on us. "What are you idiots doing? We just got finished telling you guys you're not supposed to be doing that."

"We got sniped at."

"Anybody and everybody gets sniped at."

"Yeah, well, we shoot back." We were used to shooting back. They threatened us with sending us back up North, so we said, "Oh-no, you don't got to worry about us. We ain't going to shoot no more. We'll be cool."

*   *   *

Somewhere along the line in the early stages of the war, some observation chopper pilot got tired of being shot at all the time. The guy rigged up three rocket tubes to the side of his helicopter, tied them into his electrical system and it worked. So they started arming helicopters very heavily. Basic American ingenuity.

Our gunship was a UH-1C Bell helicopter. On a really good day it was capable of flying 100 knots per hour. The later models, the Delta and the Hotel models, were faster and stronger but they weren't as maneuverable. There were two rocket pods on each side, seven 2.5-inch rockets. They were fired electrically by the pilot. Inside it also had two XM-21 systems—the Miniguns. Each gun was capable of firing 6,000 rounds a minute. But, on our helicopters they had inhibitor cards in the electronics so they only fired 2,000 rounds per minute. The guns were equipped with what was called a ten-degree pivot. The Miniguns would automatically track from side to side five degrees off center.

In training films, a helicopter with one Minigun mounted in the nose would make a pass over a football field—fifty yards wide and a hundred yards long. They'd turn a rabbit loose on the field and let him run around. Consistently, the ship would make one pass and kill the rabbit. Every time. The noise that they made was not like a gun. It was a long, deep, very loud belch. *BRAAAAAAAAAAAAAAH.*

In a light fire team, two helicopters, you dive into a position from maybe 1,500 feet up, firing the rockets and maybe the Miniguns. As you come up out of the dive, you make a very sharp turn. That's the break. Depending on who the pilot is, you could make the break as low as 100 feet above where you're shooting at. During that critical turn, the Miniguns weren't much help and the helicopter was extremely vulnerable. That's when the door gunner became important. I had an M-60 machine gun in the door. I'd do a whole acrobatic trip of shooting behind and underneath the helicopter to spray the area. By the time we were coming out of the break and I was out of range, the other helicopter would be coming in behind us and shooting their Miniguns or their 40mm cannon or whatever.

These helicopters were never intended to carry troops or supplies or letters. They were just these big pieces of death machine that flew around and that's all they did. Some of the more inventive crew chiefs would crawl under the helicopter and paint things on them like, "Be nice or I'll kill you." We had some colorful names: The Bounty Hunters, The Sting Ray Light Fire Team, Magic Turban. We were Brutal Cannon.

Most of the time, we would just hang out in the stand-by shack close to the airfield and wait to get a call. There was a lot of bullshitting, but it was fairly good bullshit. I remember talking about philosophy, the universe as a single entity with One Pilot. There was this one guy who was a real fan of Isaac Asimov, always talking about Einstein's theory of relativity.

Then the telephone in the shack would ring: "It's a scramble." It was right out of the movies. We'd go racing like hell across the airfield, dive into our helicopter, take off and go blow the hell out of whatever section of earth they had pointed us at.

Sometimes, if troops were being dropped into what was suspected to be a hot area, we'd fly in before they landed and blow the shit out of it. A lot of times, we'd

fly counter-mortar. The fastest way to stop somebody
from mortaring the base was not to hit them with artillery or to send out reconnaissance patrols, but to have
a helicopter team standing by. When the base got mortared, we race out to the field, take off like mad and
then fly up and look for the next mortar flash. When
we've spotted it, we dive in on that position and blow
the shit out of it.

The Viet Cong, being no dummies, discovered what
we were doing. They'd start to mortar the generators
and they'd allow a minute and a half to go by, figuring
that would be the reaction time for us to get out to the
helicopters. Three or four times, we'd be racing across
the airfield and they would begin to mortar us. Twice all
of us were recommended for the Distinguished Flying
Cross for running through the barrage to our helicopters.

One night we were flying pretty far south and got a
call in flight. A whole area was involved in a fire fight,
on the ground, in the air. It was really something. We
landed to pick up fuel. We're sitting there on the flight
deck and we look over to where the battle was. Usually,
it would be the gunships working out, shooting down
with the Miniguns, sporadic fire coming back up. This
night you could see the gunships firing, but even more
fire was coming back up, .50 calibres.

"Whoa, let's think this one over, man. I am serious.
This doesn't look good. Not good at all." A .50 calibre
machine gun is nothing to be fucked with. Movies have
done a disservice to that weapon. What they fail to con-
vey is that a .50 calibre machine gun is big and bad
enough that if you look around a city block, you will see
almost no structure standing that you can hide behind
safely if somebody is firing one of those things at you. It
just goes through everything.

"Hey, we're going to go over there and really kick
ass. Those sons of bitches can't get away with that." We
got into a pitched battle, the worst I'd ever been in.
When they would fire from the ground the bullets
looked like baseballs or beer cans coming up at you.
They'd kind of float up in your direction slowly. When

they'd get closer, they'd suddenly seem to speed up and whiz by. Have you ever been drunk and stood on a dark street corner where there's a lot of traffic? Your vision is a little blurry and you see all the taillights flashing by you. This was like being in the middle of the intersection with the lights flashing *at* you. They had green tracers and white tracers and red tracers.

I guess we flew six sorties. Go out, expend all of our ammunition, fly back and load up. Go out again. Finally, dawn came. The battle broke off.

There were literally hundreds and hundreds of Vietnamese fleeing the area, any way they could. Panic. The sun was up and that was it. Time to get the hell out of Dodge. This wasn't a village. It was a big swampy area. They were leaving in boats, slogging on foot, anything. I don't know if they ran out of ammunition or what, but we were taking very little fire at that point and we were just killing everybody.

It turned into a turkey shoot. They were defenseless. There were three or four light fire teams working the area. Hundreds of people were being mowed down. Bodies were floating in the water. Insane.

I was in there with the best of them. Blowing people off the boats, out of the paddies, down from the trees for Chrissake. Blood lust. I can't think of a better way to describe it. Caught up in the moment. I remember thinking this insane thought, that I'm God and retribution is here, now, in the form of my machine gun and the Miniguns that I take care of and the rockets that we are firing. It was a slaughter. No better than lining people up on the edge of a ditch and shooting them in the back of the head. I was doing it enthusiastically.

You begin at that point to understand how genocide takes place. I consider myself a decent man, but I did mow those people down from my helicopter. A lot of people we were killing in the morning were the same people who were trying to kill us that night. I tried to compensate in my head that most of the people we were wasting were the enemy. But I could appreciate in a black way that you can take anybody given the right circumstances and turn him into a wholesale killer. That's what I was. I did it. Bizarre. That's what it was. It was very bizarre.

*   *   *

We didn't have much turnover of patients on the ward until medevac planes came in. Then we could get rid of twenty or thirty at a time. You'd be sitting at breakfast and you'd think, "Oh, God, I wonder if Tracy is still there or Homer." Sometimes you almost wished that they had died so that you wouldn't have to go in. But you knew they weren't going anywhere. There was no place for them to go. The ward was always there and you couldn't get away from it.

We worked twelve-hour shifts, seven days a week. If things were slow, you'd get a day off. Or a few hours anyway.

Some days if it was really getting to us, the nurses would make believe they were the corpsmen and the corpsmen would be the nurses. Those days I'd volunteer to clean the latrines and mop the floors. I couldn't stand it. I just didn't want to look at another patient, so I'd do scut work.

Between the heat and just what you had to look at every day on the ward you were bagged. I didn't bother trying to eat lunch. I would set my alarm for half an hour and sleep through my lunch hour. Everybody did that. Somebody would have to come and wake you up. You always slept through the alarm.

The ward was divided into half GIs and half Vietnamese. We used to rotate on the ward. One day you'd have the GIs and the next day you'd take care of the . . . I hate to use the word gooks, but that's what it amounted to. When I first got there, I could see how the Vietnamese weren't treated the same way as the GIs. I thought, "Who the hell do those nurses think they are? They can't be that way. People are people."

And yet six months later, I was doing the same thing. Even though they were civilians and they just got caught in a crossfire or they had head injuries—we took all the head injuries in the area plus the civilians who got hurt by us—you just didn't want to take care of them. You really got to resent even having to go on that side of the ward when it was your turn.

If we ran short of drugs, rather than be fair and give everybody what they should get, we gave the GIs the medicine. Then, if there wasn't enough for the next day's dose for anybody, the Vietnamese didn't get theirs for that day either. We saved it for those among the GIs who were the worst. I know a lot of the kids felt bad about it. The doctors didn't even ask, because they knew there was a shortage and they didn't want to know how we handled it.

The richest country in the world and we had shit to work with. We had suction at a guy's bedside with these crummy little bottles that were the size of Coke bottles. If you were trying to suck somebody out that was bleeding where they couldn't breathe, in two minutes the suction bottle was full. Then what are you going to do? You got to take time to empty it. Where are you going to empty it? There is no place to empty it, so you dump it on the floor. You couldn't always get the suction to the Vietnamese and you let them go. People who had to be suctioned every hour and more frequently, well, you know, the GIs needed some help, so you took care of them and you ignored the Vietnamese.

We had a European nun on the ward for a while. She didn't live very long. She was about thirty. She was riding a scooter through the town after hours and there was a GI trying to get back to his unit. It was dark and he was thumbing a ride. She picked him up. Some ARVNs shot them by mistake. They killed the GI and she was paralyzed.

She arrested a couple of times and we resuscitated her. She was also a nurse and she knew she was in very bad shape. She said, "If this happens again, don't save me. Let me go. Just let me go."

She's our age and the doctors' age, so we freaked out. We'd go to the club and drink. "What are we going to do if this happens again?" It was amazing how much booze was consumed over this question, how much booze was consumed in general.

The last time she Coded—had a cardiac arrest—
everybody was really going all out for her. When that
happens there are only so many things to do. One person starts the IV and gives drugs. Somebody pounds on
the chest. Somebody keeps time for the drugs that are
being given. Everybody else knows that they're supposed to be watching the other patients on the ward.

A couple of corpsmen went down to watch the GIs.
Of course, nobody watched the Vietnamese patients.
There were no screens to protect the other patients from
having to watch these things. So they were watching the
nun, too.

At the end of the Code, not only did the nun die, but
one of the Vietnamese patients died. He got a mucus
plug in his trach and nobody noticed it. I went down to
the Vietnamese side and was looking at him. He had this
horrible look on his face, because he had strangled to
death. It was hard to tell how old the Vietnamese were,
but if I had to guess, I'd say he was fifteen, though he
could have been ten years older than that. Not only did
his oxygen tank run out, but his trach plugged and killed
him. He was practically quadriplegic because he had a
spinal injury like the nun, and a head injury, too. I
don't know if I was supposed to be ashamed or guilty or
what.

A bunch of us were sitting over in the club later. After
you have a lot to drink, you get incredibly philosophical. The final word on the boy was, "Well, he's better
off." It was stuff like that every day.

Usually when you see a five-year-old kid in a hospital
in the States, he's coming in to have his tonsils out or a
hernia repaired or an undescended testicle taken care of.
One of the first little kids I took care of in Nam, some
GI for whatever reason gave him a grenade to play with.
The grenade went off and it kind of blew his little body
to bits. He lived about a day and a night and then he
died.

Most of the GIs were suckers for little kids. They'd
always pick them up. We had a little boy that was booby
trapped. He was about five years old. Somebody had
put a bomb on him and sent him into a bar where there

were a lot of GIs hanging out. Someone picked him up and he exploded. It killed five GIs.

We had the kid only a little while. He didn't live too long. You stand there and you think, "Well, what the fuck. I don't even want to take care of this kid." Then you think, "He's only five years old. What chance did he have?" So it was just easier not to think about it. You just said, "Tough shit, that's the way it is. He's just going to die anyway." Then you went on about your business.

There was this prostitute that came in. I don't remember the exact story, but I think she had been with a couple of GIs and was caught robbing them. Anyway, two guys had been killed. She had been shot, but had survived. She was on our ward. She was about the same age as me—early twenties. I said to a friend of mine, "Jesus, she's going to die. I hope to hell she doesn't die on my shift, because I don't want to have responsibility for trying to resuscitate her. I don't give a shit what happens to her."

This guy was really cool. He said, "Why do you feel this way?"

"I hate her guts. Whether somebody uses a hooker or not, you're all in the same game and you got to pay the consequences. Only the guys already paid and she might as well pay too." I just hated her.

"When the time comes," he said, "I'm sure you'll do whatever you have to do."

"No way. There's no way I'm doing to do this shit. I'm not going to do anything for her."

So of course, she arrested on the ward when I was on duty and I *did* do CPR on her and somebody came over and tried to ventilate her. She died eventually, but not because I didn't do something. But it's hard.

I don't feel like I should have ever been subjected to that experience. You don't want to know that stuff like that exists. You don't want to know that people can get hurt that badly in those numbers. You don't want to know about little kids getting blown to bits. You don't want to know how ugly things can be, how ugly you can be. I didn't want to decide who would get medicine and who wouldn't get any. We should have treated them all like human beings and I didn't do that.

We didn't sleep at night. You got a nap in the daytime and you were set. I would do anything to keep from going to bed. We'd play cribbage until I was so blind I couldn't see the holes to put the pegs in. And I never knew if I was moving my pegs or the other player's. It got to be a joke and we laughed about not being able to go to bed. But inside, nobody laughed. It was frightening. You only slept if you were drunk as a skunk or if you were shooting dope or if you had six joints and you were near comatose.

Even the patients didn't sleep at night. When I was working nights, I'd be sitting up doing the charts and it was nothing to have six or seven patients sitting around the desk. They wouldn't talk. Oh, maybe one of them would tell you that he wanted to marry you. But really they just wanted company. They couldn't sleep. They were afraid to, even though they were in a hospital. They had no way to defend themselves and they were hurt. I was there with a light on, a warm body with a light and they weren't forced to go to bed to face whatever it was each one of them had to face when he closed his eyes.

We'd run out of blood. We'd run out of antibiotics. But we always had fruit cocktail, rubbers and shower shoes.

Every nurse's fear was being taken prisoner and not having any Tampax. You couldn't count on being in the jungle and using a leaf, because the jungle was defoliated. We were told to always have a suitcase packed, if we got overrun, we'd be lifted out. That was a crock of shit. I found out later that they never had any such evacuation plan. If we got overrun, it was just tough titties. In any case, we all packed the same things. We packed money, a camera and we packed Tampax. My flak jacket was so full of Tampax that nothing could have penetrated it.

* * *

We were right next to a little town called Dak Tho in the province of Quang Ngai, which is a traditional Viet Cong stronghold, about three klicks off the South China Sea. I was with the Calley Brigade about a year after Calley mowed them down at My Lai.

When I arrived I was automatically the ranking officer. There were three other guys who were hard-stripe sergeants,* a respected rank for a short-termer. We wore jungle fatigues, but no brass—just a U.S. on the collar and our unit designations. Jungle Warriors.

When I walked into the unit, there was a stable of twelve paid Vietnamese agents who were identified by a letter/number combination from D-1 to D-12. One of these agents would appear from time to time with information. We would pay them from what was called the contingency fund—bottles of liquor, cigarettes and cash to give them according to the quality of the information they had. Some of them were more or less on retainer and received whatever sum they were signed up to get.

The unit had a reputation for actively pursuing combat, for not only generating intelligence but also acting on the information.

Very early I began to see this reputation as some sort of justification to the infantry—an excuse—because these guys didn't have to go out in combat. Intelligence didn't have to carry rucksacks and face the day-to-day dangers of the infantry. Instead, they were allowed to create this mythology about themselves.

There was one guy in particular who was the archetypical soldier of fortune. No one controlled him and he had no control over himself. I called him the Killer.

He was from Georgia and had played college football for a while. The Killer actually had a tremendous amount of charm, but beneath that facade was a shark's conscience operating all the time.

Most of the guys in intelligence knew they were in it to avoid combat. The Killer wanted to kick ass. Me being the fucking new guy and the top banana, I had to make up my mind. There was a part of me emotionally and in-

tellectually that sided with the faction opposed to being
a commando hit unit. There was another side of me that
was unconsciously reckless and maybe a little ad-
venturous. I was twenty-four. Curious.

The day of my first patrol was a typical morning
during the early part of the monsoon season. It was just
beginning to get a little muggy, a little gray. We hadn't
taken any incoming since I'd been there. Everybody was
getting a little edgy, because we were about due to take
something. On the other hand, we were all settled in,
playing a lot of poker.

I'm just sitting in the hooch, trying to somehow
establish an administrative SOP for the whole unit. I
was very conscious of my need to cover my ass with my
own commander. Generate some bullshit and send him
paper.

The Killer gets real excited, because one of the Vietnamese agents shows up, D-9. I could see him framed
through the doorway. He's slightly larger, slightly
taller, more self-assured, more trained than the others.
He's not a peasant. He's been altered. About forty-five
years old, he's wearing black pajama pants, but he's got
on a nice tropical white shirt. There's a good 9mm
strapped to his side along with a couple of fragmentation grenades.

D-9 looks detached, like he knows what he's doing.
He isn't giving anything away. He isn't there for the
money or the bottle of booze like the other agents I'd
debriefed. D-9 has a small entourage and is clearly in a
position of authority.

He comes in to the table which is covered with a map
of our area of operations with a piece of acetate over it
and a grease pencil tied to a string. The Killer begins to
debrief him with our interpreter.

D-9 tells us that there are VC infrastructure—cadre
—in the area today. The economics chief and the tax
collector are in this particular village. If by chance there
would be a unit of Americans sweeping in that area, the
VC would take to designated spider holes. He knew this
to be true because he had a subagent working for him in
this village. That subagent would be out in the area and

he would leave little pieces of red paper in the vicinity of the spider holes.

This is all interesting, but I can't quite believe that this guy is giving us anything but a line of shit. The theatrics are a bit much.

D-9 had delivered in the past. He had a good track record. And we were all looking for an opportunity to get out anyway. It wasn't just a question of good information, it was a question of getting out and kicking somebody's ass.

If we were as gung-ho as we thought we were, we probably would have transferred to an infantry unit or the Lurps. We were punks, dilettantes. We were bullies. We really got a chance to act it out and there was no mommy to scold us, no principal's office to be sent to.

We worked with four battalions. We call up the battalion the information pertains to and make an offer to their staff person for intelligence, the S2. The S2 says he'll send a chopper for us. Every lieutenant colonel had his own helicopter—his Charlie Charlie, command control—which he used to keep track of his own troops. If there's ever action, he can get up there at 5,000 feet and watch the show.

So we go down to the helipad and a few minutes later—Whoosh Whoosh Whoosh—this Huey comes in, picks us up and takes us out to the LZ, a forward position for the battalion on a hill.

We lope down to the TOC—Tactical Operations Center, a bunker built into a hill, heavily fortified—sandbags and rafters. There's a big map on the wall, a couple of chairs and tables scattered around, like pictures you see of World War II.

The Old Man's down there and he's real lean and mean, about forty-five years old. He says to me, "Okay, Lieutenant, whattaya got?" I point out the coordinates, go through the whole spiel. The Killer endorses D-9. The S2 agrees that it's not just a bullshit joyride. The colonel says, "I'll give you a squad from headquarters and a ship. I've got a recon platoon out there right now with two or three tracks. You will rendezvous with Lieutenant So-and-so, throw a cordon around the objective and proceed to search and destroy.''

We get in the ship, take off and find the platoon down there humping around through the tall grass. We hop on the tracks, three armored personnel carriers.

I'm out there for the first time, starting to get into the Vietnamese countryside, rice paddies and fields. Every once in a while, there's a little grove of banyan trees and bamboo thickets, but mostly it's tall grass like cattails or bulrushes.

In the distance all around us are the tiny straw houses of the Vietnamese—two here, three there, all separated by rice fields. Old men and little boys are sloshing through the paddy with an old wooden plow behind a water buffalo.

D-9 stops us in a large grove of trees. The recon lieutenant puts his men in a circle with a 100-yard diameter around the area. We've got maybe thirty-five guys. Then there is the command group: me, the Killer, D-9 and his underlings, the interpreter and S2.

Finally, one of the subagents comes out of the grove with a piece of red paper. My first reaction was, "Wow, far-out. Is it true?" Then I think, "Well, of course, they just threw some red paper out there. Now we're going to look around for a half an hour and we're not going to find anything. Then we'll be back on the tracks, the ship'll pick us up and we'll go home." The more they look, the more skeptical I become.

Finally, they actually find the lid to the spider hole. The Killer low crawls over to the hole and drops a few frags down there. Then he kicks off the cover and empties a few clips into it, standing up like Audie Murphy with a machine gun.

Nothing happened. Then there's a huddle and we decide we'll throw a Claymore in. Kids go from a one-inch firecracker to a two-inch to a cherry bomb.

So they wire it up, drop it into the hole, pull the wire back to the plunger . . . *kawhoom* . . . blow the fucking thing up. Still it's mostly fleshettes,* not a lot of explosive power.

There is a tree right next to the entrance to the hole.

The demo man puts plastique right up against the backside of the tree, slaps the det cord into the charge, rolls out the det cord—"Fire in the hole." *Wham*.

By this time, I'm completely convinced that there's nobody down there. It's just a surreal game. The smoke finally clears and we stand around the hole. There's a lot of talk, a lot of indecision.

Finally, D-9 orders one of his people to go down into the hole. A few minutes later he pulls out a leg. Then he pulls out the body of a man missing a leg. He pulls out another body. And one more—a young one, just a boy, maybe in his late teens. They've died horribly. They were packed in there pretty tight. The man who lost a leg was obviously the one in the breach.

They have the look of being cadre. They're middle-aged. They have a few piasters on them, not much. It wasn't like we found the tax collector who'd just been on his rounds. They have some identification, no diaries, a few documents. We gather it all up to send back for analysis.

After the bodies are dragged out, without any command to leave the perimeter, the troopers start wandering in with their rucksacks. Out of nowhere, all these Instamatic cameras began to appear and flashbulbs began to pop simultaneously. I had a very strange feeling as if I was projected somewhere outside of it. Pop. Pop. Pop. I saw it as if it were in pantomime, slow motion. All these guys reaching gracefully and deftly into some hidden pocket in their fatigues, the strobe light effect of the flashcubes. They're smiling these big smiles of great joy, like something wonderful had just happened.

I don't want to give the sense that I wasn't elated by the whole operation. You've done the job, you've scored the touchdown. You're going to get a pat on the back. I was trying to be one of the boys. I certainly wasn't expressing the confusion and doubt that was going on inside of me. I'm standing there nodding along with everybody else. The S2 is saying, "Wow, three KIA, body count three. The Old Man is going to be so happy. You guys are really dynamite."

Then somebody notices the third guy—the young one—that his chest is moving. He is breathing.

The Killer kneels down next to him, takes him by the hair and holds up his head. He takes out his .38 snub-nose and sticks it right into the kid's temple. The Killer looks up. I guess he wanted to get some kind of consensus, some kind of permission. If he'd done it spontaneously and automatically there was no saving the guy. But the Killer wanted some kind of group involvement in this decision. He couldn't do it by himself. He says something like, "We take no prisoners, right?"

Something happened. I came back to earth. I became immediately decisive without a moment's hesitation. I said, "You can't just kill that man."

The Killer went into a tantrum, "We'll take this guy to the police, turn him in as a suspected cadre, and he will be kept there for a few days. Some relative will come and bribe whoever gets bribed and this guy will be back out again planting mines in the road. If we don't kill this guy, he's going to be killing more GIs. We have a policy in this unit, Lieutenant. We don't take no prisoners."

I said, "Well, that's not my policy. I don't know anything about that." Then I launched into this moralistic speech about how what we had done that day could be justified as a bona fide act of combat, but to kill a man like this in cold blood was something that I could not sanction. Then I let myself off the hook by adding, "Besides, this guy could provide us with some really good intelligence."

The other lieutenant called for his medic who jumped into the hole with the kid. He was shot with an IV immediately and medevacked out. For all I know, they got the kid up in a chopper, slit his throat and dumped him out.

Those guys never trusted me again after that.

*   *   *

All hell broke loose. I dived over this log and I peeked from behind it. I hear one of these guys with me screaming at the top of his lungs. His leg is all blown to shit. The dirt is popping around him. Snipers are trying to kill him. Three other fellas are up front and they're all laying in a shallow stream, face down.

The gun that was behind me, the shit should have been going off and I didn't hear it. So I just took it for granted that the gun was knocked out and the whole team was out of commission. I must be the only God damn person up here that's still alive. Everybody else is fucked up or dead.

I'm opening up with my M-16, changing magazines, trying to get that God damn pack off my back so I can work out. I know they're up there and I'm just capping them.

This wounded dude is screaming. I kept telling him to shut up and play dead. The longer and louder he screams the more they fire at him. I say, "Okay, I'm coming to get you."

I changed magazines, jumped over the log and took maybe four or five steps, dodging and capping. All of a sudden, I was back where I started on the other side of the log. A satchel charge had blown up in my face and knocked me back. I was blinded.

I couldn't see, but I knew that the gooks were all around me there. My bandolier was situated so that I knew how my ammo was doing and I'm still firing away. I was cursing them, calling them every name in the book. I don't know if I'm ever going to see the light again. I was mad. All I wanted to do was get this wounded man back and here I am getting my shit blown up.

I heard the bushes moving behind me. I spun around and I started to shoot. Someone is falling down the God damn bushes back there. "No, no, hold it. Don't shoot." It's my man Jackson. He slides in beside me. He had thought I was dead, too.

"How bad it is?" I asked him.

"You don't want me to tell you."

"Damn it, how bad it is?" I don't want to touch my face, because it's burning. I know it's bleeding because I can feel the blood running down my neck.

"Well, it's like this," he said, "there is so much blood that I can't tell you how bad it is." I just fell back thinking, Oh God, I'm blind for life. I just knew it. I figured my face was mangled too. If he can't tell how bad it is, it must be real bad.

After a while I'm dabbing at my eyes with the towel around my neck. God, I wanted to see. I started patting around my eyes. I must have been blind for about ten, maybe fifteen minutes. In a fire fight time is either very long or really short. You lose how much time is involved. It seemed like a year.

Then I started seeing blurry. The charge came off on my right side, so that side of my face was filled with shrapnel. When I started patting, that stuff was just falling in my hands. It must not have been real close to me because the shrapnel was on the surface, not embedded all the way back in my brain. It still fucked my shit up. I started seeing and I looked at him again. "Damn you, man, really—how bad is it?"

"Well, you wiping most of the blood off." He's taking it lightly and I couldn't see. I was ready to kick the shit out of him. Then I was firing again. I asked, "How many is hit? I don't hear the machine gun behind me."

"One gun team is hiding behind a rock, the entire gun team."

"What?"

By this time, I heard help running down the stream toward us. I heard somebody back there yell, "How come the God damn gun ain't opening up?" They got the gun up on a rock and they're down behind it. Ain't nobody shooting.

"Open up, Jackson," I said. "Keep yours on automatic." Now that I can see a little bit, I see movement from these guys laying on their faces in the water that I thought was dead all along. "How many is hit?" Each one of them sounded off.

"Not me."

"Not me."

"I don't know if I am."

"You bastards," I yelled.

Word came down to pull back. Most of the firing had stopped by this time. The VC were pulling out on their own. We start out. I commenced to kicking the gunner and the a-gunner for not opening up. I did almost shoot both of them.

When I got back the gunny says, "That Baldwin is a man among men." But did they medevac me out? No. If you got your legs hurt, they took you out. Arm wounds and head wounds stayed in the bush. I had to walk around with a big white turban of bandages. I said, "You got to color this sucker. You ain't leaving this big white target all over me in the middle of Nam." I stood out like a street light. They dabbed it with camouflage make-up.

We found out later that day that it was a division that our company was butting up against. But all we ever saw were a couple of sneaker marks and a couple of sweat shirts with UCLA on them. We started wondering who the hell we were fighting. We're wet and freezing in the monsoon, and these NVA dudes got UCLA sweat shirts.

*   *   *

I was following a blood trail. He was losing more and more blood. It was twenty minutes after the fire fight, so some of the blood was dry right by the first bushes I came to. The color really changes as you follow along. It gets more bubbly, frothy-looking and wetter. Which means that you're gaining on the guy.

The tension really increases. I'd seen all those stories of these fucking heroes who are badly wounded and stay behind to keep the heat off their buddies. American war movies are filled with those scenes. You figured the Vietnamese are about the same.

As the trail got fresher my steps got slower. In the beginning there was a lot of blood, but I guess he probably stemmed the flow. When I came to him, he had this tourniquet on his left leg. That's where he got shot pretty bad. He'd done a good job with the tourniquet. You would figure that—well, maybe not, I guess he was an ignorant North Vietnamese soldier—he could have just put up a white flag and I would have left him alone, you know just captured him. He could have surrendered or something. I wasn't out there to fuck with him at that point.

I heard a noise and me and a couple of guys nearby all fired at one time and put about 300 rounds in that one bush. That was it. He bought the farm. We were pretty upset when we saw the guy. He didn't have a piece in his hand, he didn't have a weapon on him. About fifteen feet from his body was an AK.

He had on black tennis shoes, black canvas with the ball on the ankles like you used to wear when you were a kid. I had seen the print of his sneakers every once in a while on the ground.

*   *   *

As a sniper we'd sometimes go out with a company, hoping to pick up any forward observers from the op-position, spot them and ding them PDQ. If the company ran into something, they'd yell for me and I'd get up front and bust caps at whatever they told me to bust caps at. Sometimes it was a gook, sometimes it was a deer. Our commanding officer got his deer in Vietnam. We lugged it back so he could have the head mounted. Spit-and-shine, nickel-and-dime Marine is what he was.

Sometimes you'd go after one particular guy. That was different. That guy has an identity. You know he has specific duties and who he is. I remember those people.

Intelligence tells you where he is, which direction he'd be coming from, what time he'd be there. And these people were punctual.

Two guys would go out after them. A sniper and a scout. They'd drop the chopper in five or six places so nobody would know for sure where you were. We'd usually set down next to a road. You'd be pretty tense then. You wouldn't be talking too much. You'd be nervous until you got a feel for your surroundings. You set up your fire lanes. What would happen if this goes down? What if you miss the hit or there are twenty-five guys following behind him? You work out the options with the scout.

You set it up, get him in the sights and drill him. When that was over you run and get his shit, rummage through his pockets and head for the pick-up. You have to call that in, too. The pilot would ask you if it was hot and you'd say yea or nay. They'd swoop in and pick you up.

That work bothered me a lot. The fire fights I had in the field, I can rationalize that for myself. You say, they knew the risk as well as you did. It was a fair fight. If I hadn't seen so many cowboy and Indian movies, I might not be so guilty about it. But TV taught me there's a right way and a wrong way to go out and kill somebody. I imbibed that shit from my childhood on. The television was my surrogate father.

You don't always fire "in anger." It took me a long time to adjust to the fact that I wasn't killing people out of anger. They didn't piss me off. That I turned my mind off to it scared me later. I thought, "Geez, if I can turn my mind off to doing something like that and say it doesn't count, wiped clean, that's freaky. You're not supposed to be able to do that. What's wrong with me?"

* * *

A colonel for the Armored Cavalry had the misfortune of having to take my men out regularly to a drop-off point from where we would go on ambush. A tank would always hit a mine and lose a track on that trip. That means a half day to a full day at the place. This fucking colonel says, "We're not going to take you out anymore."

"How come?"

"I'll tell you how come. Because you have the worst fucking record with my tanks and I'm not wasting tanks on you. I don't care what happens to your men, but I'm not losing any more God damn tanks."

"But, sir, all you do with the tanks is you drive them

up to the perimeter at night and use them like a fixed weapon. I can't see what the big deal is with a tank that won't move. As long as you can drive it up to the perimeter, what the hell difference does it make?"

The colonel didn't like that, so one morning they didn't take us out of the base camp and we got hit. At the same time that we got hit, I got a cramp in my leg. I was in a ditch, nose deep in the mud with this fucking cramp. I couldn't get around because the cramp was killing me. So I got to jump up in the middle of the fucking fire fight and start jumping around to try to get rid of the cramp. The tankers, those cocksuckers, stood up on the top of their tanks and watched us have it out.

The VC were just firing at us from a hill where we used to get ambushed from, so it wasn't as bad as it seemed. But when you first get hit you don't know where, who, what, whatever. You just hit the ground and you wait and see. We were all flat on the dirt and the colonel's boys were up there cheering. Not for us, for the VC that were hitting us. We were really fucking pissed. There are things and there are things, but your life *is* your life and you try to save it. It ain't a laughing matter.

So we wanted to get that motherfucker real bad. What can we do? We can't kill him. We can't kill his men. The best we could do was to scare the shit out of them. We decided to *really* scare the shit out of them.

Now this base camp was never hit. Never, never, never, never, because the VC would look at that camp and see all those fucking tanks and in a million years they know they ain't going through. Forget it. Eighty tanks all in a row just waiting for somebody to try something is a very impressive sight.

I arranged for us to cover the southern defense of their base camp where there were no tanks. That night I get on the telephone and I say to one of my men in the next bunker, "Hey do you see anything moving out there?" Like a fucking idiot he says, "I don't know." I'm ready to fucking kill him.

All of a sudden some other guy listening on the phone

says, "You know what? I think I might see something
out there." Only this guy wasn't one of us.

"Where?" I said. "To your right?"

"Yeah."

"Yeah!" I yell, "I saw him, too." My guys start
chiming in, "Yeah, I saw him." "Me, too." All of a
sudden we're talking up a ground attack among us on
this bunker line.

I call in to base defense. "Arizona six-five, we're
probing by fire." Voom, I hung the fuck up. I didn't
even want them to have a chance to say no. See, if you
probe by fire, you give away your automatic weapons
positions. They don't like that. But the enemy knows
wherever you have a bunker, you've got an automatic
weapon, so what the fuck is the sense of not doing it?
You'll just be giving away a position that they already
know about.

So we start probing by fire. I call up again, "Arizona
six-five, this is bunker commander. I want illumination,
illumination." Hung up the phone again. As soon as the
illumination was up, that was it. Everybody started
firing everything they had. It didn't make any difference
whether they could see anything or not.

Then I took four people and we fired across the base
camp at the Armored Cavalry Regiment that was on
guard duty on the side where nothing was happening.
Well, I want to tell you, you've never seen anything like
that in your life. Our little fire fight and a few rounds
clanking off the metal of those tanks and everything
started blowing.

The colonel calls me on the phone, "What the fuck
are you doing? What the fuck are you doing? You gave
all the automatic weapons positions away."

"Sir, we have heavy contact out here."

"What?"

"That's right, heavy, heavy contact." And I hung up
the phone like that. He starts calling in fucking air
strikes and the Cobras come in and start rocketing the
God damn place.

We're just sitting there smoking dope going, "Wow,

did you see that one hit?'' ''Whoa, look at all the colors.'' I said, ''Let me get some more illumination out here. Beautiful.''

In two and a half hours we must have burned up sixty grand worth of ammunition, easy. After it was all over there was not one body found. Because there were no bodies.

I got called on the carpet the next day. ''What the hell was going on out there?''

''Sir, we were under attack.''

''Well, there was no wire cut. There were no ladders, there were no footprints, there are no bodies. I'm getting military intelligence after this.''

''Good, that's a good idea. Maybe they can find out who's attacking us, sir.'' I walked out of his office.

We had at this particular base camp a nifty set-up. We had this barbed wire that we could move away and let the whores come in and fuck everybody in the bunkers. The next night everyone is really uptight about bringing in the whores because military intelligence is supposed to be watching the bunkers to see what we are doing. The military intelligence guy, like a real asshole, goes out in between the bunkers and the barbed wire, digs a ditch and gets in it to spend the whole fucking night.

Now we had a little problem. We wanted the whores to come in and we had this stupid bastard out there in the middle of where we brought them through the wire. But he had no radio with him—HA! We started peppering where he was with rounds. He couldn't even put his head up. We brought the whores in in the middle of very heavy fire, hitting everything around him, scaring the shit out of him. Once we got them all inside we closed the wire. Every time he stuck his head up, we laid some more fire on him and fucked the night away.

The next morning he came out shaking. And that's how we left the Armored Cav.

* * *

They didn't want salts from the field to go even near Da Nang, so we hung out at a bar halfway between there

and Quang Tri. That's where I met this guy called
Eighty-nine. Eighty-nine got the name because he killed
eighty-nine men in one day. His whole platoon was
wiped out or some shit. When they found him he had
eighty-nine confirmed kills around him and all he had
left was a bayonet in one hand and the rifle butt in the
other. He didn't have no ammo, but he had blood on
both.

When his unit came in the bar, everybody else in the
joint would shift out of the way. Hell, I'm used to the
pogues* moving because of us. All of a sudden we're
moving. I wasn't ready to move, but my buddies convinced me to get out of the way. A lot of them had one
long braid down one side of their face. Some part of
their heads was shaved. Some of them had Mohicans or
one braid like my man Yul Brynner had in the *Ten Com-
mandments*. Most of the black guys had Mohicans
because they couldn't get their hair long enough for the
braids.

Eighty-nine and his men was Marine Recon. I had a
lot of respect for them. They were all crazy, but I
respected them. They were ear collectors.

They lay these ears on the bar. The guy who had the
most ears that didn't match up in pairs, had to buy
rounds for all the rest the whole night. They were actually playing around with them to match them up. If
they didn't have matching sets, then it wasn't a confirmed kill. It meant they probably stole the ear from
somebody else. If a guy complained, "I didn't have time
to get the other ear," they would say, "Bullshit, you
must have stole that extra one."

I was fascinated with this group of men. They were all
on their second or third tour of Nam. The ones on their
third tour were told that they *got* to go home this time.
Their kinship was even stronger than ours. It wasn't
even about them saying, "Yeah, we are bad." They
didn't even think of anyone else being around. I don't
remember how I actually got to talking to this guy
Eight-nine, but I found out that he really believed in
what he was doing. That was the difference. We were
there because we didn't want to go to jail or whatever

our reason was, but he was there because he believed it.

I kind of felt sorry for them in a way. They got there and found out that their talent was killing and they were damn good at it. They had a taste of killing and they all liked it. Now when the war ended, what were they going to do? Once you reach the peak it's all downhill.

*   *   *

We were an extremely professional operation, the only troops in Vietnam who had total light and noise discipline. All the moving parts on the rifles were taped down. Trigger guards were removed for ease in firing. No noise at all. You'd never know we were moving.

On patrol we traveled stripped. There was no insignia, no identification, no cigarettes, no American anything. If we were caught, there was no way in the world—outside of the fact that we were Americans—that you could identify us with the U.S. military.

We carried cards with us saying that this person is working for military intelligence. If this person has been killed, don't touch the body. Do not remove anything from it. Report the location. We were not associated with the United States Army outside of this card. On certain missions, even that was abandoned.

We did a couple of missions that were not really kosher. Sometimes you know exactly where you're going before you go. Other times, you don't know until you get there and open up the packets with the maps and weapons. You're standing there turning the map round and round trying to orient yourself.

The idea is that if any of the Cambodia business gets out, it's all over for Nixon. So the Cambodian operations were not just clandestine, they were denied all the way to the top.

We did a mission where we wiped out a town in Cambodia. I mean, an entire fucking town. After it was over, I read some intelligence reports that said everybody there was supplying the North Vietnamese. But you got to take that with a grain of salt. Many times the recruiters for the NVA would come into a village, take the oldest person and string him up, slit his stomach open and let the wild pigs eat him alive while he was dying. Then they say, "Who wants to come with us?" God help you if you don't.

We got into this village and herded all the people together, maybe sixty-seventy people. Women, children, everybody. We burned all their homes to the ground. We thought they were being evacuated.

At the last second I broke squelch. You don't talk on the radio because the enemy can triangulate, they can hear you. You just do not talk on the radio. I broke squelch, because I thought they would move these people out, relocate them to a POW camp. Question them, find out who's doing what and release the rest of them.

A guy gets on the radio and says, "Waste 'em."

I wasn't going to talk on the radio. I broke squelch again—twice. The guy goes, "Waste 'em."

I said, "Waste what?"

"Waste everybody that you've got."

"You're talking about sixty-seventy people, some of whom may be friendlies. Are you aware of that?"

He said, "Waste 'em."

"Can I have your name and rank?" I said, because I was not going to kill all those people.

"Sonny boy," he said, "I assure you that I outrank you by five ranks and twenty years. And I'm telling you to waste 'em."

"How do I know you're not a civilian?" I said. "You may be a field agent for the CIA or something. I'm not going to 'waste 'em' until I get somebody on this fucking radio who will tell me who the hell they are and by what authority I'm doing the wasting. At that particular point, I might do something about it."

Two people who claimed to be very, *very* high-ranking officials got on the radio. One of them said to me, "By order of the Commander in Chief of the United States Armed Forces, I'm telling you that the previous transmission given you is what you are to adhere to."

"I really can't believe what you're telling me."

"We really don't care if you believe. Waste 'em."

So I got with eight of my men. The other two were guarding the villagers. I told them we'd just had an order on the radio to emulsify these people. What should we do? We had to talk for an hour.

It was a double bind. If we did it, we would be very ill at ease with ourselves. If we didn't do it, we'd be in a lot of trouble when we got back. There was no right answer.

But I had a couple of people who really enjoyed killing quite a bit. They were the ones on guard. I told them what the situation was. They couldn't wait. They grinned from ear to ear. They pulled back, made all the villagers lie down on the ground with their hands behind their backs. Then these guys wasted them. The women, the men, the children, everyone.

The pisser of the whole thing was that the next week the newspapers reported on this small village with no name, that the North Vietnamese regulars overran and destroyed all seventy inhabitants.

We came back and were fucked up about it for a while. That's when things began going bad. You see, killing is very impersonal. Pull the trigger, you don't see anybody go down. You find out later, maybe, if you did any damage. Maybe some general up in a helicopter flying over the scene sees a few people go down. But we started having a very personal contact with the people we were killing—not just these people in the village. In general, with some of the things we were doing, I started to get really bad feelings. Not feelings of morality either. Just fucking bad feelings.

*   *   *

I sent my interpreters and my intelligence people down to debrief this Vietnamese soldier to find out what he knew about VC installations within our area of operations. They came back with some hot information. About that time a plane showed up from our detachment in Da Nang. It had the payroll for my team. I evicted the pay officer and climbed into the plane. I briefed the pilot and we took off.

The pilot was relatively new in-country and had not had any experience in combat flying. The plane was an L-19, called a Bird Dog. Essentially, it's a Piper Cub with two seats front and rear. They had an extra set of controls which you could put in the back seat. Normally, I put them in, simply because it is easier to fly the plane yourself than to tell the pilot what you want to look at. This time I was in too much of a rush and I didn't put the stick in the back of the plane.

As we were flying over a river, I saw something that was perhaps a foot bridge that I hadn't seen before. I told the pilot, "Circle around. I want to take a closer look at that." He did a 360 and came in real low.

My last words to the pilot were, "You're coming in too low." His last words were, "Nah, we'll be down and gone before they know where we are." That's a technique we use on recon flights. If you fly at treetop level, even a low-performance aircraft goes over so fast that as soon as someone on the ground hears a plane and looks up, you're already gone before they can pick up a weapon and shoot at you. On flat ground, it works great. Up in the mountains where they can sit above you and shoot down, it doesn't work so well.

Although I'll never know for sure, I'm convinced in my own mind that the pilot got hit with a burst of automatic weapon fire. I believe he was killed by a bullet from the ground. I got winged. See the scar here on my face? We crashed and the plane exploded and burned.

The first thing I recall when I regained consciousness was a Montagnard tugging at the ring on my finger with one hand and pulling out his machete with the other. I decided to donate my ring. Most of the first three days I was unconscious. When I was awake, I was mainly scared shitless. I was in a lot of pain, so for the first few months I wasn't too sure what was going on. I had three broken vertebrae in my back, bad burns on my legs and some internal injuries, plus the crash had generally banged me up. I was spitting blood for a month at least.

There were six or eight Viet Cong there, none of whom spoke English. I was trussed up and carried from place to place on a litter because I was unable to walk. At that point I was very close to my camp and they had to move me deeper into their own territory. We moved almost every night. I presume they wanted to keep my whereabouts secret.

Most of the camps were Montagnard villages, bamboo and thatch huts. In the mountains of South Vietnam, it's damn cold and I never had adequate clothing or blankets. I went for the better part of a year without warming up, dressed in rags, without medication. Food consisted of a bowl of rice and a cooked vegetable twice a day. A hint of meat once a month. By my best estimate, my weight fell from a normal of 175 pounds to 90 pounds. I was able to form a ring with my thumb and forefinger around my wrist and I could slide that all the way up to my shoulder without opening my fingers. Sitting down with my knees together, I could put my fist sideways between my thighs without touching flesh.

After a while I had a beard and long hair, pretty wild-looking. They never cared how I looked unless they were planning to show me to a Vietnamese troop unit or some villagers. They did it to humiliate me and to show that they could defeat these powerful Americans. Before they would put the rope around my neck to parade me around, they would cut my hair and force me to shave. It finally dawned on me why they did that. To the Oriental, the beard is a sign of virility, power, respect and venerability. For this American to have a beard would be to accord him the same respect that an old man would get.

Eventually, we reached a place somewhat south where they had built a camp just to receive me and the interrogators. They had waited three months to begin the interrogations. That seems incredible to Americans, because we think you've got to hit them right away. But they don't want information of any tactical or strategic significance. They knew more about my area of operations than I did. They showed me that in an effort to make me break. They want things like photographs, tape recordings, broadcasts, signed statements, confessions that can be used for propaganda purposes. There was no urgency to break a prisoner right away. The delay was simply logistics. It took time for trained interrogators who spoke English to get there.

They were good. They make our interrogators look sick. They were trained in psychology, steeped in Communist ideology and they spoke perfect English. There were three of them, two who did the actual interrogating and a political officer to keep those two straight.

One of the first things they did was deny being interrogators. They claimed they didn't use interrogation or indoctrination or brainwashing techniques. They were teachers and their purpose was to teach me the truth of the situation in Vietnam. "Once you understand the truth, we will release you to go home and tell the American people the truth of the situation."

That sounded pretty good. When they said it, I thought to myself, "That's bullshit and I know it's bullshit." But on the other hand, you want to believe that part about being released and allowed to go home. Believe it or not, years and years later they were still singing the same song. They had lost their credibility somewhat, but they were still saying, "We have no need to keep you for a long time. We want to teach you the truth and set you free."

Their approach really blew my mind because I was sitting there expecting the worst and had been expecting the worst for three months—the typical interrogation with physical abuse and the whole nine yards. They began by telling me the history of Vietnam going back about 5,000 years, slightly warped to give—let's say —the Communist version of it. In simple terms, The Party claims everything good that happened in the country for 5,000 years and blames everything bad on anybody or anything other than the Communist Party. They talked about the Mongol invasions and the Chinese invasions. I'm sitting there wondering, "What the hell are they telling me this stuff for? When are we going to get down to the real reason we're here?"

Daily sessions would last about four hours. First one a day, then two a day and eventually they increased the pressure to four a day. What they were doing was trying to soften me up and see how far they could go. They wanted to make a calculated estimate of how much they could get out of me.

They didn't get very far and they never did. Everything inside me rebelled at everything they were doing and I absolutely refused to cooperate in any way, shape or form. They made every effort to get me talking about any kind of innocent subject, hoping eventually they'd get something they wanted out of me. I knew that. So I simply refused to talk at all. It wasn't long before I was called all sorts of dirty names and the treatment got progressively worse. They began to apply all manner of mental torture day and night for a little over three months. It got so bad that they would take turns or leave me sitting alone because of the fatiguing effects of the interrogation.

Towards the end my health had deteriorated drastically. I was still suffering from the effects of the injuries from the crash and I had had malaria a couple of times. Withholding medicine was another way they had of weakening you and forcing you to collaborate.

They harped on this business of, "Cooperate and we'll let you go home. Know the truth and you'll know what you have to do. As soon as you demonstrate your good faith, we'll let you go home." Demonstrating good faith was doing whatever they told you to do. In this case, they wanted me to write a political statement and sign it, which I refused to do. Eventually they wrote one for me and I refused to sign it, too.

Then the really severe physical torture started. Initially they were kind of crude, just being beaten with a heavy stick. Later on they became more sophisticated with their torture, particularly after I was moved to North Vietnam. One of their most effective tortures is one we called the rope trick. They tie your body in an extremely uncomfortable position and leave you like that for a couple of days.

Pain is a natural defense mechanism of the body. You touch something that's hot and the signals go up to the brain. The brain sends a message back to the muscles to pull back within a split second. It's an electrical system.

Just like any electrical system, the human nervous system has circuit breakers built into it, because the brain can stand just so much pain sensation before it causes damage. When the pain gets too great, these circuit breakers shut off any feeling of pain. I'm sure you've heard cases of people losing limbs in a car wreck or other accident and they say they feel nothing. Several days later when the pain begins to return, the doctor is pleased because that means they are getting better. The pain has actually subsided before they can feel it. That same principle applies to torture.

A beating is not effective torture because after the first few blows, you don't feel anything. To force a person into an extremely uncomfortable position and then make him stay that way causes excruciating pain—but not quite enough to activate the circuit breakers.

One time I was put into a cage that was about eighteen inches square and five feet long. I'm broader than that in the shoulders and well over five feet tall, so you can imagine the cramping effect that had. I was chained hand and foot with wrist locks jammed tightly together, crammed into this cage and left there for three months. I had refused to bow to them. After three months they took me out and beat the living hell out of me and eventually taught me to bow. But I made them work for it.

At the end of that first interrogation I was weak physically and worn down mentally. It finally got down to the point that I did sign the statement. The goal is to resist completely, but when you get to the wire and see that you will either go crazy or die—and those were very real possibilities—you have to decide if it is really worth dying for. It's kind of a curious phenomenon. I really can't explain it. When we got to the end of that particular session and I was forced to do something that was absolutely repugnant to me, it was almost as if I was standing off to the side watching myself sign the statement. I was over by the far wall watching this man sign my name.

Isolation was part of the treatment of all prisoners. I didn't see or talk to another American for five years. That's one of the cruelest tortures. We all developed some sort of mental exercise. One of my earliest experiences with being in solitary was remembering all kinds of things that I had long since forgotten. I found that I could clearly remember all the names of my grammar school teachers, for example. Nursery rhymes that I had learned as a kid came back clear as day. It was fun playing around with that. Something that happened in the sixth grade or a tree house I built as a boy would be enough to dwell on all day. My earliest memory went back to when I was two years old and we moved into a new house.

Fantasy life was important. I promoted myself to four-star general, jumped into Hanoi with an airborne division and just cleaned their clock for them. I also started doing algebraic progression in my head.

I spent time designing my dream house that I would build someday. Then when I finally settled on the design, I decided to go ahead and build it. So I built it in real time in my head. I would spend a day with my eyes closed and in my mind I would be standing there supervising the bulldozers while they dug the foundation. If I figured it would take three days to get the foundation poured, I would spend three days actually working on the foundation in my mind. I built the whole house that way. It took about six months.

When I got all through with it, I was real pleased. I decided the next thing I would do to kill my time was to do a cost estimate on it. Without any way to write things down, I computed the board feet of lumber, the number of bricks and concrete blocks, the amount of copper tubing and electrical wiring, all the fixtures and doorknobs and hardware. I would assign values to these things as best I could remember and add it up.

I spent a lot of time going over all the religions of the world and making up my mind whether or not there was a God. I very definitely believe there is. I built a beautiful stone chapel in my mind and every Sunday morning I'd get up with my wife and my children, eat a good breakfast and go to church. We'd sit there together in my chapel and sing hymns and listen to a sermon I'd had the minister prepare. Sunday was always a good day.

III

WAR STORIES

VICTORS

"I had a little puppy for a while in Vietnam. For a period of three days, I would take this little puppy and squeeze it until it would yelp. Or twist its little paw.

"I knew what I was doing. I knew that I was transferring something to this little puppy. Somebody or something had to suffer for all the pain inside of me, and it was going to be the puppy.

"I was so horrified by my behavior that I gave the puppy to someone else. I had to get it out of my sight. I don't think I would have killed it, but I didn't quite know where this spark of sadism was going to lead me. It went against the grain of who I thought I was. I had a sense of being split in two."

It rises like a wave of nausea in your throat, out of nowhere, uncontrolled, the dry, bitter taste of evil. You're walking the dog and in canine goofiness he insists on sniffing one empty square of sidewalk, holding his ground until you jerk the leash so hard the choke chain almost cuts his windpipe in two. A child says "No" at just the wrong time and you swallow hard when you find yourself towering over your own flesh

*and blood with murder in your eye. You actually slam
on the brakes, jump out of the car and run back to rip
the throat out of the tailgater behind you before he can
roll up his windows. An uneasy joke escapes from the
knot of petty viciousness inside you and you seem to
stand outside yourself as you watch it metamorphosize
to malicious teasing. Suddenly you're tormenting some
other human being—usually someone you love—until
he's ready to take a wild swing at you.*

*The feeling passes quickly leaving you shaking with
every thump of your heart, wondering where in this sane
and ordered world a psycho like that comes from. But
that psycho was you, the other you, the darker side, the
one who knows all the nasty things you've done or
thought in the privacy of your mind, the flipside of your
conscience that hoards the merest slights and demands
revenge no matter how petty, how misdirected.*

*No eighteen-year-old kid went to Vietnam thinking,
"Oh boy, now I'm going to be evil." But most of them
met their darker sides face to face in that war. A few of
them had an adolescent meanness which blossomed
ugly, nurtured by the circumstances they found in Vietnam. Many of them indulged the ruthlessness they discovered as part of the instinct to survive.*

*For all the glory words like duty, honor and valor,
war runs best on evil, a breeder reactor that vomits out a
hell full of pain for the little spark of sadism people feed
into it. Evil was encouraged with rewards of medals,
time off from the horror, a hot meal. How else can you
convince boys to kill one another day after day? And
when the darker side grabs the upper hand, takes control, how else can it be excused?*

*Vietnam veterans do not have the luxury of dismiss-
ing evil as a momentary aberration in an otherwise
civilized world. They have seen the ugliness humans are
capable of inflicting—that they themselves are capable
of inflicting.*

*The brutal stories are delivered with a nervous
chuckle, dirty jokes from another world that don't quite
survive translation. "I guess you had to be there." But*

there is no enjoyment in the telling. The hesitant laughter is self-defense, a shaky feint to keep the evil at arm's length. If the mortal slapstick can be kept in a cartoon life, maybe the shadow of inhumanity can be denied a little longer, the personal pain can be buried a little deeper.

I got to the rear and spent about a week doing bullshit work. Everybody that came in did that. My week consisted of making a barbecue pit.

The first sergeant there was impressed that I came in from the infantry. He said, "You seen any action?"

"Yeah."

"Then you know what it's all about."

"No, I don't know what it's about." By this time a few doubts were entering my mind. For instance, we're not doing well. I can't see any real advance being made in the attempt to secure this country. All we're doing is occasionally going out and blowing things up and wasting a few people. That's about it. There's no ground being gained.

We're supposed to be saving these people and obviously we are not looked upon as the saviors here. They can't like us a whole lot. If we came into a village, there was no flag waving, nobody running out to throw flowers at us, no pretty young girls coming out to give us kisses as we march through victorious. "Oh, here come the fucking Americans again. Jesus, when are they going to learn?"

There was some unpleasant talk that I didn't like.
There was one guy in the platoon that told me they were
searching in this hut one time and there was a really
pretty, young Vietnamese girl. He walked over to her
and jammed his hands down her pants and started to
take her clothes off. She was shivering and scared.
There were two or three guys in the hut. The girl's
mother came in and started raising all kinds of hell and
they backed off. I had the feeling that they would have
raped her if her mother hadn't come in.

I don't know what I would have done if I had been
faced with that sort of thing. I don't think I would have
taken part in it, but I also don't think I would have tried
to stop it. That would have been encouraging your own
sudden death. These are the guys who get in fire fights
with you. It would have been too easy to get blown
away.

*   *   *

I was enjoying the feel. There was a couple of guys
saying they didn't enjoy the feel. That was junk. We
had a sense that we was no longer that GI who had to
march, who had to salute. That was shit. We didn't
have to salute nobody. We dressed the way we wanted
to dress. If I wanted to wear the boony hat, I wore the
boony hat. If I wanted one sleeve up and one sleeve
down, I did it. If I didn't want to shave, I didn't.
Nobody fucked with nobody in the field. An officer
knows if he messed with you in the field, in a fire fight
you could shoot him in the head. This was standard
procedure in any infantry unit. Anybody tells you dif-
ferently, he's shitting you.

If you mess with my partner as an NCO or something
like that, in the unwritten code there, I had the right to
blow your brains out. And the guys would do it. Those
lieutenants and the CO didn't mess with nobody in the
field. They didn't say, "Hey, soldier, why is your boot
unbloused?* Why is your hair long?" Everybody just
said fuck it.

I had a sense of power. A sense of destruction. See,

now, in the United States a person is babied. He's told
what to do. You can't carry a gun, unless you want to
go to jail. If you shoot somebody, it's wrong. You're
constantly babied till you go to the grave. The only
people's got the authority is the judges or the Establish-
ment.

But in the Nam you realized that you had the power
to take a life. You had the power to rape a woman and
nobody could say nothing to you. That godlike feeling
you had was in the field. It was like I was a god. I could
take a life, I could screw a woman. I can beat somebody
up and get away with it. It was a godlike feeling that a
guy could express in the Nam.

*   *   *

I know Marines that made more gooks than they
killed, just by treating them bad. It's funny when you
don't expect to get mercy from anyone, you're very
reluctant to show it. So you really breed hideous people
over there, for the cause of National Defense. If you sit
down here on the couch, it seems ugly. At the time, they
weren't ugly. They were the things to do. Considering
what else is going on this was nothing.

*   *   *

Our base was pretty quiet. Sometimes you'd be going
up to guard mount and the commander would tell us,
"Look, we haven't had many kills in a long time. So
let's go down to the village and shoot somebody and
drag them back across the river." You weren't supposed
to shoot them unless they were on our side of the river.
He didn't say it in those words exactly, he just said,
"Hey, you know, you guys want a day off, we got to be
getting more kills." He'd kind of hint.

Guys wanted more days off. I did too, but not enough
to kill people. My squad never did it. We used to go
down to the village and shack up when we were supposed to be working on ambush. But some of the guys
would just go down to the village and mow down some

people, including women and kids, and drag them back across the river. Look what we killed.

The only way to take out your frustrations over there was to go shack up or go out and shoot somebody. A lot of guys were afraid of shacking up, because they were afraid of VD and everything. So they would go and shoot somebody.

Calley mowed down all those old women and children in that village. That's all you did find in the villages during the day. We walked into a lot of them. Ninety-nine percent of the time they wouldn't try to do anything to you. We walked in there all the time drunk and stoned, ready to have a good time and screw all the women. They had every opportunity to cut my throat and they never did. Calley went in there and mowed everybody down instead.

* * *

Too many of us forgot that Vietnamese were people. We didn't treat them like people after a while. It was hard to separate. I really didn't like to mistreat people over there. I tried as hard as I could . . . not that I didn't from time to time.

I met this woman in a bar when an American Green Beret was pushing her around and drinking whiskey. I told him to knock it off, because I thought he was being an asshole. One thing led to another and we had a fight. After that, me and the girl became friends. Later she saved my life and strangely enough she was probably Viet Cong.

In the city of Can Tho we were allowed out into the town every day between noon and four o'clock in the afternoon. Usually about a quarter to four, we'd all line up on the corner waiting for a ride back to base. We'd just jump on the back of anything headed that way.

Little shoeshine boys would also come out there at that time to polish your boots. Who the hell needed clean boots? But you did it anyway. We'd give them a dong for the job—that's like a twentieth of a cent.

One afternoon I was standing on the corner waiting to

catch a truck when a little shoeshine boy came up to me. He'd been around for about six months. We all knew his name. He had a little box that you put your foot up on. He's working on my boots and I look up and see this bar girl that I knew across the street calling my name and waving for me to come over to her. I decided to go see what she wanted. Just about the same time another little kid came running by and grabbed the shoeshine's hat. The shoeshine boy ran after the kid as I was crossing the street. The shoeshine's box blew up. It was a satchel charge that took out twenty-three Americans. I got knocked to the ground, unconscious for a few seconds, but I wasn't hurt. The bar girl was gone when I woke up, and nobody ever saw her again. The little kid disappeared, too.

*   *   *

I blew up a village one time. It was a village outside of which my squad got ambushed. Myself and my three squad leaders went in with three demolition packs, twenty pounds of C4 apiece.

We crimped the blasting caps onto the time fuses with our teeth. Stick them in the C4, load up the hooch with whatever there was. Smoke a cigarette to light up the fuse. Time it.

"Okay, we're lighting now."

"Hey, mine's not lit."

"You better get it fast, man, 'cause mine's lit."

"You got about five or six seconds. Go." Then we hauled ass out of there and BLAM. That was fun.

All the people were gone by then, so it was nothing but pigs and chickens. We got in line and shot the shit out of the livestock, pigs squealing across in front of us. It was a way of blowing off steam. We did My Lai with farm animals.

*   *   *

I made a bet with a friend of mine that I could sink a sampan with a rock. So we got radioed by a river patrol boat that there was a sampan headed our way who was probably a gunrunner. So while the helicopter pilot hovered overhead, I hooked up in my harness and leaned out. I had a good eight- or ten-pound rock. I dropped it and it went through the little boat and the boat sunk. Little Vietnamese guys are yelling and cursing . . . and swimming.

* * *

We'd move in next to a little village and stay there, patrolling every day. The only way you went to the rear was to get yourself shot.

In this one place the village people called me Wa-ky Jake No. 10. Wa-ky was the word for American and No. 10 means "the worst." What happened was, they had this one old crazy dude—sort of the town idiot —they called Dinky-dao. Dinky-dao was like mentally ill, I guess. The VC hired him to come in and fuck with our lines one night and I caught him and shot his ass. The fucking people hated me after that.

Every day we had to go down by the village and make sure everything is cool. All the mama-sans stop what they're doing and start yelling, "Wa-ky Jake No. 10. You shoot Dinky-dao. You shoot Dinky-dao. Wa-ky Jake No. 10. You motherfucker. You doo-mommie.*"

"Mama-san, you fucking shut up or I'll shoot you, too, you little VC."

"Me no VC. Wa-ky Jake No. 10. You motherfucker. You shoot Dinky-dao." I'm walking down the street with my rifle on my shoulder and my finger on the trigger guard. I'd turn on them and holler, "Pow-pow-pow," like I was shooting them, run at them kicking up that red dust all over the place. They'd take off through the village yelling, "Wa-ky Jake No. 10. Motherfucker, motherfucker. You doo-mommie." All kinds of weird shit.

I'd get a couple of them like cornered up against a hooch and I'd say, "Mama-san, what did you say? I'm going to blow your fucking head off. You VC. You VC."

"You Jake, No. 1, No. 1."

"You're God damn right and don't you forget it."

I'd go on down the street and we'd be way out of the village and you'd hear, "Jake No. 10. Jake No. 10." I used to love fucking with those assholes.

I'd come back in at evening and the little kids run up to me with those skinny little voices. "You shoot Dinky-dao, you shoot Dinky-dao. Oh, you VC. You VC."

I'd make like a monster, roaring and throwing my arms up in the air and they'd run off. "I ain't no VC, baby-san."

We drug in some gooks we killed on an ambush one night. You got to count them, right? Fucking mama-sans are all around us crying and screaming. It's some kind of religion, get all that spirit shit out. They were screaming and crying every time one of them dies. I said, "But Mama-san, Mama-san, these are VC."

"Ah, man, you No. 10," she says. "Fuck you, you No. 10."

"Fuck you. I'll blow you away, you old bitch. Old Jake out there kicking his ass, fucking gooks shooting at him and shit. Mama-san call me No. 10? I'm out there, protecting your ass here in the village."

"You kill No. 1 son," she screams. "You kill No. 1 son."

Hell, it was fucking VC.

It gave you a feeling of superiority. You walking through the village and you got your great big old flak jacket on. You got your helmet and bandoliers all over you. You got your rifle. You tower over most of these people.

It got to a point where you just didn't trust none of them. You don't sweet-talk them, because they ain't going to be sweet-talking *you*—unless when you come back through here, there's going to be a booby trap to blow your fucking ass away. So we'd just try to scare the shit out of them.

There was a couple of times when people got hurt. We had this one dude who would go out shooting people, then yell, "Snake!" Like, don't worry, I just killed a snake next to the trail.

When I was walking point he'd walk right behind me; used to carry a .45. We come across this old papa-san* dying in the dirt in a hooch. Mama-san is there leaning over him. The dude walks up, pulls out that .45 and blows the fucker's brains out. Says to me, "I was just helping the fucker out." Then he turns around and shoots this mother and her baby. Steps outside the hooch and says, "Snake." Curious motherfucker.

Mama-san is running around raising hell with the sergeant. But what happens in the field, stays in the field.

* * *

We were riding in a jeep, about five of us. The driver said jokingly, "Will anybody bet me that I won't hit that old woman walking along the side of the road?" There was an old woman walking along with a long pole over her shoulder, a big bag of rice on each end.

"Yeah, I dare you," one of the guys said. He just turned the wheel real quick and broke her damn hip.

The officer decided, "Well, I guess we better call somebody." We called a medevac. It flew overhead and I threw smoke out for it and the guys landed.

They took that old woman and threw her on a stretcher and threw the stretcher onto the helicopter. I've seen sanitation men handle garbage cans with more delicacy. One of the other guys asked the medevac crew, "Hey, what's the problem? Why you treating the old lady like that?"

It seems we interrupted their ice cream run. If you had access to an aircraft, then you had access to the things available in a rear area. There were such things as pizza, fresh ice cream, cold beer. This particular medevac crew had pulled ice cream duty. Our pulling them to this emergency, they lost their ice cream that night. I try to rationalize that, but the only thing I can come up with is, here we are in a war zone and we messed up their free time—and she was just another gook. They could give a damn.

That was the worst thing I saw over there. I didn't see

any massacres. It was a guy on a dare. He wasn't a psycho, he wasn't a nut. For some reason something compelled him to run that old lady down.

*   *   *

We didn't get into aggressive kinds of torture. But we drew this one NVA. Silverman had gotten him. We knew he was dying. He was writhing in agony. It was a belly wound, and it was pretty bad. We could have gone out there to finish him off, that might have been the humanitarian thing to do. You knew he wasn't going to live, maybe another few minutes. It would have been better to just put his lights out.

We didn't do it. We took turns posing over him with a bayonet aimed at him—shit like that. We didn't poke him or anything else. Just posed and snapped pictures. Each person had a different kind of picture because he was rolling from side to side. It must have taken him about twenty minutes to die.

In retrospect I'm ashamed of it. I'm glad I don't have any of the pictures. I'm a lot more ashamed about it now than I was then. I guess we did it just to prove we were real tough motherfuckers. We won and he lost. The thrill of victory, the agony of defeat.

*   *   *

First time I was over there and they'd go beating up on people, I said, "God damn, you guys got to be nuts, man." But, you see a couple of your buddies get blowed away and you don't give a shit about nothing or anybody else. You don't.

You see fucking VC bodies laying there and think nothing of it. You say, "Fucking dead gooks." But you look over here and see jungle boots sticking out from under ponchos with helmets laying on top, and you get a feeling inside I can't explain. You say, "Whew, fucking American is dead, man. For what?" There they are, lined up, poor sons of bitches. Probably didn't even know what hit them.

I got close to being court-martialed in Vietnam for shooting some kids. Of course, we thought they was VC. We were out on an ambush. Headquarters called and said they were getting sniper fire from this village and we were to go over there for a little Search and Destroy mission. They said, "Sweep through it." So we did.

I was the squad leader. Burned all the rice and burned down a few hooches. We shot two or three kids that were running across the rice paddies, because it was dark and we thought they were carrying rifles. I beat up this old man. He was giving me a hard time. I beat him up and I was getting ready to shoot him, when somebody came over and told me that he was the fucking village chief.

When we got back my whole squad had to write up like a statement. But the CO told me, he says, "They had all better coincide. They better match up to what you said." So we all got together and we made up the same story and it was cool. We had brought a couple of prisoners back that time. The CO, he told me, "Next time, remember, dead men tell no tales. Don't bring back no prisoners." That's what got me in trouble.

It wasn't too long after that, one of our platoons got in a fire fight with the ARVN by mistake up on some hill. Platoon leader killed the Vietnamese captain by mistake. Then some other company attacked a church full of people, killed them and burned down the church. The CO comes over to me and says, "Well, now you ain't the only one that's fucked up. They're going to forget about you now."

That God damn Search and Destroy. They send you out to do it, then they want to fucking bust you for it.

*   *   *

My base camp was made up of twelve Special Forces people and eighty-seven Montagnards and their families. We were really out. I mean way, way out. We used to be visited by a general once a month. I would send my men out in the field to shoot at his helicopter. The pilot would say, "We're getting very heavy ground fire."

The general would yell, "Turn back, turn back." We only got visited about four times the whole year that we were there. The rest of the time I was kind of on my own, which was good. I was able to give my men three in-country R&Rs and a few other little bennies.

One time when this general came into our base camp, we didn't shoot at him. We had heard that UPI or CBS was going to be with him, so we let them land. That morning we had dragged six bodies in off the wire that we had killed the night before. Two or three times a week you'd get two or three bodies off the wire. This time they must have told the gooks that if they got inside our wires and overran us, they could eat all our food. They all had P-38s, the ration canopeners, around their necks. Sick fucking war.

Anyhow, we had these bodies. Of course, right away, my men would chop the ears off. They dry the ears and wear them around their necks. The CBS and UPI guys got there and the bodies don't have any ears. The schmuck general went fucking nuts. He said, "You get your men and you get those God damn ears and you have them sewn back on the heads. I won't stand for this."

Our medic was this guy named Grizzly. Big, six and a half feet tall, but gentle. Grizzly the Gentle Giant I used to call him. He happened to be a motherfucker in a fire fight—the meanest one of them all—but a gentle person, too. With the same hands that would take the butt of a weapon and bash somebody's brains in, he would repair our wounds, do minor surgery, patch people up, give physical exams. Grizzly tried especially hard to take care of the Vietnamese children and send them where they could get treatment.

Grizzly goes around and gets some ears—they weren't even the right ears. Then he sewed them on—upside down. When the general came back and saw the ears sewn on upside down, I was fined on the spot. On the fucking spot.

*   *   *

I had a patient who was supposedly an NVA courier. He had been picked up outside town with documents on him. He'd been shot in the chest, so he had a couple of chest tubes in and a little sump tube that was just used for drainage.

There were two MPs guarding him. Guarding him meant sitting across the hall with their chairs tipped back reading books. We all figured that he's sick, he's not going nowhere.

The nurses' shirts have this little pocket slit on the left front where we carry our scissors. I was kneeling by his bed milking the chest tubes. That means I was stripping them, to make sure that there weren't any blood clots. He pulled the scissors out of my shirt. I looked up from the floor by the side of the bed and he was coming down with the scissors, ready to stab me in the chest. I had hold of his chest tube and his sump tube. I just ripped them out of the guy's body. Needless to say, he dropped the scissors. The MPs were just looking for an excuse to do him bodily harm. They took him off the ward.

They came back a few hours later. One of them came in the ward and said, "Hey, Lieutenant, come on out here. I got something to show you." The MPs had peeled the guy like an apple. I didn't say anything. I didn't know what to say. They thought, in their own way, that they had done something for me, because this guy had tried to kill me. I wonder what those guys think about that now.

It wasn't unusual for people to be interrogated on the ward. People from intelligence came on the ward with maps and would try to question patients. If a patient was due to have pain medications, they'd say, "Don't give him any. We want to talk to him and we don't want him to be sleepy." They didn't care about his sleeping habits, they just wanted him to be miserable.

But the guy who tried to kill me was still alive and they peeled him like you'd peel an apple. Then they hauled him off in an ambulance. I don't know what happened to him.

*   *   *

When I was wounded they brought this Viet Cong casualty into the field hospital. He was about four beds away from me, attached with IVs and bottles, out cold. They were pumping dextrose into him and blood.

The doctor was working on this Australian soldier. As fast as they put blood into him, it went out, he had so many holes in him. They must have given him sixty-seventy pints of blood plasma. The Australian was dying anyway. A few hours before someone is about to go, there's a look that comes over the body. You just kind of know from the way they breathe, the color of the skin and the way the flesh hangs that they're on their way. This Australian was lying there dying.

The Viet Cong woke up. All of a sudden he saw that he was in an American hospital and he freaked out. He ripped the tubes out of his arms, broke the bottles on the side of the bed. He staggers over and slits the Australian's throat with the broken bottle.

The doctor, who had been working on this Aussie for hours and hours and hours, went crazy. I've never seen a doctor do this in my life. He grabbed a .45, put it in the Cong's mouth, picked him up off the floor with the .45. Then he pulled the trigger and the VC's brains went all over me. The doctor totally forgot about his Hippocratic Oath. He was just really pissed. When he saw what happened, he went insane.

*   *   *

After an ambush the VC and sometimes the NVA would drop their weapons and run. We'd pick them all up. We would take the rounds apart, put a little bit of C4 in the bullets, then put the bullets back together. The loaded weapons were dropped on the trails that we knew the enemy were using. Once in a while, you get hit with a ground attack and they'd be coming in. One of them would put his weapon up to fire and *ka-whump*—he blows in place.

Americans were taking Kalishnikof rifles for trophies. We mined so many that they had to make an announcement in the *Stars & Stripes*, "If you find an

AK-47 don't fire it with the ammunition that is in it. The Green Berets are mining the weapons. Use your own ammunition. Caution." Americans were picking them up and getting blown away, too.

At one point, the NVA were throwing shit bombs at us. They take advantage of the ammonia in the shit when it breaks down as an explosive. One guy pops up with the bright idea, "Why don't we collect all the Montagnard shit in the camp and make bombs to use against the NVA?"

"What the fuck are you talking about?" I said. "Shit bombs! This is what the Viet Cong use when they can't get anything else." I said, "Do you want us to become like them?"

One asshole says, "Well, sir, we are guerrilla fighters."

"You want to go out and do it, go ahead."

We had so much stuff. We had two different types of Thermit* grenades, fragmentation grenades, concussion grenades, Claymores, mortars, rockets.

Fu-gas is the best. I've seen things: B-52s doing air strikes 150 yards away, so close that they blew all the tubes in the radio and knocked all the buildings down. Powerful shit. I saw the shells from the battleship *Arizona* that sounded like a subway train pulling into Times Square. But . . . the best is the Fu-gas.

It's very simple. You take gasoline and you pour soap into it. That creates a sort of napalm when the soap and gasoline get together after four or five hours. You have to stir it around to get more or less the same consistency throughout so that you get a better dispersion rate. Then what you do is, you take a Thermit grenade and put it on the front of a fifty-five–gallon drum and you take a stick of dynamite and put it under the barrel. You put a No. 2 cap on the Thermit and a No. 4 cap on the dynamite. The dynamite pushes the gasoline up, then the Thermit ignites it. Everything for 200 yards left, right and in front is burnt to a crisp.

We made a lot of our weapons ourselves, besides the shit they gave us. We did our own booby trapping. We would take 500 or 600 pounds of cement and put metal rods through it like a mace from the olden days. We'd cover the rods with feces and then hoist it up in a tree, cover it with leaves and trigger it with a little spring. Somebody comes walking down the old trail and *wham*. Even if you only get him halfway, he will have such a raving septic infection inside it doesn't matter. Either you get them one way or you get them the other. We would fight fire with fire. What they did, we did. We just thought that we did it much better.

I would take C-ration cans and booby-trap them with pressure-released devices. Very small. You put the explosives inside the C-ration can, turn it upside down so it doesn't look like it's been opened. Then you put it on top of a pressure-release device. When somebody picks it up—*whoosh*—it's all over. We used to love to do that.

I have to admit I enjoyed killing. It gave me a great thrill while I was there. My attitude was, the less of them there were, the better my chances of making it. Of course, after a while that was forgotten. There was a certain joy you had in killing, an exhilaration that is hard to explain. After a fight, guys would be really wired. "Wow, man, did you see that guy get it? Holy shit. Did you see that?"

During ground attacks, a guy is dead and just as he is about to fall over, the volume of outgoing fire can be so intense a couple of rounds pick him up. He starts to fall over again and—*whack*—they pick him up. We would have contests to see how long we could keep the bodies weaving. For most people, seeing this, it's a horrible, horrible sight. We were so sadistic that we were *trying* to make it happen. The person was already dead twenty or thirty times over and there you are trying to keep him up.

* * *

The U.S. government told the Vietnamese government, "We're going to do something nice for you. We're going to buy these five-horsepower water pumps for you people. Also included will be ten feet of firehose

for the intake, and another ten feet of hose for the
exhaust. They got gas tanks on them, too." That unit
cost $200, at least. The U.S. government did that so that
the Vietnamese could drop one hose into the river or the
creek or the ditch and pump water into his rice paddies.

Some bright GI came by and said, "Hey, man, pull
that out of the rice paddy and spray my tank off." He
probably threw the farmer a dollar in U.S. scrip.

"Hey, Marine. Hey, Marine, come here. Washee-
washee." Soon you see all kinds of six-bys and jeeps
lined up. They set up a car wash on the side of the road
and they charged a dollar to wash your vehicle. The
people still used their old paddle wheels to pull the water
out of the river.

*   *   *

The kids in villages would see us coming up the canal
in this huge armored gunboat, and they would start
begging right away. They'd jump in front of the boat
and would not let us pass until we threw out some food.
They were willing to sacrifice those little bodies just to
score some C-rations.

I began to hate them, because I couldn't stand the
idea that we were coming into these people's lives and
totally disrupting them. You began to sense that these
people wouldn't give a shit if we were there or the Viet
Cong were there or anybody else. All they wanted to do
was to farm and to be reasonable. And we would come
in there and have their kids jump in front of the boat for
food?

*   *   *

We had what they called Kit Carson in our unit. Kit
Carson was a guy from the Vietnamese Army who was
assigned to American units. When we went out to search
and destroy a village, he would come in and talk to the
Vietnamese, find out if they seen any VC in the area.
Then he comes back and translates it to us.

Ours, he was scared. This guy was more like a show-

boat than anything else. He was a Charles, you understand. Like, you could see the resentment when we
destroyed a village. But there he was, with us.

When we had to interrogate some of the prisoners, we
used to take three gooks up in a helicopter about a
thousand feet. We're with an intelligence officer, G2
section from the general staff. He's in civilian clothes.
We got our Kit Carson up with us to do the translation.

He grabs the first one and says, "Talk." We say,
"*Crackadill, sakmile, crackadill.*" *Crackadill* was "to
kill."

The first gook wouldn't talk. Intelligence give you the
signal, thumb toward the door, and you push the guy
out. The other two gooks look to see this guy going out
the helicopter door.

If the second guy didn't look like he wants to say
something or he's lying, the intelligence officer says,
"This guy out the door." You'd kick him out, because
you're supposed to do what these intelligence officers
tell you to do. They're speaking for the Army. The last
prisoner is crying and he's like a typewriter. He's talking
Vietnamese like crazy. That's human nature. This guy is
running his mouth. You can't keep him from talking.
You'd have to gag him to make him shut up. The Kit
Carson is translating all this thing.

Before we get back to the base camp, after this guy do
all the talking and the intelligence officer document
everything, they kick him out the door anyway. Even
the good gook, they'd give the word on him and throw
him out the door.

We went up with three prisoners and we come back
with zero prisoners. Nobody looks around and asks,
"You went up with three prisoners, what happened to
them?" We come back, and the intelligence officer goes
back to wherever they go back to and carry the information to the command.

I could never understand how these guys survived, the
Kit Carsons. To me they're like traitors. They working
for the South Vietnamese Army, directly assigned to an
American line unit. Yet they see things going on against

their people—atrocities against Vietnamese—and they're right there. He's doing the interrogation. He knows what they're going to do with that last guy.

* * *

You take a group of men and put them in a place where there are no round-eyed women. They are in an all-male environment. Let's face it. Nature is nature. There are women available. Those women are of another culture, another color, another society. You don't want a prostitute. You've got an M-16. What do you need to pay for a lady for? You go down to the village and you take what you want. I saw guys who I believe had never had any kind of sex with a woman before in that kind of scene. They'd come back a double veteran.* These were not men who would normally commit rape. They had not had psychological problems. Being in that kind of environment, you give a guy a gun and strange things happen.

A gun is power. To some people carrying a gun constantly was like having a permanent hard on. It was a pure sexual trip every time you got to pull the trigger.

I remember riding down to Hue City with a couple of guys and one officer one day. I had a .45 in a shoulder holster and a grenade launcher in my hand. I was making eyes at all the Eurasian women, the children of the French. Most of them spoke more than one language and they were educated women. I'd annoy them all to hell. Finally, when she'd say something to me, it would be in Vietnamese. And it would make me crazy. I'd want to kill her. The problem was, I could have.

* * *

I once was with a Cambodian whore in the field on an operation. She spoke no English. Her entire vocabulary was fuck and suck and yes and no. We talked for the entire evening, believe it or not. We were totally able to converse.

She would go, "Me no suck-suck. Me fuck-fuck."

I replied, "Me no want you to fuck-fuck. Me want you to suck-suck. You bien?"

"No-no-no-no-no, me no suck-suck. Me fuck-fuck."

"Listen, I want you to suck-suck first, then we fuck-fuck later. Okay?"

"No-no-no-no-no, me no suck-suck, me fuck-fuck." That's how we passed the whole evening and I had a marvelous time. I swear to God.

The whores were amazing. We would sometimes take tremendous pains not to discuss our missions because they were so secret. We would be flown in by Air America. Two minutes after we landed you'd hear, "Putt-putt-putt-putt." The whores would be coming on those fucking Honda motorbikes, in the middle of the fucking jungle. It was unbelievable how these hookers found us. I don't even know of any roads that were near where we were.

Sure, there were missions where they wouldn't pull up. They would find us later on. But, usually, you would land and there they were, "Candy, soda, dirty pictures, boom-boom, dope." Not necessarily in that order.

I never got the clap and I always went in bareback. I was insane. I never had crabs or syphilis. Even when I got back and was going to marry my wife, I said, "I don't want you to get uptight, but I'm fairly certain that I'm going to fail this blood test. In Nam I fucked some of the dirtiest whores you have ever seen in your whole life and there's just no way I can pass it." But I did.

I know that some of the whores were putting glass up their vaginas and other ones were infected with a strain of syphilis that was very virulent. The spectrum of the antibiotics they were using at the time was not wide enough to get rid of it.

The Viet Cong and the NVA figured a combat loss is a combat loss. It doesn't matter if a guy can't go to war because he's got the clap and it hurts when he takes a leak or if he can't go to war because he's got a bullet through his head. Either way it's a loss.

*   *   *

We were a mobile assault group, so we had helicopters at our disposal. I would get command on the radio and say, "We're going on a long-range reconnaissance patrol to coordinates Yankee Zulu one-nine-fiver-seven. We will be breaking squelch every two hours." Depending on how many times you break squelch, you can communicate without really talking on the radio. They would listen for the break. Then I would get my men together and we would go to Vung Tau or Saigon. I'd have a whore blowing me and I would reach over and hit the squelch button a couple of times and roll back. When we got back, I'd file phony troop-movement reports. That's where it was at on many occasions, not all the time. But I did it, I filed false reports. They phonied up what we gave them anyway. It really didn't matter that much as far as I was concerned.

The place where I spent many an evening when I could get away from the war was the Hung Dao Hotel, a three-story, dilapidated shack in the middle of Tu Do Street, Saigon. The first floor was almost like a hospital ward, they had rolled about ten beds into it. The second floor was the kinkier stuff, so they had little rooms. That was also for officers or people who just wanted to fuck alone. The whores cooked and lived on the third floor.

We had some hot times with the whores at the Hung Dao. They really catered to you. Actually, they didn't give a shit about you other than your money, but as long as you had cash, they catered to you. I didn't care. I didn't want the hassle of establishing a relationship. I just wanted to get it on.

There'd be a dozen of us in the place and somebody would yell, "One, two, three, switch," and everybody would jump up, run into somebody else's room and start fucking whoever was in there. The whores were so nonchalant, they'd be smoking a cigarette while you were fucking them.

There was one girl who was about twelve years old

who was great. She was one of my favorites. Although there was another woman there that I swore I'd marry. She stole a ring from me, so I didn't marry her. They would steal you blind, but they always had a big ball of opium for you to smoke. The opium was one of the best parts of the Hung Dao Hotel. In fact we were at the Hung Dao so much and they loved my team so much, they made us T-shirts—Hung Dao No. 1, Hung Dao No. 2. Each one of us had a numbered T-shirt.

*   *   *

We were running security on a road in a free-fire zone. In Vietnam you had a friendly zone and you had a free-fire zone. Anything that crossed into the free-fire zone was fair game. Any gook—woman, man, boy, girl —it was game to you. Anybody come along with a cart or just walking and we would go through their stuff.

We was in the field twenty days or so. Up in the depots in the rear they got steaks. We didn't get steaks. We ate mainly C-rations, lousy C-rations and dry things that came out of cans.

These gooks are riding by in a Lambretta, which is like a motorbike except you sit people in the back. We say, "Hey, let's stop these gooks." So we came out of the bush and we pulled them over to the side.

"What you got there? Hey, you VC? What do you got?" It was a baby-san and a papa-san. I guess she was a teenager, maybe about fifteen or sixteen. The papa-san was forty, a mature man.

They had a can of pears! American pears in a big green can marked with a big U.S. on it in large print. We say, "Isn't this some shit. Here we are in the field, we don't know what pears is. They got pears! And *we* don't have pears." I'll never forget the guys' faces in the unit from the GIs up to the captain. We are shit in the field, and the guys in the rear have given these gooks pears, man.

Right away a guy took a bayonet and he opened up the pears. We're fighting, literally fighting, to eat pears. Food! It wasn't fresh, but it was something other than the shit they put together chemically and pressed into a can. It was like the man brought me steak and potatoes and I was back in my mother's house eating Sunday dinner.

Most of the guys didn't get any pears. I got a few pears and I got to drink the juice in the can. So we turned around and we said, "Hey, ain't this something? These gooks is riding around with pears. How did you get pears?"

"GI give them to me." He worked in a mess hall back in the rear somewhere.

"The GIs gave you pears? Oh, yeah? For that, we're going to screw your daughter." So we went running, taking the daughter. She was crying. I think she was a virgin. We pulled her pants down and put a gun to her head.

Guys are taking turns screwing her. It was like an animal pack. "Hey, he's taking too long to screw her." Nobody was turning their back or nothing. We just stood on line and we screwed her.

I was taking her body by force. Guys were standing over her with rifles, while I was screwing her. She says, "Why are you doing this to me? Why?" Some of the gooks could talk very good. "Hey, you're black, why are you doing this to me?"

We turned back to the father and we said, "So you got pears. GIs are nice enough to give them to you." All the Vietnamese carried this ID card. Big old plastic ID card with a picture on it that says that they are okay in the Republic of Vietnam. So we ripped up the ID card. "Hey, we got a VC here, fellas. A VC stealing government stuff, huh? So you must be an infiltrator." We shot him.

As I said we was in that *free-fire zone*. We just started pumping rounds into him until the guy just busts open. He didn't have a face anymore.

Baby-san, she was crying. So a guy just put a rifle to her head and pulled the trigger just to put her out of the picture. Then we start pumping her with rounds. After we got finished shooting her, we start kicking them and stomping on them. That's what the hatred, the frustration was. After we raped her, took her cherry from her, after we shot her in the head, you understand what I'm saying, we literally start stomping her body.

And everybody was laughing about it. It's like seeing the lions around a just-killed zebra. You see them in these animal pictures, *Wild Kingdom* or something. The whole pride comes around and they start feasting on the body. We kicked the face in, kicked in the ribs and everything else.

Then we start cutting the ears off. We cut her nose off. The captain says, "Who's going to get the ears? Who's going to get the nose? So-and-so's turn to get the ears." A good friend of mine—a white guy from California—he flipped out in the Nam. The dude would fall down and cry, fall down and beg somebody to let him have the ears. Captain says, "Well, let So-and-so get the ears this time. You had the last kill. Let him get it this time." So we let this guy get the ears. We cut off one of her breasts and one guy got the breast. But the trophy was the ears. I had got a finger from the papa-san. That was about it, what I got from the incident. We let the bodies stay there mutilated.

The next day we're doing some Search and Destroy. We went through a couple of villages we had to sweep. It comes over the air, "There's VC in the village of Phu Hip, so many klicks up. Go take a look."

We go through their village like harassing the women, shooting the guys. Now this is a guy that you just don't like the way he looked. His eyes were slanty and you just didn't like it. We shot him even though there was no VC there.

If the people don't treat you right when you walk through that village you can give them hell. They give you that snotty look. They won't say nothing to you, but they're a little cold. We expected for them to run out and welcome us like that World War II type of thing. "Hey, GI. Yay, you the Americans." But they were a little standoffish.

As soon as we step outside the village, the captain radios in, "We're under heavy contact." Then right away, those Phantom jets come in and drop those 500-

pound bombs. The village is leveled down and we go on to the next one. That's our Search and Destroy. If there wasn't an enemy out there, we made it be the enemy.

The slicks come and move us out, take us back into Long Binh. The colonel is there to congratulate us, "You in for a commendation, trooper. You had nine killed in that campaign, so you in for a commendation."

I had nine killed. I think I killed more than that. But like I say, we going into the village, somebody I don't like, you understand, I shoot them down. But they had written up that it was combat, heavy contact. That there was no American losses, but there was heavy losses by the enemy.

*   *   *

You can't tell who's your enemy. You got to shoot kids, you got to shoot women. You don't want to. You may be sorry that you did. But you might be sorrier if you didn't. That's the damn truth.

*   *   *

"Hey, Lieutenant, you want to see my pictures?"

"Yeah, sure." This usually happened at night, because then everybody was asleep or at least quiet. I'd go over and sit at the side of some guy's bed and he'd pull out a cardboard box full of pictures. I knew from the start that we would get around to the atrocity photos. It happened every time. They took pictures of the things they did. I don't know if it was to justify that there was a reason for it or what. If I was in a field unit and my best friend was peeled and had his penis cut off and stuck in his mouth, I might do the same thing if I ran across a gook. That's what a lot of these guys did and then they took pictures of it.

Showing them to a nurse in a hospital, it was like they had to tell somebody. After I'd seen the pictures the first couple of times, I thought, "Maybe I should say something. Whether or not I can do anything about it, if he's got something to say maybe he'll feel better for saying it.''

Then again, some of it was curiosity. You figure you've seen it all, everything, and suddenly you've got another picture. Something that freaks you out all over again.

He'd always start out with, "This is my best friend. And this is my lieutenant, and this is my sergeant. He's pretty cool. He's a lifer, but he's cool." He would go on and on. Then he'd get to those pictures.

"Oh, we ran across some NVA." There's a girl with the NVA who was probably their nurse—a version of me. Someone would have stuck a grenade up her rectum or a few guys gang-raped her, stuff like that. Then he'd get around to the fact that he was the one who did it, himself.

"I never thought I'd do anything like that, Lieutenant. But I guess you do stuff like that in war, don't you?"

"Yeah, you do things you never thought you'd do. You see things that everybody thinks about, but never has to face."

"Oh, yeah . . . sure . . . I guess that's cool." He'd put his stuff away and go down to the latrine.

When it came time for bed check, I'd find him still down there, sitting in the john, lots of times with the needle still sticking in his arm. He'd shot up for the guilt or so that he could go to sleep or whatever. Or he'd put so much up his nose, he couldn't even walk. I'd drag him back to bed.

I remember one kid who was eighteen. He had a lot of pictures and all he wanted to do was kill gooks. "I got to kill gooks. I got to kill gooks."

"My God, you're only eighteen years old. Don't you think there's anything more to life?" He had malaria. He'd had it before, a couple of times. His picture book kept getting bigger and bigger each time I saw him in the hospital. I thought, "Eighteen. What does a guy like that do when he gets home?" There were a lot of guys like that.

*   *   *

"Come on back, it's the Bell Telephone Hour. We're wiring somebody up." I was the big cheese and I was acting like the big cheese. I would go down to inspect the interrogation of the prisoners of war. I was always hiding behind my rank, more to protect myself than to really do numbers on other people. Basically, I didn't want to be bothered.

I'd go in and there'd be some poor woman or some old man, some kid even. They didn't attach the wires to the genitals or the breasts. They always attached them to the pinky fingers. Wrap a roll of wire around one pinky and wrap it around the other. Then they ask the guy a question, turn the crank on the field telephone and give him a little taste of it and he'd say, "*Khoung biet, khoung biet, khoung biet*." "I don't know, I don't know."

There were standard questions we were supposed to ask. When was the last time you saw Viet Cong operating in your village? Who among the prisoners that you were rounded up with is the head of the woman's organization? Who's the head of the fisherman's organization? Who's the head of the farmer's organization? There was a whole litany of questions that were supposed to be asked.

They would put people through a fair amount of pain. It wouldn't last very long and it was halfhearted in a way. There was a quality about it of adolescent viciousness that has no purpose other than its own satisfaction. Beyond reason. Putting cans on cats' tails.

I focused on a way of justifying it for myself: the transitory quality of it, the impermanence of it, the fact that it did not damage them. I don't even know if it did any damage. What happens when you run a jolt of relatively high-voltage electricity through somebody like that? Does it do any damage to them? I didn't know anything about psychology, so I didn't consider that. I'm sure that it had a tremendous impact on people, maybe not physically but certainly psychologically. It sure didn't make us any friends, I can tell you that.

Often the person we were wiring up would be a young woman who was maybe comely. There were all kinds of

sexual overtones to that. Domination. The misogyny of
war is being denied women, and then having your only
contact with women in some sort of subjugated positions.

I turned the crank a couple of times myself. I feel bad
about that. The thing that I feel the worst about was
that my own humanity was called into question, my own
values, my own sense of myself as a moral, righteous
person. I was defrocked. I was exposed as another bar-
barian along with all the rest. My experience and my
class and my education had insulated me a little bit, so I
didn't have to worry about the dirty work. Now I was
pitching in.

Everybody had their limits and mine were if somebody were being completely destroyed right in front of
my eyes, that would be where I'd draw the line, I guess.
Somehow I thought my moral equity was a little bit
higher, that I would have drawn the line before that.

The war took my measure. Not just me, but me and
my culture. The culture had given me a framework, a
point of reference for understanding myself, my religion
and my parents, my background and all. And I was not
that person.

*　　*　　*

I didn't really speak the language. I could understand
a few phrases, though. One day during a fire fight, for
the first time in my life, I heard the cries of the Vietnamese wounded, and I understood them. When somebody gets wounded, they call out for their mothers,
their wives, their girl friends. There I was listening to the
VC cry for the same things. That's when the futility of
the war really dawned on me. I thought, "Jesus Christ,
what a fucking waste this whole thing is."

VICTIMS

"This is a story of long, long ago, when the world was just beginning . . ." a resonant voice booms out of the darkness. The makeshift movie screen explodes in a vortex of lava fire like rolling napalm. The following quiet is filled with the rattle of the old projector and the very real night sounds of Southeast Asia. "One Million Years B.C." Dadumm.

Gar hadn't seen a movie in a long time. In fact, he'd been in the field almost four months straight. But Da Nang was a big base. They had an outdoor theater with a wooden wall painted white and rows of benches for the men to sit on. Gar couldn't complain about the choice of films either—cavemen clad in animal skins, grunting, fighting, hunting with their hands, chased by giant iguanas that smacked their scaled lips. It seemed particularly relevant to his life these days. When Raquel Welch appeared, a lynx bikini slung low on her hips, cascades of red hair billowing over bare shoulders, a whoop went up from the crowd. "Oh, yeah! Shit, she look good," Gar yelled.

In the distance, someone else yelled, "Incoming! In-

coming!" Raquel faded and vanished as the projector
clacked to a stop. Most of the men ran for their
bunkers, including the projectionist in spite of a voice in
the audience that threatened, "Turn that thing back on
or I'll blow you away."

Only Gar and a few other grunts from the field were
left. In the red glare of the rockets, with mortar shells
bursting all around them, they flipped the projector
back on and settled in for the rest of the movie. Beyond
the flickering light somebody called, "They're infil-
trating!"

"We shot our rifles off all around us," Gar told me.
"Everybody knew not to come in there while we were
watching the film, because we would shoot them. Everybody was enemy at that point."

The primitive hate, anger and fear that the war wrung
from men didn't just end when a fire fight was over.
Soldiers became violent, dangerous men and any enemy
would serve as a recipient of their aggression if the of-
ficially designated enemy wasn't handy.

It is difficult to understand the strength of those emotions and the way they change a person without experi-
encing them oneself. One veteran only half-jokingly
offered to take up a collection to finance a trip for me to
the African-nation-in-turmoil of my choice. He sug-
gested that I might learn more about the men I was
interviewing from a stint as a mercenary. At least then I
would be able to answer the two questions people most
often ask Vietnam veterans: How many did you kill?
What does it feel like to kill somebody?

I declined. I was getting plenty of those kinds of war
stories, and I was beginning to understand the frustration and pain behind them. Even more intriguing were
the fragments hanging fire, the unfinished stories about
another emotion which seemed very alien to war—love.

In the middle of a blood-and-guts tale about an artillery barrage at Khe Sanh, the man telling the story
disappeared into his bedroom and began rummaging
through the dresser. I could hear the drawers sliding
open and banging shut. He returned with a watch face,

*the crystal so scarred I could barely see the hands. He
had picked it up near the body of his friend who died in
the barrage. The exact time of his friend's death to the
second was frozen in that small machine. He had kept it
all these years as a sort of personal monument to their
friendship.*

*"They always get more worked up about the people
you killed than over your friends who died," he said.
We devour the death and destruction with morbid
curiosity and then turn our backs in embarrassment
when the storyteller reveals the love men shared and the
tears they shed.*

*The veterans themselves seem confused by the com-
munion beyond fellowship they experienced in Vietnam.
Ten years later, many of them attribute the hollow ache
inside to an overhearty slap on the back in Nam—or
they don't mention it at all. But the friendship, the
honest human love is all they wanted to bring back from
there, and it was the one thing they couldn't seem to
hang on to. The guilt, the pain, the scars are intact. The
lessons of friendship and compassion are lost.*

It was the Fourth of July. The weather was lovely. Almost every night, after chow when the guards were settling in and the sun hadn't quite gone down—early twilight—there was usually a general burst of M-16 firing, some machine-gun fire and a few grenades tossed off during the mad minute. But the Fourth of July it wasn't a mad minute, it was a mad night.

The mad minute went on and on and on. It would start on one side of the perimeter and it would spread. A couple of rounds would go off and there would be a few tracers. Then it would catch. On the other side of the post, flares would be going up. Every kind, the red ones, the white ones and the green ones.

Everybody knew that the red flares didn't mean anything, it was just color. We were all stoned and everybody was goofing on it. People would fire in great arcs across the base. The holiday was a good excuse to get more drunk than usual or more stoned than usual or more of both than usual. That was mostly the way I did it, spent the evening drinking beer and getting stoned.

There was a unit of the Armored Cav in from the field. They had been into some heavy shit somewhere near the Cambodian border north of us. They were parked across the road on the other side of the diesel dump, bivouacked on the hillside. Several of the guys from that squadron came over to our EM club* for some booze and hung around.

I had met this guy who was a TC* on a self-propelled howitzer, attached to his cav squadron. He was a sergeant, I guess. A really nice guy. He had an almost completed college education and for some reason we had studied some of the same things. He reminded me of me, and I suspect I reminded him of himself. We were hanging out in my hooch sort of pretending that we were sitting in a fraternity house. But we were really getting very stoned and drinking a lot of beer, getting off on each other. We also had some whiskey that somebody had "found." There was a lot of boisterous carrying on.

At about ten-thirty at night there was a commotion from the enlisted men's club. My hooch was just up the street, two bunkers and three hooches.

There was a short burst of M-16 fire, right beside us. Everybody hit the floor immediately. There was shouting from the club. This sergeant and I were the closest to the door and we crawled to the doorway to look out.

Here is this guy standing out in front of the club with an M-16 in his hand. I'd been living with him—this black guy from Alabama whose name was Cream. He had a reputation as a mean motherfucker, but was okay if you didn't cross him. There's a guy on the ground screaming his head off. Cream is cursing and yelling unintelligibly. I couldn't even make out what he was saying. The guy on the ground was clawing at the dirt. People were standing in the doorway of the club. We all knew that Cream had shot this guy. Somebody came out of the club who was a good friend of Cream's—if anybody was a good friend of Cream's—another black guy who was obviously trying to calm him down. "Give me the weapon. Leave him alone." This exchange went on for about five minutes and nobody moved. Cream was absolutely berserk.

This man on the ground is screaming like you never

want to hear screaming. No words. Just sounds. Finally, the other guy talked Cream into going back inside the club. At this point another three guys appeared from inside the club and rushed to their fallen buddy. Cream came rushing back out, fired off another three rounds or so into a Conex container, screaming and yelling again. Then he stopped and stood there and let the weapon fall to his side. His friend came up to him, took the M-16 away, took him by the arm and walked him to his bunk in the hooch next to mine. Everybody waited. The medics arrived with the MPs on their heels. The wounded man was still screaming in the dust.

I still don't know what the cause of the argument was. But they were drunk and the guy Cream shot was white. It wasn't specifically racial—that much I found out—but there was an insult of some kind.

What I do know is this: Cream was married and had a couple of kids. The guy he shot lost his legs and he only had nine days left in-country. Nine days. He was going back to wherever he came from to a football scholarship. It was his last day in the fucking field. That was the Fourth of July.

*   *   *

I went out for three days with a killer team on my birthday. I came back and I had a note from the rear to report to Phu Bai. They sent me to the rear for a big box that my cousin had sent. I saw that box and thought, "Cake, hey. I better take this back up in the bush and turn some of my partners on to it." I got a hold of it and thought, "This sucker is light. How can it be this light?" I popped it open.

Them dudes in the rear had the audacity to open that box, eat the entire cake, leave me one slice about a half an inch thick, seal the box back up and tie the string around it. It was a joke.

I picked up that one slice. I couldn't even eat it. I crushed it, then I picked up my .45 and went after them. I was a bushman and them in the rear didn't trust bushmen with weapons. I went and kicked in the door to the office they were supposed to be in, but nobody was there. I would have gone to the brig that day, because I would have shot them.

I'm out in the bush busting my behind trying to stay alive. They're back here on theirs giving theyself medals, giving theyself extra R&R time. Then they got the nerve to ruin the only pleasure I got when my family sends me something. All of them suckers back there were fat anyway. They didn't need that shit. They stayed out of my way the rest of that day and they made sure they sent me right back to the bush.

I decided that someone was going to pay. Maybe I won't shoot them. But somebody was going to pay, physically. There wasn't going to be no browbeating them or cursing them out. Somebody was going to pay physically. The guys in my squad understood where I was coming from.

They might have beat me for one or two packages, but after they beat me for that cake, they knew I was coming down to hurt if I got down to the rear again. Every one of my packages made it through. Never fail. And they made sure that I wouldn't have to come to the rear to get them either.

I finally got ahold of one of the guys that took my cake. I broke his ankle for him. He tried running, but he headed right into a friend of mine. My friend tripped him up. When the pogue hit the ground I reached down and stepped on his ankle for him. I says, "Where's your friends?" All he could do was cry, so I said forget it and walked away.

See, over there it got to the point, I didn't play games. I didn't like what they was doing. Too many guys could remember their letter from home saying, "How did you like the package you got? You wrote two or three times and you didn't say nothing about the package. You could at least thank us for it."

*   *   *

We were in the monsoon season, in the middle of a driving rain. Monsoon rains didn't start, they arrived. I

was about to go get something to eat and somebody
came running in and told me that I had to go fly. "Shit,
not again. Don't we have enough time to get some dinner?"

"No, we got to go right now." I threw on my clothes,
I didn't slow down long enough to put on any underwear.

I jumped in the helicopter behind Lieutenant Carver.
Carver was a bullshit artist from Texas, bucking for
command pilot, so he was flying on the right side of the
helicopter today. Warrant Officer Tyler was flying on
the left side. Normally, their positions would have been
reversed. I didn't like Tyler. Not that he was incompetent, I just didn't like him personally. There was no love
lost there. He didn't like me either. The crew chief,
named Blake, was seated on the left in the rear.

We sat there for about half an hour. There was no
way we were going to take off in that rain. You can't do
it. I'm moaning, "We could have had dinner. It's not
going to let up for another half an hour. Any idiot can
see that. You could let us go get dinner now. You're not
going to take off."

"Nope, we've got to be ready."

"Fuck. Jesus." The roof of the helicopter was leaking and I was bitching because the water was dripping
on my machine gun where it was laying on the floor. I
didn't like that. So I leaned forward to move the
machine gun out of the drizzle.

At that point, lightning struck the helicopter behind
us, charging the ship. The rockets in the helicopter were
fired electrically, so seven rockets were set off. Coming
out of the tubes the fins on six of them opened. They hit
each other and knocked around all over the place at ran-
dom. One rocket went straight forward and entered the
tail boom of my helicopter. It came tearing through the
transmission and through the fire wall of the cabin. Had
I not been leaning forward it would have torn through
the left side of my chest and ripped my left arm off. As
it was, it passed over my shoulder.

There was a tremendous explosion. Weird. No warning, nothing. One second I was leaning forward, the

next there's this loud noise and the world was gone.

When I opened my eyes, I realized that I wasn't dead. Carver's chest was torn away, clean as a whistle, but his spinal column was intact. His head was still on top of the spine. It was bowed over backwards, kind of bobbing there with his eyes open, weaving in front of me. His left arm and shoulder were in my lap.

Blake and his door were picked up and thrown out about ten feet away from the helicopter. He wound up standing on his feet going, "What? What happened?"

Tyler just had one side of his face wiped away. He was a mess. Part of his arm—thumb, forearm from up to the bicep was cut down to the bone—all of that was gone.

I didn't even realize that the door on the other side of the helicopter was just gone. I was panicked, because I could see fire all around. That was the solid propellant from the rocket burning. I didn't want to be in the helicopter when the fuel cell exploded. I didn't want to burn to death. My door was jammed on its tracks. So I was beating on the door, thinking I was trapped. My door wasn't about to be opened. I was clawing at it. Crazy. Finally—I don't know how—all of a sudden, it just fell off.

I did this flying spasm to get out of the helicopter. But an ammunition can with 1,500 rounds of 7.62 ammunition in it had been picked up and bounced around and was wedged on my foot. So there were a few more minutes of panic getting that thing loose.

I got out and kind of wandered off down the active runway. It was still raining. I just limped away in a state of shock. I was deafened.

The crew of the other helicopter grabbed me and Tyler and dragged us off the airfield. They dumped us in a truck and rushed us to the hospital. I didn't realize it at the time, but I looked like I was at death's door. All they could see was blood and garbage. They didn't realize that most of it was from Carver. I was spattered with lung and everything.

I had some fractured bones in my leg and spent a couple of weeks in the hospital. I got a Purple Heart out of the deal. I'll never know why. We weren't in a combat situation. I woke up and it was pinned next to my pillow—sort of like a visit from the Tooth Fairy. Not many of the guys in the hospital wanted to talk to me. I was in an extreme state of shock, compounded with guilt. Unreasonable guilt, "I should have done something for Carver." He was gone. I don't know what I could have done for him. But I felt guilty.

There was a big delegation of my buddies from the company who came down to see me in the hospital. "All right, what job do you want?"

"What do you mean, what job do I want?"

"Well, you know, how would you like to be . . ." They offered me easy, easy jobs.

I said, "I'm a door gunner." By this time I have to admit that I was really into being a door gunner. I loved it. I loved flying. I liked shooting people as long as I wasn't too close. Those little things on the ground were okay to kill. It was okay that they were shooting at me—that's part of the game.

I must have liked it. I've got fifteen medals. I was part of the elite. I was a big, bad door gunner. We had had too many wild, maniac times, drunken revelry. One time we pissed on the officer of the day when he came by to check our billet late at night. He was looking up at us on the roof with a flashlight asking, "Who the hell is that?" All he can see is a gun pointed at him, and a flashlight shining back down. "Get the fuck out of here or we'll blow you away."

Nobody screwed around with you. We were the tough guys. We were like brothers. It was a nice feeling. We were the heroes. We got to fly the helicopter.

Occasionally the copilot would say, "I'm a little bored. I want to shoot the machine gun." And I'd say, "Well, I want to fly the helicopter." We'd trade. There I am at twenty years old and I'm flying this machine worth hundreds of thousands of dollars.

When we're not shooting the shit out of something, we're playing games like smoke bombing the whore-houses. We'd go into the enlisted men's club on the base and, by God, nobody better fuck with any one of us or we'd kill everybody else. It was like Sgt. Rock* and I didn't want to leave that. I didn't want to become one of these noncombatant, anemic types.

I told my buddies that. I was a hero at that point. "Son of a bitch, the guy goes through this and he still wants to fly with us. Jesus, what heart. What a great guy." I felt on top of the world.

I spent a month or so in a cast. I pulled away part of the inside and rubbed it so that I got an ulcer on the front of my shin. I talked the doctors into cutting the cast off early. I went back to flying. I was crazy.

*   *   *

I was company radioman, so I didn't usually go out with the individual patrols. But one of the radiomen was a friend of mine so I went out with him, right? His name was Whitney and he was from Brooklyn. We were in boot camp together maybe three months before we found out that we lived six blocks away from each other back home and he went out with my sister. So me and Whitney are pretty tight. I got him into being a radioman. We even tried to take out insurance policies on each other with Hawaii Mutual, but they wouldn't let us do it. You know, I'd pay his premiums, he paid mine. That way, if I get it, he'd get it. Friends make out, right?

I went diddy-bopping* out there with them. We went past this village and it was sort of getting dusk. The next thing you know—pow-pow-pow—we're taking rounds. So we're firing it up. But the fuckers ain't moving, and there's only about a squad of them. They were really hardcore, so I figured we must be up against NVA regulars. We're trying fire-team rushes and they are, too.

I called the rear and told them what was happening and was begging for support. I'm trying to get artillery. I give the grid coordinates and they say, "It's no good, we can't do that. That's friendlies."

I says, "What? Hold the phone a minute, man." Then I yell out, "Yoh, you speak American?"

"Aaww, shit," I hear from the other side. My finest

fire fight is with another Marine unit.

But then—they don't want to stop. You got both squads knowing that they're shooting up Americans and they're still firing at one another. Pissed off. Fucking jungles are hot and nasty, the whole world is against you, and these guys were pissed off. So calmly, me and maybe two fire-team leaders, we just sat and waited for everybody to run out of ammo. Finally they ran out, and we went over there. They had two KIA and maybe four or five guys wounded. We had three guys wounded. They wouldn't stop and they wouldn't let us approach them. It gets that crazy. They were still hot.

*   *   *

Pilots came down from LZ English and they wanted nurses to come up for a party. I thought that would be great—just to get away for a while. I wasn't much of a party person, but I said, "If you guys let me fly the chopper, I'll go." They said okay.

I didn't have the slightest idea how to fly the damn thing. There's pedals on the floor and this little stick. I've got this chopper full of nurses, a couple of guys in the back. It was at night and the guy said, "You see that light way over there? Well, just fly for it." I was all over the highway—everything but upside down. The guys in the back are screaming, "Take it away from her, take it away from her!" But I got up there fine.

They had a few little landing lights out. "Okay, put it down there." I put it down, but I couldn't keep it down. It kept hopping like a rabbit. I hopped all around the parking lot. Finally, the guy had to land it.

That was the stage where I thought I could do anything. The Army was in the process of giving me that confidence. There was nothing that I couldn't do. Well, I couldn't keep the chopper on the ground, but I could at least get it to where I was supposed to go.

The guys had put on an incredible feed for us. There was even lobster. It got to be time that I had to make a pit stop, so I was running around looking for a place to go to the bathroom. I stumbled into this room full of mattresses, wall to wall. Right away my antennae go up. I thought, "Uh-oh, I better warn the girls."

I go back and I say, "Hey, you know there's a room full of mattresses back there and some of the guys are getting the girls pretty drunk." There was also a lot of opium and a lot of dope. "We got to get out of here."

We tried to put up a united front. Those of us who were reasonably sober practically carried the drunk ones to the chopper pad and tried to get someone to give us a ride home. The guys were furious. We thought it was going to be a gang rape, that's how bad it was. I didn't think we would make it out alive. The GIs called nurses round-eye tail, and suddenly that's exactly what we were. This was the enemy camp. They had had enough to drink that they were really angry and simply refused to take us home. The plan was to feed us, get us all hopped up and have a big old time. Then I spoiled it for them.

Finally one guy broke down and agreed to ferry us back to the hospital. Thank God for him. His mother must have taught him right. I was pretty naive and stupid back then, but I was on the first chopper home.

I went into the Army drinking half a can of beer and falling asleep. I never smoked marijuana before I went to Nam. I'm sure there were a lot of people in my situation.

A lot of the helicopter pilots, whether they were gunships or medevacs, I used to see them come in after they drank all night. They passed out and puked their guts out and then they got up and went and flew. I've seen guys go out and bring in a load of patients and they'd be puking their guts out by the chopper because of what they had to see or because of what they had to drink the night before. Then they'd get back in and do the same thing.

Everybody there smoked marijuana with a few exceptions. There were the big drinkers. If you tended to drink, well, you drank, and if you smoked, you really smoked. Everybody did it to extremes, just to get their act together to face the ward the next day or whatever they had to do. By the time I left, I knew doctors who had done heroin. I knew two nurses who went home hooked on heroin.

I tried it about a dozen times. Although I liked the high, I puked my guts out every time. It was a great high. You know that feeling when you're nodding out and you can't keep your head up, I can remember thinking, "Everybody knows what I've done, because my head won't stay up." But once that nausea wore off, I can see why guys got high—you don't care what happens. You let corpsmen go to lunch and if they were drinkers, they'd go over to the club and have a few belts. I'd go off the ward and have a couple of joints— my eyes are fire-engine red—and that got me through the day.

*   *   *

When I changed divisions, I started catching all kinds of shit. First I was wearing a bush hat, which they weren't quite ready for. Plus I had a Fu-Manchu and they said that was too long. What about my boots? They weren't shiny enough. And I had something around my neck that wasn't my dog tags. My dog tags were stuck in my boots. You unlace your boot and put one dog tag on each foot so they don't make no sound at night when you're moving.

These guys all thought that I was a short-timer. I *was* salty. But you could also tell the difference in the units I had been with. By the time I got there, I had seen a lot of action. I got me a Bronze Star. I forgot how many fire fights I'd been in. Some of these guys could count their fire fights on one hand without using three fingers. Never saw anybody. Some of them had no kills. And they was tedious about the boots and uniform. That seems like a small thing, but it annoyed me.

The first fire fight, the gun squad leader panicked. He don't know if either one of his guns opened up. He don't know where he is supposed to set up his guns at. The gunner was stationary doing nothing but freezing.

Instinct for survival took over. I snatched the gun out of his hand and started working with it. I told the a-gunner, "Get up and walk with me! Do something! But get up and get me some more ammo." I yelled, "Ammo up! Ammo up!" There's no ammo coming to me. They are shooting from behind these little rocks—but nobody is bringing ammo to me. I had to run around back to where they were and tell them, "Give me this God damn ammo."

I got recommended right there and they made me the squad leader. They demoted my man and got rid of him.

Later, the gun-team leader, name of Browne, and his best friend and brother-in-law, White—they both had these funny color names—came over to see me. They was from the same neighborhood, real college kids, the whole works. Browne didn't like me being the squad leader, because he thought he was going to be promoted automatically when the guy that panicked left. He said, "Well, you're short, so I'm going to get squad leader anyway. You're going to leave soon."

"I ain't that short," I said, "I got me awhile to go." Come to find out we came in-country a month apart. I had him by a month. "But don't worry," I told him, "one day you can have the gun squad. I plan to get the fuck out of here. I don't want the fucking machine gun anyway."

I started working my gun squad. They were breaking down the guns and cleaning them, but they would take their time and bullshit around, always cleaning them in daylight. I had them breaking down and cleaning the gun blindfolded. "Why we doing this?" they ask me.

"Because I say so. If I get any lip, you suckers are running."

"We're what?" I was a madman to them.

"You're not going to get me killed. I already seen what you guys can do in a fire fight. Which is nothing."

The gunny was with me, so pretty soon the whole platoon is cracking down their weapons and putting them back together, doing what they're told and not questioning, responding to sounds, listening. The lieutenant we had, he thought it was kind of funny. I looked at him and thought to myself, that fool is going to get killed. I knew he wasn't going to make it. He didn't.

The captain started volunteering us for a lot of bullshit. Any time something came up—like going to find somebody to kill—he volunteered us. Before, the company wasn't really finding nothing. So the captain was getting desperate. He wanted to make major and he could only do that by getting into fire fights and getting the body counts.

I just wanted my men to survive. If I got to count on these men and all they know how to do is hide behind rocks, they are going to get me killed. I ain't ready for it.

About this time, a kid came in-country and for some reason I took him under my wing. He was one skinny fellow, Stanley. He was a rich kid, sure-enough rich. He would tell me about when he turned eighteen his family bought him a home on so much acres, about his Jaguar XKE and shit.

I couldn't understand this guy. He would take his drinking water and wash his hands before he'd eat. I said, "When you run out of water, what you going to have to drink? You're going to be sorry. What you going to do, ask somebody for some of their water? They ain't going to give it to you. It's one thing if you drink your water. If you need more, they'll give it to you. There's no doubt about that. But you take your drinking water and waste it washing, that's different. You're going to have to learn to eat with dirty hands."

"Well, okay. I'll see," was all he said. He was funny because he couldn't grow a beard—had this scraggly beard. Stanley didn't drink and he had had sex once in his life up to that point. The only black person he remembered seeing in his life was the maid and the chauffeur. He claimed there was three black brothers in his school, but he said you couldn't tell they were black.

"I saw your guys rioting and stuff on TV," Stanley said, "and that's all I know." It tickled him that when we sat down and talked, he found out, hey, we were people just like him. We had different life-styles, but we're still people. He got an education that he would have never got if he hadn't been in the service. It was beneficial to him. He started understanding.

For instance, the Vietnamese used to ask us, "Why are you over here fighting when you can't even live where you want back in America?" That was a true statement. We all understood it, but Stanley couldn't understand. It was a matter of me trying to explain to him and trying to get him to not see color when he sees me or any of the other men in his platoon. His life depended on that. If he sees color, then he's never going to help some black dude. "Oh, that's just a nigger, I don't know if I'm going to risk my life for that." If he let the black dudes know how he felt, then they may say, "Why should I help him? He's into the prejudice thing." We didn't have time for that. Color over there was petty. I had pride in being black. But I also had pride in being a Marine. A lot of men had to have their lives thrown on the line to relate to that.

I made corporal when we took this hill called Razor Back about three times. We would go up there, spend a week and leave. Each time we lost men. There ain't nothing on the stupid-ass hill. It's out in the middle of bullshit. Walk up it getting killed and walk down the other side again. We did that three times.

Then we decided to do our own Tet on that area. Our recon had spotted units all over the place and we were going all out on a Search and Destroy. When we pulled into the staging area, as far as the eye could see was Marines and the sky was full of choppers. The choppers were picking them up and taking them to the damn hills, running out and running back as fast as they could.

You could hear sniper fire hitting the chopper as we came to the LZ. The chopper gunners were firing down. I did my praying. Everybody was making the Sign of the Cross or closing their eyes to pray like me. I said, "This is the big one now." I been in a lot of fire fights, but this one scared the hell out of me. I was more scared than I had been in my very first fire fight. And I was *scared* then.

As we ran off, we hit the ground. I seen gooks running up the hill firing, our guys running after them like a damn movie. They'd pop their heads up, guys were taking potshots at them. Everybody had 200 rounds of ammunition for the machine gunners, one or two rockets, M-16 ammo and one mortar round. We were throwing the mortar rounds over to the mortarmen, taking the M-60 ammo to the gunner, trying to get the rockets over to the rocket men. They were going to get us killed delivering this crap to each other. The guys were in their holes. We were losing a lot of men but there were gooks falling a lot, too.

We finally wound up securing the hill just as it's starting to get dark. I looked at Stanley and this other kid named Donald who wasn't in-country even three months. Stanley had taken a liking to him, tried to take him under his wing. I was just telling them, "I want you to keep your heads down. Keep your eyes open. We got snipers up here."

Stanley responded like I was telling him. Donald took his time and was laughing. They were sitting behind a little knoll. Donald sits up facing away from the outside of the perimeter. As I was telling him to keep his eyes open, all of a sudden there's this pow!

The bullet went through Donald's upper shoulder, came out his chest and went through Stanley's arm. Stanley panicked.

When it hit the kid, he didn't die right away. His guts were hanging out his mouth and his nose. He like coughed them up when he was shot. That hurt me. I didn't really have a chance to be working with him, to teach him how to stay alive, because by the time he came, we was on the run constantly. He didn't learn how to do what you told him instantly, when he was told to do it.

He looked at me and all I could see were the tears in his eyes. It was like he was saying, "I'm alive, but what do I do? I'm dying."

I debated whether I should put a bullet in his head and take him out of his misery. For some reason, I couldn't do it. I looked at him, he was a young kid. He was seventeen when his parents signed for him to get in the service.

Stanley went into shock. I yelled at him, "Get down to the chopper, get out of here! You're going home."

Stanley was groggy. He kept asking, "What? What happened to Donnie? What?"

I was getting Stanley out of there, because I took a liking to him. I grabbed him by his collar and started yanking him and running him down to the chopper. He yelled, "No! Wait!"

"There ain't no waiting," I said. "There's nothing up on this hill that you want." He kept looking at the other kid. See, Stanley got close to him. If Stanley had stayed there, he would have died.

I ran him down to where the chopper had landed to pick up the wounded. I threw Stanley toward it and said, "Write me one day. But now you're going home." The chopper took off and he looked back at me and started to wave. I turned away. You know, fuck it. Lay down. Then I got the fuck back up the hill.

By then Donald was dead and we laid him over and got him in a poncho. I said, "Get him out of here. I don't want him up here. Get him down." I wanted him away from the top of that knoll . . . So I could have somebody else up to cover that spot.

We wound up getting the sniper and a couple of others.

The next day, Browne, the lieutenant and that particular squad he was hooked up with went on patrol around the area. Our mortars sitting up on top of the hill said they saw movement in the valley but didn't check with a living soul to find out if we had a patrol out or not. They opened up on them.

They fucked up Browne and killed the lieutenant and a couple of other guys. When we tried to get to them, the Viet Cong had their snipers nearby. Every time one of our people got near, the snipers would pick them off one at a time. So we had to leave Browne down there overnight, alive.

When we went down the next morning trying to get Browne, he was trying to wave the corpsmen off, like don't touch me. But before we could tell them not to touch him, they flipped him over. He was booby trapped. It blew out his side. They didn't mean to hurt him. They thought they was doing right. They had on gas masks because we had opened up the tear gas. The glass in the eyepieces of the masks busted on their eyes, so about four of them were blinded instantly. Besides that they killed Browne really. He was still alive when we pulled him out—but he was dead. His whole side was blown out, there was nothing there.

I'll never forget Browne's eyes. He looked at me and he tried to smile. White, his brother-in-law, looked at him. I had to send White home—he cracked. They had been too close. I felt sorry for both of them. But Browne was eventually going to be out of his misery. White, his man, was going to have to live with the whole idea. They thought they was going to go home together. A lot of guys got hurt bad trying to take that stupid hill.

*   *   *

The convoys had to go through the An Khe Pass and there were a lot of places in there where the boys would get ambushed. Nobody was too crazy about driving those big trucks through An Khe Pass. This eighteen-year-old kid was celebrating one night, because the next morning was going to be his first time through there. He was going to do it up big, get drunk and get himself a prostitute and spend the night doing whatever it is they do.

She was a sweet little thing. She brought a satchel charge into his APC with her. They did their thing. She went home, and shortly thereafter the charge blew up. Of course, being in a confined area, he not only got the shrapnel, he got the full load. He came in with no arms and his legs were gone below the knee. All he had was a head and a trunk.

I was the lucky one. I got to take care of him. He was so bad, he got a "special": one nurse just for him.

He had these huge gaping holes and he had lost so much blood. You give somebody a lot of blood and they have problems coagulating. They couldn't stop this kid from bleeding. So he's got these big dressings on his stumps that are bleeding and his arms are bleeding. He's recovering from the anesthesia. Yet, you don't want him to recover, because he's going to freak out when he sees what's left of him.

Plus, there were some other guys on the ward who knew him and they are waking up. They see him and they're going nuts. There's nothing you can do for them. All you can say is, "If you don't like it, man, you can just look the other way. I'm sorry, but there's just nothing that we can do about it."

Every time the kid tried to open his eyes or even lift his head to see how he was, we just gave him a blast of morphine. It took him two days to die. What an awful price to pay for a one-night stand.

It was a big thing to be a man in Nam. They went out and they got laid and they used to brag about how many times they got the clap. I'd be walking down the ward with the big syringes of penicillin right out of the refrigerator. I'd roll it between my hands to try to warm it a little bit. It used to be a big joke about who was going to get it. Well, hey, you're a man if you got the clap. The more times you got it, well, even better. The fact that you were going to take it home to your wife or your girl friend, they didn't think about that.

That poor kid, eighteen years old. After a while, it got to the point that I didn't even let him open his eyes. If he even looked like he was coming around, I just blasted him.

*   *   *

There was rumor of a regiment of NVA in the area. Our new base commander, who was obviously nervous, doubled and in some cases tripled the perimeter guard. Bunkers that normally had two or three people on them now had as many as nine or twelve. It made no sense to me, but it happened.

A heavy alert had been called, so we support troops were supposed to be taking our inner defensive positions. I was in my flak jacket with my M-16 and my bandoliers of ammunition. Lots of people in the two units that I lived with were called up as extra guards. A couple of them even volunteered. This Armored Cavalry battalion was also on the base so there were lots of APCs and tanks and a couple of Big Boys.*

At about midnight the entire perimeter just exploded with activity, rounds of outgoing constantly firing. Those of us who were behind got really nervous and ready for a fight. The rumor was that there was incoming, but we didn't hear any incoming. You could tell even when the entire line was firing. We knew the difference between incoming and outgoing. There wasn't a single fucking round of incoming that whole night.

In this massive hysteria at about 2:30 A.M., somebody on a guard tower—maybe stoned, maybe not—thought he saw NVA coming through the wire, headed for a bunker. Radio messages went out. Somebody on a Sheridan tank went zipping around the lower perimeter road, took position approximately seventy-five yards from that bunker and fired into it with a beehive round at more or less point-blank range. A beehive round * is filled with fleshettes, a 90mm shell filled with little nails with fins.

Nine of the twelve people on that bunker were killed. Nine GIs. Four of the nine people on that bunker that died were people that I lived with.

Somewhere around 3:30 in the morning a radio message came to our captain that several of his people had been hit. That's all.

Heavy firing went on until about 5:00 in the morning, endlessly. Everybody was shooting at nothing, thinking that they were being shot at.

At about 5:30 in the morning, the captain got the word that the bodies had been delivered to the medics. As usual I was unable to sleep when there was all this going on. Everybody else had sacked out saying, "There's not a fucking thing coming in here. Man, I'm going to go to bed. Fuck you." But I stayed up. When the captain came running to find somebody to ride shotgun in his jeep on the way to the medical company, I was there ready to go, sitting on my sandbags and watching the nonexistent war.

We drove around the base to the medical company.

The lights were off on the jeep, because the captain was nervous. I wasn't nervous because I felt sure that nothing had happened.

We arrived at the medical company at dawn. There was just enough light to see. This deuce and a half pulled up, a flatbed truck with no canopy and an open tailgate. It had eight or nine bodies on it.

The medics started off-loading the bodies. I stood there and watched them and one by one these four people I knew were off-loaded, quite dead. Not very much blood. Little red holes all in them. The medics just went berserk—quietly berserk, but berserk nonetheless—knowing that it wasn't "Them" who killed these guys, it was "Us." They looked at the puncture marks and they knew. They'd seen too many before. The bodies were like puppets. Rigor mortis hadn't really set in, so they were like rag dolls, these four people that I knew.

Later that morning, my captain came around after breakfast and he and I drove around the perimeter to the bunker and just looked at it—that was such a typical scene. By this time, because of the other guys in the next bunker who had seen what had happened that night, we all knew exactly what had gone down for sure. We also knew that the particular tank involved had been sent off the post hastily that morning.

We also knew that it happened somewhere between 2:30 and 3:30 in the morning and it had not been until about five o'clock before medical help even arrived. That one of the guys who had been killed had been alive and might have been saved if the medics had gotten there when it happened instead of two hours later. This man happened to be the NCO in charge of the GR Point at that time. He was a young guy. He had received word in the mail the week before from his wife that his first baby had been born. Senseless, needless. All wars are filled with that. But there was more of it in Vietnam. Or maybe, because the whole thing was so senseless, every time something like that happened, it was just another insult.

All that information was in by the time ten o'clock rolled around. We were called into a formation in the

yard for a memorial service for those guys who were
killed, conducted by the lieutenant colonel chaplain
from the Armored Cavalry regiment, one of whose
tanks had been responsible for this event. We stood
there at attention in the morning sun and the dust,
listening to this fucking asshole do a little memorial
service about how "These people did not die in vain."
If looks could have killed, that man would have been
dead. In fact, that man would have been dead if we had
been left alone with him. We'd have jumped on him like
crows on a corpse.

I still don't know exactly what that did to me. It is
something that I haven't gotten over and don't expect
to, somehow. And shouldn't really, not just because of
the insane waste of it all, but because of the way in
which it was dealt with by people in positions of authority. It's the same as seeing people argue about the shape
of a peace table in Paris. It's the same as calling annihi-
lation, pacification. It's the same as Watergate. It's the
same as oil company profits. It's called business as usual
and it's what this country is or what it has become.
Maybe it always was.

I could hardly keep myself from shouting at that
chaplain. I was crying because of my friends who had
died and I was crying because I was so angry, like a child
cries when he's angry. At least, that's the way I cried as
a child. I was totally helpless in a fight, because I got so
angry that I would cry. I felt exactly that way at that
moment. I was so angry and hurt that I was crying.

I wasn't the only one. I looked around. I always look
around, I always keep my head up when everybody else
is praying. There were a lot of people standing there
with tears running down their faces. Not everybody, but
a third of us.

We all got into trucks and were driven off to chow. It
was close enough to walk, but everybody took a ride
that day. We were sitting there like we were in basic
training on the way to the rifle range, lined up in the
truck, not saying a word. Not a word at all.

Whatever it was that passed among us that day was

one of the most intense sharing experiences of my life. It's easy and it's true to say to myself, "Well, it happens all the time. That's what war is about. Whether they're killed by friendly or unfriendly fire, the reaction is similar." But in personal terms, it was one of the times when I was there that taught me the kind of communion people are capable of. I have never in the rest of my life experienced anything even remotely like it.

*   *   *

I had a dog in Vietnam. His name was Pussy. In Nam you know you have a capacity to love, but there was no one else in the fucking world that loved you. The only thing I could love while I was there was a God damn dog. So I was very close to Pussy.

We had a rat epidemic and rabies, so they were going around killing all the dogs. There was a bitch named Ralph that had had puppies at Christmas. When the MP was killing all the dogs in the base camp, he shot Ralph's nose off. Ralph ran down the road and we had to hit her over the head with a shovel to kill her. I said to myself that there was no way this was going to happen to Pussy. When the MP came to kill Pussy, I just yanked back the bolt on my M-16 and said, "What do you want?"

"I've come for your dog," he said.

"No, you haven't. You've come for me."

"No, I just want to shoot the dog." He wore gloves and was shooting them with a .45.

"I'll tell you what," I said. "Shoot the dog. I shoot you. That's the situation. Go ahead. There's the dog." He walked away.

*   *   *

I never saw so many guys cry as I did while I was in Vietnam. Some of those corpsmen and men from the field amazed me with how gentle they were with their buddies. One of the big fears the guys had was of dying

alone. A lot of guys came into the hospital really badly
hurt and they did die, but their buddies stayed with
them.

"Don't leave me, please don't leave me." And they
didn't.

About the time I'd get fed up with being there, I'd
walk into the ward and see a paraplegic who could still
use his arms, feeding the guy next to him who had been
blinded. I'd think to myself, "You may hate it here and
you may feel like shit and look like hell and think you
just can't stand another day, but at least you're not one
of these guys. If that boy with no legs can get over to
feed his blind friend, you can do what *you* have to do."

I went over to Vietnam thinking Army doctors were
hard-asses. It's just not so. We had a Vietnamese girl on
the ward. She was the same age as I was—twenty-one.
She was cleaning the barracks. They used to clean the
floors with kerosene or something to get the wax off.
Some smart guy flipped a match on the floor while she
was down there scrubbing it. *Whoosh,* she was gone in a
puff of smoke.

The surgeon taking care of her was named Paul.
When he got to her, she was 100 percent second- and
third-degree burns. Plus she had inhaled a lot of smoke.
Usually these people are going to die, so you let them.
The thing was, she was still conscious and talking, and
her kidneys were still working. So he had to try and save
her. He started an IV on her and she came up to my
ward.

Burn victims shed the inside of their lungs. It's like
getting sunburned on the inside and peeling. She would
cough up her lungs and she'd be bleeding and slowly
choking to death. She could speak English. She would
hold on to Paul and beg him not to let her die.

It was getting to the point that she was really bad and
he had to make a decision. Either you trach her, so that
you can clean her out and let her breathe, or you just let
her die. Paul said, "I've got to think about it. I'm going
to leave the ward for a while. I'll be back in an hour."

An hour went by and he didn't come back. Another

hour went by and he didn't show. Finally, I went looking for him. He was in this place that was our library—it was about the size of a walk-in closet. He was in there crying his eyes out. He said, "What am I going to do? I never should have started that IV on her. I never should have put that catheter in her. But she was alive when she came in and I had to do something. I can't trach her. She'll live six weeks and then she'll die horribly. What am I going to do with her? What am I going to do?"

He didn't do anything. He was going to let her die. We had to go over and change the dressings on her. He didn't want to do it any more than I did. But he helped me. The whole time she just cried and begged him not to let her die. But it was inevitable; she was gone in another day or so.

The doctors used to help us with the dressing changes quite a bit, because they knew how ugly they were. You've got a guy and you've got to change his whole body when you change the dressing. You have to give the guy morphine just to take the edge off, because he's so badly injured. The doctors felt bad for us. There were days when there wasn't a dry eye in the house, what with the patients screaming and us crying, trying to get the job done.

We had this patient for a while named Sam. I took care of him. He got hit in the chest with an armor-piercing shell just as he was about to leave for R&R. His wife was already in Hawaii waiting for him. Nobody expected him to live, but he made it through OR. He was in the recovery room all night, and he lived through that, too. So they brought him to the Intensive Care Unit.

It was a typical nightshift. I was the only nurse. There were a couple of corpsmen and a bunch of almost dead people. Sam was right across from the desk. He had a trach in and he had a big dressing and a lot of tubes coming out. I went over, took his blood pressure and sucked him out. Fresh trachs you always had to watch, because they bleed pretty easy. Everything seemed okay.

He wasn't doing well, but he was still with us. Considering he got hit with an armor-piercing shell, he was doing real well.

An hour went by. A corpsman came over and was taking Sam's vital signs. There was a tube leading from the trach to the ventilator where you get a build-up of water, CO_2 and stuff. You have to empty that periodically, or eventually it could back up and drown the patient. The corpsman emptied that and he said, "Hey, Lieutenant, come over here and take a look at this."

The water was sort of rust colored. I didn't think anything much of it, except that it was probably blood from his trach that was leaking a little bit. I pulled the plug out of his trach to check to see if he was bleeding. Foam and blood came pouring out of his trach tube. I started sucking him out and sucking him out, but it just kept pouring. It comes up and up and up and I keep sucking and sucking.

Then I had to hook him up to the ventilator to help him breathe again. But you can't really ventilate him, because he's got all this shit in his lungs. I was thinking, "Oh, man, we're in trouble now." He hadn't put out any urine. The amount of urine that somebody puts out is a pretty good indication of their volume status, how well their kidneys are doing and whether or not they're in shock. A shot glass is about 30cc of fluid and if they put out that much an hour, that's acceptable. Sam hadn't put out much the first hour, and he hadn't put out any the second. We usually let a patient go two hours and then called a doctor if they still hadn't put out any urine. Sam was still borderline.

It was after midnight. We didn't have many monitors to measure the heartbeat and stuff, but for some reason, Sam was on one. His EKG was changing. All of a sudden his eyes went back in his head. "Holy shit, he's going out on us."

When you told a doctor to get over to the ward, they usually did. But if they were playing poker, you had to say, "Look, you better get over here. So-and-so is *fucked up*." It sounds funny, but if you said the words "fucked up" they put down the cards and they came.

I told the corpsman, "You tell John to get over here right now. This guy is really *fucked up*. I think he's going out."

The doctors lived in the next building over from the hospital. But the corpsman had to go over in the dark with a flashlight and find the doctor's name on the door, bang on it and hope that he wasn't with a nurse or something—that he was in his own bed. This time the problem was more serious than that. The doctor that was taking care of Sam was in the process of having a nervous breakdown.

In the meantime, Dave who was the nurses' supervisor, had come through the ward. I told him what was going on and he said, "Jesus, what's the matter?"

"We've either got a trach that's bleeding a whole hell of a lot or he's in pulmonary edema," I said. "He hasn't put out any urine and he's been getting plenty of fluid. Maybe that's what the problem is. Lots of fluid in, none out." In our very unsophisticated way of handling pulmonary edema at that time, we pulled Sam upright in bed to make his legs a little more dependent, to get fluid down there. We put rotating tourniquets on his arms and legs to keep extra blood from returning to his heart and give the heart time to clear out the fluid in his lungs.

I said to Dave, "Well, now what are we going to do?" We really couldn't do much without a doctor.

"Where the hell is John?" he asked.

"He's supposed to be coming. I sent a corpsman after him a long time ago."

John, because he was in the process of having a nervous breakdown, was dressing himself like he was getting ready for inspection. He put on his uniform, buttoning every button he had. He laced his boots all the way to the top. He walked on the ward twenty minutes after we called him.

Dave and I were frantic at this point. John asked what was going on and I said, "No urine, no blood pressure and EKG is deteriorating. He looks like he has massive pulmonary edema. He's stopped bleeding, but all this stuff is coming out of his trach tube."

"Give him some ringers," John said. Lactated ringers is a volume expander that's just an IV used in any operation. Even if you just had a tooth out, they'd give you ringers. It's a salt water solution to keep you hydrated while you're having your operation. But it was the last thing that Sam needed. I looked at Dave because I knew the doctor wasn't right. "Hang it!" John shouted. So I hung a bottle of ringers and opened it wide. It was like drowning the guy.

We didn't realize it at first, but John couldn't bear to look at the patient, so he concentrated on the fact that there was no urine in the bag. "He needs fluid. Hang another bottle of ringers."

By this time, just by looking at him, you could tell John was in another world. The doctor had really stepped over the line. One of the corpsmen took him and sat him down at the desk and Dave—who didn't have a hell of a lot more experience than me—decided that we had to do something fast. Sam had a cardiac arrest. Just a straight line on the monitor. One of the corpsmen was doing CPR on him and I started to give him a diuretic to try to get the fluid out of his lungs. But he had so much fluid in his lungs that we couldn't ventilate him and we couldn't suction him. Then right in front of us, his color goes bad and he's dead. So I gave him six shots of intercardiac epinephrine in the chest.

The doctor just sat there at the desk. He was gone. He'd had a bad week or two. He'd lost a lot of patients. They weren't his fault. He was a fine doctor, but he'd reached his breaking point. He just sat there watching. By now all the lights were on and the sad thing was all the patients were watching, too. Dave was crying. I was crying. The corpsman was crying. What a mess.

Sam died. To add insult to injury, he was real tall, so we had a lot of trouble getting him into the body bag. It was a real struggle to crunch him in there. I couldn't imagine what it must be like for his wife to be waiting for him in Hawaii and get nothing but a telegram.

A few months later a friend of his came on the ward, walked up to me and said, "How is Sam doing? I heard he got hurt real bad and was here for a while. I was in the field with him. He was going to Hawaii and I just missed him while I was out on patrol."

I knew who Sam was, his name will stick with me forever. I said, "Well, Sam is dead." The guy started crying. This great big guy with tears rolling down his face.

The doctor that took care of Sam, that had the nervous breakdown, his friends are all surgeons. They don't recognize mental illness as a problem, because you can't see it and you can't cut it out. If you can't cut it out, then it doesn't exist. They knew that he wasn't eating, that he stayed in his room, that he was getting more and more seclusive, but they didn't want to believe he was in trouble. It could happen to them, too. He was taken out of there a little after that and was sent back home.

*　　*　　*

I had a real good close friend in Vietnam. You never should make close friends. Never. You live together, you find out everything about everybody else, but you have to avoid getting close. We had been together from Day One: smoked dope, dropped acid, everything.

We went out on an ambush. The VC and NVA march their people through the woods in threes. They figured one guy alone might *Chu Hoi*, "surrender." Two, they both might *Chu Hoi*. But with three, one would be loyal to Ho Chi Minh and keep the other two from *Chu Hoi*-ing.

We were at an ambush site in a primary area. Two or three groups of three go walking by. All of a sudden, a column of twenty move through. So we figured, this is it, this is the main force. We blew them away. It turned out they were the point for a battalion and we got creamed.

My good friend caught it in the guts. His guts were pouring out all over my hands. I took a poncho and tightened it around his waist and tied him to my body. He kept saying, "Put me down, let me die. Just let me die."

"There's no way," I said. "You're not going to die. You're going to make it."

He was dying. There was no two ways about it, but it was something I wouldn't admit.

There were only four of us left after that whole thing. Everybody else was dead. We started walking through the jungle. He was fucking moaning and screaming. We had no morphine, because we'd used it to get high. It was just a sick situation. After a while, he stopped talking. You get hypnotized by the heat of the jungle. You keep walking, and you're just too tired to talk. He was a light burden. I didn't feel it at all.

I guess at some point he must have died on me, but I wasn't aware of it. We got to an ARVN outpost. When they cut him off me dead, I went ape shit. I started swinging, I hit the person that cut him off, I hit my own man, I hit everybody around me. They poked me with I don't know what, four shots of some shit. I was still hyped up and didn't go to sleep for forty-eight hours. Then I slept for a day and I was okay.

*   *   *

A corpsman that I got to be friendly with said one of his friends was coming in from the field and would I like to go downtown with them, almost a date? I thought that would be fun. They got me all dressed to go. I had a helmet and a flak jacket. They gave me a knife and I had an M-16. Little-girl nurse disappeared and I looked like one of the guys, a tall skinny guy with long hair.

We borrowed an ambulance and drove to the outskirts of town. There were these little buildings that were combination temple and hospital all along there. This particular corpsman used one of these places to park the ambulance. We pulled in and he said, "I'll be right back. I just want to check with the nurse in here to make sure it's all right to leave the vehicle for a while." The only reason she was a nurse was because she was wearing white.

All of a sudden, he comes running out and he's screaming, "Get in here! Hurry!" I go running in like a fool locked and loaded. We were in this dark and dingy little room. There were a half dozen beds. Each bed had at least three patients in it. The corpsman says, "You've got to look at this little baby. This baby is really sick."

It was hard to tell how old the baby was, probably six months. The father was sitting there holding the little baby's hand. I touched the baby and he was hot—I mean, really hot. I asked the nurse how long the baby had been like this. The baby had been sick for a few days.

"What have you done for the kid?" Obviously, they hadn't done anything for him. He had a diaper on and he had a little sweater on, like any baby here would wear. A little knitted sweater with a hood. They'd found an oxygen tank somewhere and it was turned on, but it had been empty for I don't know how long. They'd put a small green catheter up his nose for the oxygen. But it had gone all the way to his stomach, because his little stomach was all bloated. And they had a little catheter sticking out of his rectum. I don't know what they thought that was going to do.

We didn't have any light, so one of the corpsmen went back to the ambulance and got a flashlight and a first-aid kit. I clapped my hands in front of the kid's eyes and by his ears. He didn't close his eyes, he didn't move. Oh shit, he's been like this for a few days and he's probably blind and he's probably deaf and he's probably going to croak.

Here I am, Mrs. Albert Schweitzer, right? I said, "Go call the hospital and tell them that we're bringing this kid in." I told the papa-san that we're going to take his kid to the hospital and he was so happy that he started to cry.

I picked up the baby and pulled this ridiculous tube out of his nose and his rectum. In the ambulance we had those chemical kits that get cold when you open them up. We took all the clothes off the kid and laid him on a stretcher with the cold packs all around him to try to get his temperature down. The papa-san was sure that we were going to save his son.

Back at the hospital, there were no patients in the emergency receiving area. I found out the doctor was on sick call, so I went to get him. There's a bunch of guys

with him. They've got runny noses and toothaches or
the clap. They're all waiting to be seen by the doctor.
I put the little baby on a pair of saw-horses with a
stretcher between. I ran up to the doctor and yelled,
"Hey, you got to come out here. We got a real sick kid
here." And I ran back to the kid.

I put a tourniquet on him to try to get an IV in his tiny
arm. It never dawned on me to check to see if the kid
was breathing or not, but at this point, if he wasn't
dead, he was almost there.

The doctor didn't come out. There have been very
few times when I've been out of control, but this was
one of them. I just could not believe the doctor didn't
come running. So I took my M-16 and I went right up to
him and I jammed a clip in the weapon and I shoved the
barrel right in the doctor's nostrils. I told him, "You get
off your ass and get out there to look at that baby or I'm
going to blow your head off." Needless to say, he got
up and came with me, but he hollered at the corpsman
to call the CO and tell him what was going on.

I was crying and I never cry. Tears, so many that I
couldn't even see. The corpsman who had first found
the baby was crying, because he couldn't believe that
this doctor would not see a sick child. All the guys that
were on sick call came over to see what was going on,
whispering, "This nurse is really fucked up, man. She's
going to do something crazy." But most of them were
crying before the thing was over.

I started screaming at the doctor, "You could start an
IV or something! You know, we have aspirin. We can
give him some oxygen. We don't have to just stand
here." He just stood there looking at the kid.

The commanding officer came in. Luckily for me, the
guy I was with took the gun away from me. The CO
said, "Do you think you can just drag every sick kid in
here that you see? What do you think this is? I suppose
we'll have to do something, now that you've got it
here."

They were looking for a place to put the IV in the
little kid and couldn't find one. The kid gave a couple of
little gasps and he was dead.

The doctor whose nose I'd stuck the gun into looked like he'd exsanguinated, he was pale as a ghost. The CO told him to go back to sick call. The guy could barely walk. Then the CO hollered at me, "You get this kid back where he came from and you take his old man with him. Don't let this happen again!"

We picked up this poor little dead baby and put his sweater back on him. We gave him back to the father. On the way back to the ambulance, we looked around for the guy from the field who had been with us. He was just wasted, laying in his bed crying. He had gone and shot up right away. He was so gone he couldn't have ridden back into town even if he had wanted to. He just wanted to get high and forget about it all. The corpsman and I snorted smack all the way back into the little hospital where we dropped off the father.

*   *   *

It was Christmas Eve and the truce was supposed to begin at six o'clock. At that time everything shuts down and we have three days of Peace on Earth. There was a fair amount of pressure put on commanders that troops should not be fighting then, since we were the good guys.

A ground unit in the Delta stepped into it. They were getting the living shit kicked out of them. These guys were trapped. It looked grim for them.

There were fifteen light fire teams in the area—thirty helicopters. Any number of Navy jets were flying in, just trying to blow the shit out of the enemy and save these guys. A one-star general is circling in a helicopter directly above us overseeing the whole operation. He was trying to hustle us along, because at six o'clock, we had to break it off. Otherwise, we would be violating the cease-fire.

He's doing this whole number, "All right, gentlemen, we've got fifteen minutes before it's six o'clock, so let's get those gunships rolling in there. Navy jets, you stand by. I want you to clean up with the napalm afterwards." Like some sort of commentator, his voice is coming in from way the hell up on top.

Next, there's the fire-team leaders who are coordinating all the other fire teams. "All right, we're going to roll in on azimuth number so-and-so such-and-such. Let's line up. Bounty Hunters, you're five-seven. You go first. Five-six and five-five will be right behind you. One good solid pass. That's all we have time for."

The Navy jets are calling, "Okay, Army light fire teams, you better stay the hell out of the way, because as soon as you get done with your roll-out, we're going to come in pitching some hot stuff right behind you."

On top of that, you've got the guys in the helicopters who are talking to each other. "Gunner, be sure to cover us hard on the break. Keep those guns strong underneath us."

Everybody is talking, including some poor bastard on the ground, who is saying, "Save our ass, please." There's another radio operator down there who has managed to get his ass shot. He's laying next to an open mike, moaning and begging for help. Mostly it's that one word over and over again. "Help, help."

You've got this bullshit general dealing with the aesthetics of the truce. You got the guys actually going in, dealing with the mechanics of the run. You've got the guys in the helicopters sorting out who's going to do what and when, on a personal level. And you got this guy on the ground who is bleeding to death.

I'll be damned if at six o'clock we didn't break off and leave. This is Christmas Eve. I can't speak for the rest of the support on the operation, but our fire team left. We had expended our ammunition, we had a couple of really hairy passes and we were low on fuel. I was flying the lead helicopter and our fire-team leader said, "Well, what are we going to do? By the time that we go and get refueled and get back, it's going to be after six. So we're going home."

Behind us napalm is burning. You can still hear this guy on the open mike as we're going away, this guy laying down on the ground bleeding and yelling into the radio.

I took my machine gun off the cable and slammed it on the floor. Bam! The other guys in the helicopter looked at me. I reached up to my little control panel on the ceiling with all the switches to the four or five frequencies of radio and turned them all off. I just sat there in the silence. It was getting dark. Flying along.

I didn't realize it but I had missed the cabin communication switch. Nobody said anything at all for five or six minutes. Somebody finally turned around and said, "Hey, what's wrong? Why are you acting this way?" I was surprised. I didn't want to hear from anybody. I didn't even answer him. I damn near tore the control box down trying to get to that one switch I'd missed.

Their reaction made me start to realize things were not right. Later that night the crew chief, a good buddy of mine, came over and said, "What have you been doing?"

"What do you mean?"

"You're acting really weird. The pilots asked me to talk to you. You on any drugs?"

"What do you mean? You were just there. Didn't you hear? Are you deaf? Don't you realize what just took place? We left those guys to die. Because of a fucking six o'clock truce which nobody really gives a rat's ass about, except maybe in Paris where they're sitting around arguing about the size of the table. You're asking me if I'm stoned out on something? You think I'm weird? How weird are you?"

"Hey, okay, sorry we asked. Take it easy. Never mind. You're not on drugs. All right, we'll leave you alone."

They thought I was skulled out on something. That was the only logical explanation they could come up with. I saw that things weren't right. Maybe this wasn't Sgt. Rock after all. I still liked flying and I liked being a door gunner, but from that point on, I felt something was really wrong here. I couldn't pick it out. It was just strange.

*   *   *

A lot of the area where we were was defoliated. At Christmastime I came off the ward and I smelled a Christmas tree. I hadn't smelled anything in so long but the stench of urine and garbage from the refugee city, plus the smell of the ward, that I thought, "Oh God, I'm hallucinating." I followed my nose and, sure enough, we had *two* Christmas trees. One was put up in the emergency room where the guys coming in could see it. The other one was put over by the nurses' quarters. We all made decorations to put on the tree. I remember the night before Christmas, sitting under the tree playing cribbage with one of the guys and that Christmas tree just smelled so good.

That was the best Christmas of my life, because I didn't have anything to give anybody. A couple of people bought little gifts—you ran out to the ville and got them something. But mostly all you had were the people there. I didn't have to go, "Oh, shit, this one wants a sweater and that one wants a book. What if I can't find the book? Oh God, then what am I going to do?"

We had a service the night before Christmas and all the patients that could go off the ward went to it. We had patients in the hospital who could play the guitar, so they played for us. I had my doubts about God when I went over there, but now there are no doubts in my mind that there is one.

We all got care packages from home that had food or little presents in them. Everybody shared with the patients on the ward. We all chipped in our money, went to the PX and bought wine so every patient in that hospital got wine that night, unless he was dead or in a coma. Even the guys who had tubes in their stomachs—they were going to drink the wine and it was going to be pumped right back out, but they all had a glass of wine.

The only sad thing was that we got this nineteen-year-old kid in that lost both his arms. It was early Christmas morning by the time he came from the Operating Room and was in Recovery. We had put stockings on everybody's bed with stuff in it—a few pieces of candy or something. We were desperate, because we had run out of stockings and we didn't have one for this kid. I had gotten a care package from a friend I had known in nursing school. So I said, "I'll go open that now and maybe there's something in there." Sure enough, there was this little fuzzy, red stocking. So we put it on the end of his bed and put some stuff in it. When he woke up, all the guys had their tiny Christmas presents spread out on their beds. The guys in traction had tinsel hanging off the frames. It was so ugly, but it was something. It was Christmas.

When the kid woke up and saw his stocking, he knew he couldn't open it, because he didn't have any arms. Let me tell you, did we feel like shit.

One of the corpsmen came on the ward who wasn't on duty till the night, but he had come to help open the presents. The kid was crying his heart out. There wasn't anything we could do, so the corpsman just held on to him for a couple of hours. The kid just cried and cried and cried. He didn't even have enough left to put a decent prosthesis on. It turned out that his wife had just had a baby, but he was never going to get to hold it.

Other than that, Christmas was pretty good, because everybody shared and you had nothing to share.

"Hey, man, next year has to be better."

"Yeah, maybe we'll be in Laos."

*   *   *

The battalion commander saved my life. He called me into his tent one time after an operation. There was a big stack of papers on his desk and he said, "Do you see these? These are all charges against you."

"I don't care," I said.

"Who do you think you're talking to?" he yelled. "I've been going through wars for more years than you've spent on this earth. Sit down." He pulled out a bottle of whiskey and we sat down and talked. "I'm pulling you out of the line and I'm sending you to Saigon for your last three months. You're going to sit around and guard generals and you're going to get fucked a lot."

I had figured I wasn't going to make it back. So what? I just wanted to kill as many VC as I could.

But the battalion commander handed my life back to me and said, "Here. You did a good job. You did all you could do. You are nuts. I'm going to try to save your life, because you're a good man." He took all the charges against me and ripped them up and dumped them into the trash can.

I was leveled when I walked out of there. I didn't know what to make of it. There was something unresolved, in that I wanted to stay and get back at the VC for all my friends. There was a constant process of rerunning the mental tapes of your friends who had gotten killed. Never left my mind. I wanted to kill. I couldn't get it out of my mind. But I suddenly had a chance to stay alive. It was an alternative that I hadn't considered.

IV
THE WORLD

HOMECOMING

The nose lifted abruptly and the wheels bounced over the last hump on the runway. As the plane pulled hard over the trees, a brief cheer reverberated through the cabin.

A few men on night ambush several kilometers away looked up as the airliner wheeled and climbed. They watched until the navigation lights, red and green and flashing white, disappeared into a cloud bank over the South China Sea. The words that pulsed in each of their minds were, "They're going back to the World." Their thoughts diverged as each man quickly calculated his own remaining time in-country.

The men aboard the plane were quiet and within an hour most of them were asleep—a deep childlike sleep, mouth open with saliva collecting in the corner, dead to the world. Bodies conditioned to tropical heat shivered in the cool air. A stewardess busied herself putting blankets over the sleepers, tucking them in.

The in-country flight had been hectic with too many loud jokes, the aisles blocked with young men roving from card game to card game, upset stomachs excused as airsickness. The return trip would be serene, unless a bad dream rocked one of her passengers out of his lounge-backed cradle.

The Big Bird to Paradise was flying home, straight and true. A GI could leave the foot-sucking muck of a rice paddy and within thirty-six hours find himself in civilian clothes, walking down Main Street of his hometown, searching faces for a glimmer of recognition. But they never returned to the world they had left.

People, buildings, cars, dogs, everything looked like clever imitations of the real world. The World that they had talked about and dreamed of every day in Nam was gone, replaced with a flat, lifeless forgery of reality. They didn't belong; couldn't fit in, find out. Nothing worked. No one wanted them. "I went from a free-fire zone to the twilight zone."

Simple things change in a year—clothing, hairstyles and television shows—but nothing had changed as much as they had. They had seen too much, done too much. And now they found out they had hoped for too much.

Me and my buddy Al rotated out at the same time. We left from a place called Freedom Hill. A big chopper came down and picked us up and dropped us on the flight deck of the *New Orleans*, a small carrier out in the middle of Da Nang Harbor. We looked back in at land, where we spent a year. I had never thought about getting killed, but I never thought about coming back either. I knew if you thought about coming back, you'd buy it, for sure.

I looked at Al and I started laughing. I said, "Al, I think we made it." He started laughing. We laughed so hard that we were crying. We couldn't stand up. My sides ached. We made it.

Yet people we'd hung around with for months were gone, gone forever. You were real glad that you were you and not them. You felt so good to see the people that had survived with you. It felt so good to look into their faces after it was all over and you could just exhale, take a breather, just taste the time, taste the life.

It was love. It was true love of being alive and being thankful for the joy of looking into their faces. It

almost made what you had been through worthwhile.
But, I guess, not quite.

After rolling across the Pacific for sixteen days,
seeing this country was amazing. I cried. I wanted to
kiss the dirt. It was home. I had been a foreigner in a
strange place. Out there, outside the United States,
you're in Indian Country. There was only one place that
meant anything and that was my home.

I was really looking forward to coming home, but
after three or four days, I was climbing the walls. I
dropped back into the old neighborhood and nothing
had changed. They were the same people in the same
situation with the same head. There's been no time passing for them. It was like I never left. But I *did* leave. I
wasn't the same anymore. I didn't feel comfortable doing what I used to do. I didn't know how to *spend* time.

I was geared up for dealing with a hundred thousand
dollars worth of equipment and a lot of responsibility
for human life. I've come back here . . . to do what?

Civilian level is bullshit. You make a mistake, nobody's going to die. Big fucking deal. It's really hard to
get excited about what's going on over here. You see
politicians lying to you, it makes you want to throw up.
Send them over there. I see people in business who never
had to put their ass on the line or really extend themselves and they're making it. It's not fair.

In Nam, they called grunts kings. I walked with kings.
These people were going to get shit on when they came
back here, but in Vietnam they were kings. There was
no bullshit. You get in a fire fight and you see exactly
who's who. There wasn't anything phony. It was all
very real, the realest thing I've ever done. Everything
since seems totally superfluous. It's horseshit.

People don't understand. They hate you for being
there, like you should feel guilty for it. "You went to
Vietnam? Oh, wow, man, where's your head at?"

"Go throw some wheat germ on your yogurt. Fuck
you, I don't want to hear your bullshit."

When we were over there, I thought, "My God, if I
ever get back to the World, I'm going to tear the place

apart. The World will be my oyster and *nothing* is going to stop me. I'll have it all." Here it is going on twelve years later and what the fuck have I done?

* * *

I'd been living in the boonies for six months and flew right back to the States. So I was very disoriented. At El Toro Air Force Base a guy says to me, "Where you want to get stationed?"

"Marine barracks, Brooklyn," I says fucking around with him.

"We got one in New London, Connecticut."

"That's close enough." Bang, bang, bang, he stamps everything on my papers. I had no idea what Marine barracks was. I just wanted to be near the neighborhood, hang out. I was a hot nineteen years old and been to Vietnam.

I went to the Marine barracks in Connecticut and I found out—uh-oh, it's all embassy Marines. They're all covered in blue with red stripes down their pants, spit-shined boots, orders. None of them has been to Vietnam and this ain't grunt stuff. These guys may be the finest in discipline, but they don't look out for each other. In Nam the grunts learned to look out for each other. You look out for your boys, you fuck over the officers. Here, it's just the opposite. Everybody is doing everything they can to nail you. The Marine Game—you *will* obey regulations or you *will* be written up and you *will* go to the brig. I didn't want to hear that, I just came back from a war.

I signed in wearing my civilian clothes. I'm all alone and I was feeling discombobulated. It was just too much, too quick for me. I said to myself, "No, man. I don't want no part of this." There was only one thing in my mind: Get back to Vietnam where I felt at home.

I was there two hours and I flipped out. I started walking down the corridor knocking all the frames full of rules and regulations off the walls, throwing down all their little trophies and commendations. No words. Nothing.

There were about ten guys there coming toward me, and I started going at blows with them. They beat the shit out of me, cuffed me and threw me in the brig. They gave me a shot of dope which fucked me up, too.

After I got out of the hospital, I went over to see the major. He looked at my records and said, "You're a grunt. What are you doing here?"

"I don't know."

"Do you want to leave this unit?"

"Yes, sir."

"Do you want to go back to West Pac?"

"Yes, sir, I just want to get back to Vietnam, where I belong." I really felt that I belonged there.

No problem. I was out of that barracks in record time.

My second year in Nam I got into the Air Wing. All I fucking did was smoke pot and ride gunner on helicopters. But they were beginning to send Marines back, and they were trying to push me back to the States again. I wasn't having any of that. I had to go up in front of a full bird colonel and lie to him about why I had to stay in Vietnam. Here I am, an Italian boy from Brooklyn, New York. I told the colonel that I took some money from loan sharks back home and I'm in trouble, they're going to kill me and hurt my family. As the colonel can see, if he checks my records, I've been saving my money and I ain't been on R&R—which luckily was true. He fell for it. What does he know? He's from Fishbite Falls somewheres, right? He let me stay.

I was going to stay a third year, but they gave me a year early-out and made me go back home. Some guys they had to lock up because they wouldn't leave Vietnam. A lot of guys wanted to die there. I mean, I wanted to die there. All my fucking friends died there.

I felt so much like I didn't belong in America. What are you going to do? How are you going to talk to somebody? I went back there to get it over quick, but it never came. It was suicide, trying to kill myself, going back. I didn't know that's what it was then. I just wanted to get back and be around people I knew. I didn't care if I died around people I knew.

* * *

Finally my day came and I made the big swoop. Big Bird to Paradise, we used to call it. They said it was time to go and I started crying. One dude gave me a bracelet. I said, "I'm going home to the States, but you fucking dudes are still going to be here." I got my shit and throwed it on the truck and said, "Let's go." I left the fuckers $20. "Go ahead and buy a case of beer on me whenever you can."

On my way out I was assigned to some rinky-dink headquarters battalion where the office pogues sit around on their fat asses. They took all my stuff away from me. I reported in the field hat that I had had made by some of the villagers. A sergeant takes it away from me and gives it to some other dude sitting in the office. They didn't want me to be too salty. If I'd have had that motherfucker in the field, I'd have had his ass. But I didn't want to make no trouble. I was going home.

Then on Okinawa, they took all our gear away and gave us new fatigues, all too big and didn't fit. Put us in some big old barracks somewheres and wouldn't let us go into town. Just out of fucking combat and you can't even go and get a few beers, and have a little fun. They had us picking up cigarette butts for three days. That was "rehabilitation," so we would come to our senses. This chickenshit staff sergeant, younger than we were, who was making us pick up cigarette butts, said, "Just because you been to Vietnam, you ain't no God damn heroes."

We didn't want to be picking up cigarette butts, we been picking up bodies for fifteen months. Give us a little slack. We practiced marching. We had formations. Alls we wanted to do was go home.

When I first got back, I was at my brother's house in California. The first week I was there, I slept on the floor because I couldn't get comfortable in a bed. I'd drink cold beer and get a sore throat. I had to wait for my beer to get warm before I could drink it. I ain't shitting you. I ate like a fucking animal. They asked me all kinds of questions. "How many did you kill?" "How does it feel to kill somebody?" A hell of a lot better than if he had shot me, that's what I told them.

I was an MP for a while in Quantico after that. I wanted to be a cop when I got out of the service. But the police told me I was too small. Hell, they didn't tell me I was too small when they sent me over to Nam. They didn't tell me I couldn't fight. They don't give nobody a chance to do nothing.

I didn't know how to act, didn't know what kind of clothes to buy, didn't like long-haired people, didn't like nothing. I carried a gun on me. People seemed to be messing with me all the time. Hey, I'd seen enough of that fighting shit. I didn't need that. You get back though and they say, "I see you made it all right. Big fucking deal." Some fucking ass asked me, "How come you didn't get killed."

*   *   *

When I got discharged, they had the nerve to demand $600 from me. They were saying that they overpaid me in Vietnam. How the hell was I supposed to know they were overpaying me? They said, "Well, you was getting rank." But we didn't know what the pay scale was over there. An officer came up and said you were due this amount of money. You'd sign the chit. They would give you so much in Vietnamese money or scrip and then you would put the rest in a bank down in the Da Nang area. You'd send X amount home. That was it. I'd send $100 home, take $20 out in the bush and the rest send down to the rear. It was a set pattern with me. I had to threaten to get civilian lawyers. We settled on $300. I had to pay to get discharged.

*   *   *

When I got my honorable discharge, I thought it would be really nice. It comes in the mail and it's a computer printout with my Social Security number on a piece of cardboard, so I just threw it away. I was really disappointed. I thought I'd at least get a little plaque or something.

* * *

When I came back about six of us were walking through the airport and a girl—maybe eighteen or nineteen, about the same age as me really—she asked me how many women and children did I kill. I told her, "Nine. Where's your mother at?" I thought it was great fun putting her down like that. But inside I felt, "Gees, why is she treating me like that?"

I thought I would come home as a war hero, you know. I didn't really want to be a war hero, but I thought I'd get a lot of respect, because I'd done something for my country. Somewhere deep in my psyche I thought that people would react to what I'd done, and say, "Hey, good job. Good work."

My family did. "Hey, great. How many people did you kill?" That wasn't right either. I didn't tell them when I was getting home, because I didn't want a party. But it happened anyway. I couldn't stay at that. I hung out an hour or two. Then I went out with my friends and got fucked up out of my face.

* * *

I landed at Travis Air Force Base. My brother was living in Berkeley. I didn't think anything about that. All I knew was that my brother lived there and I was close by, so I might as well stop and see him. The first day back, I had survived. I had made it.

I took a cab from the base to Berkeley. We were riding down Telegraph Avenue. I told the driver, "I want to get out, I want to walk."

"You want to walk? Here?" I was in full dress

uniform with decorations, medals.

"Yeah, man, pull over. I want to walk."

"Okay, it's up to you." So I paid him and got out.

Walking down the streets of Berkeley, I felt like the man from Mars visiting the Earth. Everybody was looking at me. All kinds of comments. People spit at me. I was more scared walking down that street than I had been in Vietnam. There I had my weapon and I could protect myself. But they had taken my weapon away. These people looked like they wanted to kill me more than the Viet Cong did.

I immediately went to a bar to call my brother to come and get me. Kids in the bar started throwing peanuts at me. Then my brother showed up with a bunch of guys and hustled me out of there.

*   *   *

After I was wounded the third time, I went home on leave from Vietnam. I was really shot, blown up emotionally. Things were very good for me in Long Island for about two weeks. I spent a couple of hours staring at the refrigerator, flushing the toilet and turning on the hot water. I did have a little trouble sleeping. It was too quiet. I loved to hear the artillery going off at night. It meant that somewhere someone's getting his ass greased.

I went to a party. For some reason, a lot of people from my childhood that I really hated seemed to be there. I just couldn't handle it, so I walked out, stoned on hash. But I wanted to call the girl whose party it was and apologize, let her know it wasn't her fault that I left.

I stepped into a phone booth a few blocks away, put in a dime and the phone started dialing itself. I tried again with another dime. I got some garbled recording. I put another dime in and another one. The phone started spitting them back at me.

I see a Ford van parked across the street with the side door cracked open just a little bit. Up on the corner there is a little group of people all dressed up. I was convinced that I was on *Candid Camera*, that this whole thing is one of their routines. The cameramen are in the truck and the people on the corner are part of the crew. I said to myself, "I'm going to give them a real *good* film clip." I ripped the receiver off the phone and started beating the machine. I pried off the dial. I started pounding on the glass of the booth, breaking the glass with different parts of my body, my elbows, my knees, one with my head. I took that phone booth apart.

Then I step out grinning. I'm waiting for Allen Funt to run up and say, "Smile, you're on *Candid Camera*. Sign the release."

Nobody comes.

I realized then that it was me, that I was all fucked up. I freaked out, totally paranoid. I didn't fit in anywhere. The thing with the phone booth triggered it all. I knew I couldn't go back to Nam. I couldn't go back to the Army. Woodstock was happening then, so I went there AWOL.

I figured, fuck it, I'm going back to Vietnam. A few extra days, what are they going to do? Fuck them. After Vietnam, Woodstock was great. I had four or five blow jobs, I was fucking my brains out. There were tons of drugs. I was grooving out. After Woodstock, after this loving type of thing, I just couldn't go back to the Army.

I told my parents that I wasn't going back. They went nuts. They weren't all that patriotic, but they wanted me to get out of the Army and I had so little time left to serve. I said, "I'm never going back. I don't care what I have to do. I don't care what you have to do. I'm not going back to the Army."

At first I tried to get out of the Army by playing crazy. I went from one Army base to another making up wild stories.

The whole time I was AWOL I was getting paid. Once I got paid three times in one week. They didn't know what the fuck was going on. I would go on sick calls two or three times a day at different Army bases. Although I had a lot of trouble getting in, I spent two weeks in the Ft. Dix psychiatric ward. I tried to be depressed, but I was so fucking happy I wasn't in Vietnam that I had a ball. I had the greatest time of my life on that nut ward.

In the mornings they would lock razors into the razor handles and a beautiful broad would stand over you while you shaved. She was always rubbing herself all over you. I was really fucking getting off on it. I shaved every fucking day just for the shaving nurse. But, if you didn't want to, you didn't even have to get out of bed.

What they would do is sit and take notes on how you interacted with the patients. Twice a day, we would sit in a group and tell each other how fucked up we were in front of everybody else. One woman who was brought up there had tried to commit suicide. She would be crying and the psychiatrist would be saying, "And Mrs. Smith is with us now. She's very depressed." Mrs. Smith would let out a yowl. The whole scene made me laugh. Of course, I was on mood elevators, too. I was trying to be depressed and I just couldn't do it.

I had a couple of wild fights up there. I was playing dominoes with this guy they had brought up from Valley Forge. Every time I put a domino down on the board, he would start breathing heavily through his teeth and glaring at me with "Kill" in his eyes. I'd say, "Sergeant, I think you'd better get over here." Finally, the guy exploded and tried to hit me. Of course, I took a fucking chair and smashed him over the head. The nurses locked themselves inside of the nursing station. Somebody else tried to attack the nursing station. The violence spread like a plague up there, once it started.

We would go bowling at Ft. Dix. They would clear the whole bowling alley out so the nuts could bowl without disturbing the regulars. I laughed a lot. I played dominoes and the guitar. I basically had a good time. At the end of two weeks the shrink said, "What do you want me to do?"

"Well, listen, Doc. I can't go back to Vietnam. Do you understand what I'm saying?"

"I understand what you're saying, but there is nothing I can do for you. You're saner than I am. You could be running the ward."

"I can't go back."

"I have to do this. I'm sorry." He signed the orders for me to go to the overseas replacement station to go back.

They had two privates who escorted me to the station. I was halfway there and I said, "It's okay. I know where it is. I've already been to Vietnam. You can leave." As soon as they left, I went AWOL again.

This went on for four or five months. I got really fed up. I decided to go to Canada.

*   *   *

The day I got discharged, I flew into Philadelphia Airport. I got two and a half rows of ribbons. I'm very proud. I'm a meritorious sergeant and I got an honorable discharge. How do you like that shit?

I got off the plane and I went into a bar. The only thing I knew how to do was drink. I order a shot of CC and a beer and I'm standing there with a big smile on my face. There was a guy over at a table with two kids and a woman. The kids were about my age—nineteen or twenty.

"Home on leave, are you," the guy says to me.

"Nope, just got discharged."

"You just got back from where," one of the kid says.

"Vietnam."

"How do you feel about killing all of those innocent people?" the woman asks me out of nowhere.

I didn't know what to say. The bartender got a little uptight. But, I didn't say anything. They told me when I got discharged that I was going to get this shit. But, I didn't believe them.

"Excuse me," I called the bartender over. "Could I buy them all a drink?" I felt guilty. I *did* kill. I tried to make amends somehow.

"We don't accept any drinks from killers," the girl

says to me. Now I'm pissed. The bartender tells me to take it easy and goes over and chews out this girl. She says, "How does it feel being in the Army?"

"He's not in the Army, he's a Marine," the bartender said.

"You bet your fucking ass, I'm a Marine."

"Oh, you going to get nasty now?" They were harassing me right in the fucking bar. I paid for my drinks, left the bartender a tip and walked out. Forgot all about it. I got in the car with my brother and his wife and I was just too happy being home to let that bother me. But now it does.

Later when we got home, my brother said, "Don't wear your uniform." What kind of shit was that? I wanted to wear the fucking thing. I had my ribbons. I was proud of what I'd done. I'm a king. That didn't hurt me then, but it hurts me now.

*   *   *

I spent eleven months and twenty-six days in Vietnam. I was flown to Japan. The first night there, I realized how much tension I had been under the whole time. "I'm going to go to sleep tonight and, unless there is an earthquake or a fire in the hospital, I can just sleep straight through."

From Japan I went to San Francisco. The first meal that you get after you land Stateside is steak. No matter what. For us it was breakfast, so we had steak and eggs. My hands were still in bandages and I was against having anybody cut up my meat. We were in the hospital cafeteria where all the enlisted personnel eat, not just the patients. So you had all these women technicians and all these Air Force nurses. The way that all of these women were acting, they were looking strangely and sliding away.

I'm having a hard time eating my steak. And I'm hungry and I want to eat it. The other guys are kidding me, "You want *me* to cut up your steak for you, Mikey?"

I got irritable. We'd been up for a long time, short on sleep, and my hands were hurting me. Everyone was staring at us. I thought, "You're looking at me like I was an animal. All right, I'll give you a real show." The medium-rare steak goes in the bandages and I'm cramming it in my face. The juice is running down my chin and I'm making grunting animal noises. People are fleeing the area. All my buddies are laughing their asses off.

That was the first time I noticed that people were treating me funny, like I was a psycho, like a slightly retarded child who had a history of violent outbreaks. "I want you to be nice now. You're not going to cause us any trouble now, are you? We know you've had it rough, but just relax and take it easy."

"What the fuck are you talking about? I don't have any machine guns on me. Why are you treating me like I'm going to blow up in your face? I promise, I'm not going to get into my helicopter and mow down the entire hospital." It was kind of fun for a little bit being the psycho. But it never lets up.

There were a lot of guys who were really disturbed. On the flight from Vietnam to Japan I saw this guy laying on a stretcher with a blanket up to his chin. I thought that here's someone who's really caught it. But he's got a beard. We started a conversation and I asked him, "How did you talk them into letting you grow a beard?"

The guy changed right before my eyes. He started raving, "They want to shave off my beard! They're not going to do it! They keep on giving me these shots! I don't like the shots!" He got louder and louder. One of the corpsmen on the plane came over to him to check him underneath the blanket. He was handcuffed, strapped down with leather belts across him with padlocks on them. The guy is doing a good job trying to get out of all this restraint. They gave him a shot and he sank into a stupor.

The corpsman looked at his folder. The guy was an infantry man. Somebody had called him a motherfucker and he took the barrel of an M-60 machine gun and beat three guys to death with it.

So, I have no doubt there were some psychos shipped back. But they were a small minority of us. Why were we all treated like that?

You did your duty, you didn't run off to Canada. You didn't fake some head case to go 4-F. We all know that you've been a killer. You're a little strange. We don't trust you, not all the way, because you've been through this terrible, harrowing experience. You did what you were told to do and you did it very well. You've just been fucked.

*   *   *

I wonder sometimes whatever happened to those guys. Some spinal cord injuries and guys that had stepped on these things called Bouncing Betty. They explode and get your thighs, take your penis, your rectum. So big deal, you get a guy to the hospital and you save his life, but if he's not a quadriplegic, he's got a colostomy, he can't have sex, he can't have kids.

A lot of those guys committed suicide on the way to Japan or in Japan or in a VA hospital. I know of guys that had drugs smuggled on the ward to kill themselves before they were being evacuated. They'd say, "What time does the plane leave? I got to tell the guys in my unit. They're bringing my pictures. They're bringing my stuff."

"Well, it's not due till eleven. You know with the Army, that probably means noon or so." They were waiting for their stuff to come in and they would commit suicide on the plane to Japan. Especially the bad ones. What nineteen-year-old kid wants to live like that?

*   *   *

I spent about four days in the hospital in California. I went AWOL every night, the first time that I'd ever done that. The commanding officer tried to come down on us. "The commanding officer wants to see you, right now."

"Hey, you go tell the commanding officer to get fucked. I'm tired, I'm drunk and hung over. I'm going to sleep."

"You're going to be in big trouble."

"What are you going to do? Send me to Vietnam?"

* * *

I had extended for another tour, but the military decided to send me home early because I was "unstable." They were right. I had trouble taking orders. I had been there so long, I thought I knew a lot more than the officers around me.

I was a patrol boat captain. Our main job was to patrol the rivers and keep Charlie from using them as supply routes. We were sitting ducks. I had a crew of five people and I was determined that all those guys were coming back alive. If anybody gave me an order I didn't like, I just didn't do it. I wouldn't go down rivers that I didn't think were safe.

They got annoyed at me because I called in too much air support. I was a firm believer in air support. We had all these nice airplanes and lots of bombs. If I saw something I didn't like, I wasn't going to go down there and find out what it was. I called those beautiful Phantoms and let them drop the tons of bombs they were dying to drop anyway. Maybe it's just a water buffalo. I'll float down there later and let you know.

In thirty-five hours I went from Vietnam to San Francisco. I left from a place where you took a shower if you felt like it, but it didn't matter because the water was black anyway. Clean clothes were a luxury. If you found any, you saved them for special occasions. We all talked pidgin English.

When I walked into a bar when I first got back, I banged on the bar and said, "Boy-san, *bami-bam*." In a Vietnamese bar, there's always a boy behind the bar, because everyone over seventeen has been drafted.

Bami-bam was beer. The bartender looked at me like, "What the fuck is wrong with you?"

I found myself at San Francisco Airport sitting at a table eating eggs. It was like going to Disneyland. I hadn't seen real eggs for a year and a half. It hit me that I wasn't carrying a gun and I didn't have to watch my back anymore.

I wasn't back more than five and a half hours and I was truly cruising. I was lucky; I came back with relatively long hair, so I didn't look like the typical Army freak. I met a girl in the bar and we rapped and got high. She decided to take me home. We were getting undressed and she saw this red, ugly scar on my elbow. She asked me what was going on with it. I told her offhand that I took a piece of shrapnel in Vietnam. She kicked me right out of bed and out of the house. That devastated me.

I hooked up with some other guys who had been on the flight with me from Vietnam. We decided to hit Vegas on the way home. At Caesar's Palace, we checked in and tried to blow some bucks. We hadn't seen the World in a long time and we wanted to be cool. One of the floorwalkers found out through our conversation that we were fresh out of Nam within two days. He got us our hotel room for nothing and arranged for us to see all the shows. We even gambled with casino chips. He was dynamite. We stayed for five days.

One reason we picked Vegas was because it's such a fantasyland. Vegas is what we needed. If you're on a merry-go-round and you feel like you're spinning, everything is okay. But if you're just standing on the ground, and you're whirling, you're in trouble. The war in Nam hadn't touched Vegas.

*   *   *

When I came into California after fighting in Nam for two years, I hooked up with this guy from the Coast. He bought a brand-new car and we went to Vegas. Fine, I got $3,000 in my pocket, let's go to Vegas. I'm twenty years old, short hair, the whole bit. I never been to Vegas in my life. I've never picked up girls in my life. I don't know what that's all about. I was seventeen when I started with the Marines.

I'm playing this slot machine. There's this beautiful broad about three machines over and she keeps looking at me. I figured, "Ah, go ahead. All she can do is tell you to go fuck yourself, right?" So I walk over with the dumbest line, "Excuse me, is this machine taken?" She looks at me very nicely and says, "No, it's not." So I'm talking to her, "How are you? Do you live here?" About the third quarter I put into the slot, I hit the jackpot. I pretend I do it all the time. I scoop it up, put the money in my pocket. This lady from the casino comes over and she takes some numbers off the machine and she pays me a little money.

I'm talking to the young lady playing the machine and again, after about the third quarter, I hit the jackpot. Oh, I know I'm scoring and not only with the machine. I know I'm going to fuck this bitch, too. So I act like I do it all the time.

This time the casino broad comes over, takes the numbers off the machine and asks me for ID. She thought I could be a pro, one of those guys who puts weights on the machine or something. I showed her my ID and she saw I was only twenty years old. She says, "Oh, I'm sorry, but you're going to have to leave." I looked at her and said, "Give me the rest of the money from the machine." She did.

"I've got to leave, huh?"

"Yes, you have to be twenty-one to be in here." So I felt *bad*. The fucking broad I was trying to pick up heard this, and all of a sudden I'm a little kid again.

* * *

We had a corpsman who we sent down past the USO to the end of the runway to get his plane time after time. He'd be back a couple hours later. He missed it. "I don't know, Lieutenant. I went to the men's room, and when I came out, the plane was gone.'' He was afraid to go home.

I thought that was kind of nuts. Yet when it was my turn to go home, I got sick the week before. To this day, I don't know whether it was psychological or not. I had dysentery and I lost about fifteen pounds in a week. But I also was getting more and more anxious. I couldn't eat. I couldn't even swallow. I had a hard time breathing.

At the time, I didn't think it was connected with going home. The natural reaction is to look forward to going home, to getting out of there. But as bad as it was in Nam, I knew exactly what to expect there. I hadn't been home in fifteen months. It was kind of nice over there in a way. Your parents couldn't get to you. They could write you a letter but it wasn't the same. Nobody could get to you. Even the Army couldn't get to you. What are they going to do, send you to Nam? I was more afraid of going home than of staying there. Within a little more than a day, I left Vietnam, was discharged and found myself sitting in my parents' house having breakfast.

My dad had this toaster that was very touchy. You had to drop the English muffins in just right for them to go down automatically. I couldn't get the English muffins to drop in. I'd stand there and drop them in easy, and then drop them in hard, then I'd slam them in. My father would say, ''Look, just like this.'' He'd pick up an English muffin, drop it in the toaster and they'd go down right away. I was bullshit. I was never like that before I left.

I got downstairs one morning before my folks got up and those God damn English muffins would not go down. I threw the toaster against the wall. I picked it up and threw it against the wall again. I kept throwing it against the wall until I couldn't throw it anymore. I'd been home about a week when that happened. There were a billion trillion crumbs everywhere.

My dad never said a word. He just looked at me. I

said in a small voice, "The English muffins wouldn't go down. You know?"

I was a nurse in a hospital in Nam. What about the guy in the field who was home within twenty-four hours?

When I first got home people would say to me, "Oh, far out, you been to Nam. Did you kill anybody? Was it really true that there was such a thing as Black syphilis?" I'd start to say, "Well, there was no such thing as Black syphilis. There was some that was hard to treat, but . . ." I'd look around at them and they weren't even listening. They didn't really want to listen. They didn't even wait for an answer. I could have read off the thirty-one flavors at Baskin-Robbins and it wouldn't have made any difference.

I didn't know what biodegradable was. My sister-in-law and I were doing the dishes. I washed out a jar and was going to throw it away. She said, "Don't throw that in the garbage. It's not biodegradable." I'd missed a little piece of American culture while I was away for a year.

I went to the supermarket. They're all lighted up and cold. First of all I couldn't stand the cold. Second, you get into the habit in Nam of watching everybody all the time. I got in the store and I couldn't stay more than five minutes, because I couldn't keep an eye on everybody. I told the others that I would wait for them in the car. What made it worse was they made fun of me.

My hometown is a small college town. The main street is not very big. But when you're not used to being around traffic, you lose your ability to judge oncoming cars. I'd step off a curb and see cars coming and not know whether I had enough time to make it across the street. I'd either wait until there were no cars coming or I just ran like hell across the street.

Friday nights were the worst part for me. Friday night here was Saturday morning in Nam. If you had the day off, you went out with the doctors to the leper colony where we had surgery and clinics. Friday nights I'd sit around the house and I just knew that it was eight in the morning and the guys were going to get in the jeep and go over to the Lep. They were going to work all morning and then the nuns were going to feed them lunch. Then they would go to the beach.

The beach at the leper colony was beautiful. It was so peaceful. Charlie never bothered you there, because they were afraid of the lepers. You could lay out there and know that you were probably as safe there as you were ever going to be. The water was as warm as a tub. But twenty-four hours and a couple of international datelines and the whole thing changed for me.

* * *

I came back from chow one evening, walked into the yard and I noticed a Red Cross jeep in front of the captain's hooch. I didn't think very much about it—except a little shudder ran up my spine since one didn't see them very often in general. I went into my hooch, shuffled around deciding whether I was going to take a shower then or later.

Suddenly, the captain appeared with a slip of paper in his hand. He said, "Can I speak to you?" I said sure and he motioned me to come out behind the hooch by the bunker. I didn't have an inkling of what he wanted. He did a little hesitant dance and he said, "There isn't any real way for me to say this."

My heart dropped. I knew before he said anything what was up. It wouldn't have been that way had it been my grandfather or my brother or sister. It had to be my mother. Then he said, "Your mother died today." And he gave me this little piece of paper he was holding. It was a sloppily typed message on Red Cross stationery. She had had a cerebral hemorrhage which was called a sub-arachnoid cerebral hemorrhage in this little piece of paper.

I knew immediately that it meant that I was leaving Vietnam and that I wasn't going to come back. I was as affected by the thought that I wasn't coming back as I was by the fact of my mother's death. I didn't want to leave. I would get out of the Army on a hardship discharge, and I was going to have to take care of two teen-agers. At twenty-six, I was not prepared to be a father. My anticipated three years of avoiding responsibilities of having to go earn a living or make choices about my future were suddenly rubbed out. My chance to be alone was gone.

I couldn't get out of there that night. The captain was very solicitous and tried to get me out on a chopper or to find out if a medevac was leaving, anything. Nothing was going anywhere; there was not a whole lot of flying at night. I had to spend that dreadful last night there.

I wandered around in a daze for a little while. I wasn't able to cry. I wanted to, but I couldn't. I took a shower and tried to cry in the shower all by myself. It didn't work. I figured I'd feel better if I could make myself cry. But another part of me was operating that said, "If you cry now, you're not going to stop. You're going to lose it, because you're going to cry for everything."

People didn't know how to deal with my grief. I was not spraying it all over the place, but, my God, my mother had died. There was polite compassion. But I was going to be leaving, and guys were protecting themselves from the loss of a friend. You were careful about the depth of the investment that you made.

I remember thinking at the time, "Where are they all?" I had trouble finding people that night. Everybody was somewhere else. I had the distinct feeling that a couple of people were avoiding me, partly because they genuinely didn't know what to say. It was something that had happened in that place called Home. Home was hard to deal with. It was very far away, alien and increasingly strange and removed. Men and their mothers, that's heavy duty stuff as well.

There was also the knowledge in those people that I was closest to that I was not going to be there by that time the next day. If they were going to miss me nearly as much as I was going to miss them, they didn't want to deal with it. And I don't blame them. I didn't want to deal with it either. In effect, what I was leaving was a family. It was a real small one and it was populated by people who were also about to leave, but it was all I had.

I didn't sleep. I just lay awake on my bunk. I walked around outside and looked at the flares. I looked it over for the last time. I packed. The next morning I got on a Caribou* from the base to Bien Hoa. My emergency orders were supposed to be waiting for me at the flight desk there. I didn't even have to go through my unit. It was all done as fast as it possibly could have been done.

On the flight home, I sat next to a chaplain. He was a real asshole who was carrying his dress uniform in a plastic bag, hung over the seat. He had been a chaplain in Saigon or somewhere. He spent half the flight talking about parties he'd been to. I couldn't even talk to him. I just did not want to be next to him. I didn't tell him why I was going home. I didn't want to hear anything he had to say. I didn't want any pats on the shoulder. I didn't want any Be-a-brave-young-man bullshit.

I didn't want anything from those stewardesses either. I didn't want their smiles, I didn't want their boobs. I didn't want anything. I was so angry. I kept thinking to myself, "How can you fucking people have *this* job? How come you're stewardesses on *these* flights? What's the matter with you? How can you deal with this? I can't deal with it and I've been there. How can you deal with all of us week after week after week? You must know how crazy I am." They were doing their best to be really nice.

I left Vietnam and thirty-seven and a half hours later I was home. Home, in the middle of fucking November, drizzle and 32 degrees. No transition, fucking weird.

I was met at the airport by my stepuncle and a woman I'd had an affair with for a couple of years. Waiting for me at home were my seventeen-year-old brother and my fifteen-year-old sister who had lost their father and their mother in the space of four years. And my eighty-three-year-old grandfather who had flown up from Florida. My mother was his only child.

I stood on the same hillside where I had said goodbye to my mother the past Easter weekend and was plunged headlong into being an American again. A mourner and an angry one. I wore my Class A's to my mother's funeral, by God. I was tan, mean—by their standards—and angry.

Everybody was getting into Christmas. Christmas! I haven't been able to deal with Christmas since I got back from Vietnam. I go into a funk about two weeks after Thanksgiving and I stay there until it is over. There were a lot of people that I knew still over in Vietnam, while all these other people were doing their fucking Christmas shopping as if nothing else was happening in the world. That's trite, but that's the way I felt. I wanted somebody to pick a fight with me. I was ready to hit anybody who got in my way over anything. I stayed angry for at least two years.

*   *   *

I went home straight from California to O'Hare Airport in Chicago. I got home about three in the morning. Everybody in the house got up and said hello. Then they all went back to sleep. At 8:30 when my father left for work, he woke me up to say, "Listen, now that you're home, when are you going to get a job?"

I packed up and left. I haven't been home since.

*   *   *

I've been in job interviews trying to get a lousy job, and some guy looks at me like I've got two heads. All you want to do is grab him by his tie and drag him across the desk. It's frustrating. "Well, what can you do? You can't type, you've never been a file clerk. You're unemployable." One moment I was a king and the next moment I'm the dregs of society. Nobody wants to know shit from me. They'll do anything to get me out of their offices. "Lots of luck in the future.

What's your name again? Whew, I'm glad that guy is gone. Don't send me any more like that fucking guy that just left.''

*　　*　　*

I had always heard that you got to have your job back. When I went to them for my job, they said, "What you want to do? Put somebody out of work? They got families and kids." After their little song and dance, I ended up working in the stock room where I had started the first time around. The only way I got that was to threaten to take them to court.

They told me that I couldn't have the seniority that I had built up before I left until I had been back physically for one year. In the second week of the eleventh month I was fired. With my seniority, I wouldn't have been fired. But they resented the fact that they had to take me back. I had already worked back up to my old job.

I went to the VA and told them I needed some assistance or a job. They sent me to a factory paying minimum wage. I went there and it was a sweatshop. I ended up without a job.

I went to the power company and I had to take a physical. The doctor and I were talking and when he found out I was a veteran he asked me if I went to Vietnam. After that he started looking me over like something has got to be wrong. When he was taking my blood pressure, he took my arm and lifted it up and started looking it over, from my armpit to my wrist and back again, turning it over and back. I knew what he was doing, but I tried to ignore it. Then he grabbed the other arm and I had to say, "How dumb do I look to you? Are you trying to tell me my blood pressure has changed from one arm to the next?" He's still twisting my arm. I said, "Get your hands off of me, man. The physical was going all right up till now."

He was looking for tracks and it pissed me off. I wasn't going to be put in that position. I told them what they could do with that job. The telephone company told me to get on the waiting list and that it wasn't their fault that the service only taught me to use a gun and didn't try to teach me a trade. I got on the waiting list for federal jobs, the waiting list for UPS, for the Post Office, for correction officers. I wound up taking a parking agent's job. From the very beginning they said to me, "Oh, so you're one of those veterans. Well, there are no special privileges here for you because you were in Vietnam." Now, I had just walked through the damn door and this is what I got thrown in my face. I didn't come in there asking for nothing but a job.

So I bought a gypsy cab and rented out three others. The cops gave me such a hassle, they wound up pulling my license. So I went and did the thing that most of the guys did. I was out on the street running numbers, selling some smoke, some coke. I had to survive. I had to take care of me and my family.

* * *

We were all strapped in. They figured you might act up on the plane and grab at a window or a nurse. But they would hype them up, put you out automatically with morphine. Psychos coming back, amputees coming back, guys that wanted to die.

I came back with an I-don't-give-a-shit kind of attitude, on a military medevac jet. They connected for me to go into the VA hospital back home. They had a VA representative to talk to everybody. He was telling us all about our benefits. I didn't want to hear nothing from nobody. My scheme was, "Just let me get out of the Army." I had an honorable discharge. I had medals coming to me. They showed me this big paper with all the medals numbered on it. I didn't want to see shit. I said, "You can keep your uniform. You can take the medals and shove them up your ass." I had forty-four days that was coming to me and they paid me for that.

I got back to the World, but this wasn't the World that I had left. I was born again. Like the Christians say, "Be born again." I did not fit into the real world anymore. For that twelve months in the Nam, I used to sit down and imagine what I would do in the World when I got back. I'll be with this woman, I'm going to do this and that. I came back to the World and I see people rioting about Nam. People hated GIs for being in the Nam. They was blaming us. I flipped out. I couldn't believe it.

I was in a VA hospital the first time I heard anybody saying, "Those fucking guys over in Vietnam. Look what they're doing." Man, it did something to me. Like I was guilty. I was a criminal. You had sentenced me to die. These are the same people from when I left the year before. I'm back but I don't belong. I wanted to go back to the Nam. I would have re-upped, but I was all wounded. This world was alienating, what people was talking about, what people was liking.

When my mom came to see me, she was a different person. I didn't hate her or nothing like that. But it was a different person. I couldn't communicate with her. I just looked at her. We talked and it was over.

I would just sit in the room in the hospital and my mind would flash back. I would have dreams about the Nam, the Nam and action. I could see myself fighting, when I'm actually sitting in a VA hospital on the bed. I could see myself back in the Nam.

This is not the World. Lord, how can they do this to me? How can they bring me back to a World where I don't know what they're talking about? The United States is saying one thing. The people are saying something else. President Nixon is talking about the Silent Majority. The people are in the streets protesting. Who are these people out here protesting while there are guys in the Nam going through psychological and physical hell? Walking in monsoon when it rains for months at a time. Being sniped at. Being killed. Stepping in booby traps. Catching jungle rot. Getting eaten up by leeches. How can they say the war is unjust? How can you walk out of Nam and leave guys out in the field or missing in action?

I wasn't thinking they were un-American, but man, somebody pulled the rug out from under us. Somebody stabbed us in the back. The average person in the peace struggle didn't understand. We got stabbed in the back by the Army, while we were in the Army. We got stabbed in the back when we got back to the United States by the Peace people. We got stabbed in the back by President Nixon. He's talking nonsense. Henry Kissinger is talking about peace and ending the war. All this is garbage.

I felt a guilt trip. I said to myself, "I can't let people know that I've been to Vietnam." I knew they could look at me and tell that I was different.

I got out of the hospital. I used to sit in my room at home and I would just drink and be quiet. I just couldn't imagine myself going to parties, being with women. I was totally disoriented. I just could not adjust.

That first Fourth of July was the hardest thing for me to get through. I was in a big store and somebody threw firecrackers. I crouched down. People laughed at me. I felt like somebody dropped a safe out a window on me. "They know that I'm a Vietnam veteran."

I went back to school that September. I paid my own way to school. I didn't want to get my GI benefits because I didn't want nobody to know that I was a veteran. I was ashamed, because everybody in the U.S. hated GIs for being in the Nam. I was trying to hide myself.

I thought maybe if I go to school I can adjust. I go to school and they're saying, "Those fucking GIs over in Vietnam." The professors would shake their heads, "It's a shame those GIs are over in Vietnam killing innocent people." I wouldn't say nothing.

I walked into the classroom and the professor told me to write a report. I'm sitting there and my mind clicked. All I could see was I was in Nam and the professor standing up there, he was a gook. He looked like a gook to me. He wasn't even Oriental. But I wanted to kill this man. "I should kill this professor." My mind said,

"Kill this dude, man. This is the enemy. What's he doing out in the field?" My mind was flashing back.

I would hear kids talk, "What's going down in Nam is a shame. We going to join the peace movement. Let's go on a demonstration." These guys are trying to kill the people that is my World. These are enemies. I got to kill these mothers.

Now a lot of vets back here in the World just picked up rifles and started shooting people. I can understand that. They could not adjust. They just threw us back into a place that we were untrained to live in. They should have had to train us to come back into the World. It took me *years* to understand that I'm part of the United States.

CASUALTIES

Wasted.

    "After a hump, you were wasted."

    "Jesus, we wasted them gooks."

    "I got really wasted on that dope."

    "Geezer got wasted up on some hill."

    "What a waste."

    Americans were wasted in an amazing variety of ways in Vietnam. When they returned home, they were wasted again, like greasy paper plates after the picnic. Disposable soldiers, men and women who were treated like so much human refuse to be lugged to the dump.

    Some of them are still on the streets, beating feet, wearing faded surplus field jackets with someone else's name sewn over the pocket, fatigues precisely bloused in spit-shined combat boots, down at the heel. At the VA methadone clinic there are a couple of guys who have been slapping each other on the back and giggling over pecker checks for ten years without missing a week.

    Prisons, from county work farms to federal pens, have provided bivouac for thousands. There are more setting up individual defensive perimeters in a different

*town every few months, sandbagged into a bare room
with a hot plate until they feel the compulsion to saddle
up again.*

*But the majority of Vietnam veterans are snooping
and pooping in the mainstream of American life, lonely
guerrillas in company coveralls or three-piece suits. "I
have two resumes. One of them includes my military
record." "When I was on the phone with you today
confirming our interview, the guy sitting two years at
the desk across from me said, 'You in Nam?' He's a vet,
too, and I didn't even know it." On their own again,
they're making the best of a bad situation.*

*Most of the veterans I talked to had never discussed
their experience with anybody. "God, I've never talked
this much about the Nam." "I've told you things I
haven't even told my wife. She wouldn't know how to
handle it." When they came back to "the World," no
one wanted to know about their war. It was carefully
ignored or rejected outright. One veteran told me,
"Bringing up the Nam was like farting at the dinner
table. Everybody looks away embarrassed and acts like
nothing happened. Well, pardon me."*

*Besides, telling war stories hurts. The defiant shrug
that says, "I've seen even worse, but I ain't telling
you," doesn't veil the pain. Veterans' eyes still give
them away. I saw the pain in their faces over and over
again. Most of them haven't cried yet. The fear of not
being able to stop crying is still too great.*

*I played dispassionate interviewer, cajoled and
prodded. I was alternately anonymous confessor and
devil's advocate. I poured the booze that washed out the
big pieces. I walked to the john to get Kleenex for them
to blow their noses, careful to stay in there a few
minutes to give them time to get themselves back
together. I was a little surprised at my own composure.*

*Then early one morning, on the highway between
Providence and Boston, hurrying from one interview to
the next, thinking more about deadlines than anything
else, I was suddenly sobbing. The road disappeared in
the tears and I had to pull onto the shoulder and stop*

the car. No one interview, no particular story made me cry. None of the veterans had really spilled his guts on me. It was just the accumulation of too much vicarious, second-hand pain, broken voices and broken spirits. What a waste.

My first impulse was to call my wife. I pulled into the first Holiday Inn I came to and got on the pay phone. "Hi, honey. How are you?"

"Fine. I'm fine. Are you all right?"

"Yeah, I just wanted to tell you that I love you."

"I love you too," she said, "very much."

"Good. I'm glad. Well, goodbye."

The war in Vietnam left a wound on my generation that hasn't healed. It has closed with the infection still raging inside. The longer we ignore it the worse the infection grows. The healing process seems so simple. All we have to do is open the stinking thing up, wash it out and keep it clean until we're well again.

I'm tempted to say, "Go out and grab the first vet you see. Love him and cry your eyes out together." That's too sentimental. I know love is too much to ask in our busy, busy age. "Give peace a chance, all you need is love." We outgrew all that and got down to business—as usual. Sympathy marred with the least trace of condescension comes out pity and the veterans of Vietnam aren't looking for that.

This is what I will ask. Look around you at all the people you know who are about the right age to have been involved in the war. Ask, "Were you in Vietnam?" Some three million people served in the Armed Forces in Southeast Asia between 1964 and 1975. You'll find a Vietnam vet much more easily than you think. Try to get him to tell you about his experience if you are genuinely interested. Once he starts talking, just keep your mouth shut and listen. You both may learn something about that particular conflict, about the human spirit, about yourselves. At least it won't be another waste of time.

If you don't think about it and just keep right on going, it doesn't bother you. But if you stop long enough, it gets to you. I went almost eight years without any trouble. Oh, I had my nightmares and those nights I couldn't go to sleep without a light on, but I dealt with it.

Then about a year and a half ago, I was assisting with some surgery when the patient for whatever reasons didn't make it. I had no control over the outcome and didn't cause the death. The patient happened to be a little Chinese-American girl.

This happened in December. By May, I was almost unable to work, unable to get out of bed. I was depressed all the time. I felt terribly guilty. I thought it was all my fault, when really I wasn't at fault or in control. Legally and morally, there was nothing I could have done except what I was told to do. The people in my department knew that this incident bothered me, but they didn't know what to do about it.

I wasn't going out, I wasn't doing anything. I'd come home from work and I would forget to buy food, so I

wasn't eating. I had a friend come up to visit me from
Missouri. She saw me and said, "What's the matter
with you?" I told her that nothing was wrong. But I was
at the point where I could barely talk. I could function
at work enough so that my work was acceptable, but it
was all I could do to maintain my composure. I was in
such an anxiety state all the time—I was afraid that
something else was going to happen—that I could barely
manage the most minor cases. On the outside, nobody
knew.

We had a shrink talk to us about the problems that
cardiac patients had. So I said, "Maybe I need a vacation or maybe I'm tired." So I went to talk to him. He
was pretty cool. He said, "What's the problem?"

"I don't sleep or it takes me three hours to get to
sleep. When I do sleep, I'm awake two hours later. I
don't know. I had a friend who told me I was acting
depressed. I don't feel depressed."

"Well, what do you do?"

I thought for a minute. It turned out that I wasn't doing anything. It took every ounce of energy I had to get
from my home to work. Being suicidal didn't enter my
mind. When you're really depressed, you don't have
enough energy to carry it out.

I've been going to see the guy three times a week for a
year now—because I did eventually try to kill myself. I
asked him if I had not gone to Vietnam would I have the
problems that I have now. He said, "You've got survivor syndrome and I think your problems were triggered by the fact that the girl who died was Oriental.
The guy who takes a gun and holds off the police from a
tower, something precipitates that attack. Your problems were precipitated by the Oriental girl. She's
Chinese, but she could have been Vietnamese. You were
totally out of control and you were doing what you were
told when she died. How many times did you do what
you were told when you were in Vietnam?"

He's been tying all this in. I was within a breath of
being put on the funny farm. The only thing that keeps
me out of the hospital right now is seeing this guy three

times a week. I was on antidepressants for a year. I feel pretty good now and I've been off the drugs four months. A lot of things are falling into place.

It feels good to tell this guy, "Yeah, one day I watched this monk. He was really pissed off that Americans had desecrated this cemetery. I was standing right there when he burned himself up right in front of me."

"How many people did you tell that to?"

"I didn't tell anybody. Who are you going to tell that to, anyway?" Although combat veterans have few people to talk to about their experiences, I have maybe even less. How many nurses could I walk up to and say, "Oh, yeah, I denied people medication. I saw patients being poisoned because we had no beds and we needed beds for the GIs. That's murder."

I have a lot of nights I don't sleep and I refuse to put the light on. "What's so wrong with turning on the light?" he asked me.

"Well, that's like being a little kid."

"When you were a kid, did you have nightmares?"

"No, I never had nightmares until I came home from Nam. I never had trouble sleeping before that."

It's getting better, but I should have had this guy ten years ago. He is on my side. He is my friend. I also have an empty medicine bottle on the kitchen counter just to remind me that I took the contents of it one night. That was enough to kill ten people.

*   *   *

The girl I had been engaged to had gotten pregnant by somebody else and had married a third guy. That blew me away. We had stopped writing after I was wounded. I had a very fatalistic attitude. I stopped writing to everybody.

I ended up living with my parents. From July until late September my entire activity consisted of coming-to in the morning. In the late afternoon, I'd get cleaned up and sobered up, until early evening when I would go out drinking. Night after night, I would just drink until I was senseless.

I was terribly shy with women. Evidently, I could only approach women when I was extremely drunk. In the mornings, I would find all kinds of bits of paper in my pockets with cryptic notations and telephone numbers on them. "Janet with the red scarf 555-6868." I never called any of them.

I went back to work. I went to work for the city of Minneapolis in their testing labs. I was a materials tester of concrete, asphalt, steel rods. I was making about $500 a month. My drinking just went on and on. I would spend days not showing up for work. I wouldn't call in sick.

I was severely depressed. I could accomplish nothing. Most of my friends felt that something was wrong, but they had no idea what to do. My family was very concerned. This was before they put a label on post-Vietnam syndrome. I felt cheated. I felt bad about myself. People treated me funny.

*   *   *

I didn't cry until April of 1970 for any of it. I didn't cry until the day that would have been my rotation day, the day that I was due to have returned had things worked out otherwise. That was spooky. I woke up April 6, 1970, in tears and cried all day. That's exaggerating. I cried from 8:30 in the morning until five o'clock in the afternoon. Pretty much nonstop. Perhaps three hours of that were hysterical uncontrolled crying. I was crying for everything.

Things were a little better after that, but not much. I was not equipped to deal with any of the things I had to deal with. I probably did okay, but I was walking a fine line the entire time. None of it was what I wanted to be happening. There was no solace anywhere. There was nobody to talk to. Except Rebecca whom I married. I would pick up the phone and talk to her for two or three hours at a stretch.

She knew the kind of trouble I was in emotionally. The way she describes it is that when I came back, I was dead from the neck down. My mind functioned and I went through the motions of getting through my life, but there wasn't anything going on. I was really dead. The first crack in all that was when I finally cried. Then for the next two years it was a climbing out, which she had an enormous amount to do with. She finally put me in touch with my body again, she put me in touch with myself sexually again.

Then in the fall of 1972, almost three years to the day after I came back, I had a nervous breakdown. It was a small nervous breakdown. It wasn't straitjacket time. But it was serious. Everything came to a complete halt.

It was a lot of things. It wasn't all Nam-related, but much of it was. There was lots of accumulated baggage and guilt—lots of guilt. Guilt about being in Vietnam. Guilt about my mother's death, guilt about leaving the other guys, guilt about surviving. Wondering where really my life was going. Feeling out of synch. Feeling I was living in a berserk culture, which I was. Knowing that, but not having anybody to agree with me.

Finally, I got into a place that I have never been in before in my life. I woke up one morning knowing beyond a shadow of a doubt, for all of my prejudices against psychiatrists, that I ought to go somewhere for help.

I was not able to get out of bed. I felt completely out of control. The fear that that inspired was paralyzing. All I wanted to do was stay in bed, not go to work and cry a lot.

I was very lucky because Rebecca was on top of the situation and got me where I needed to go quickly. She took care of all the details of my life, let my boss know what was going on.

Many people who knew me very well were wondering when it was going to happen. My wife wasn't surprised. I was walking some kind of razor's edge and something was going to give. I look at photographs of myself at that time and I see how rigid and tight I was. I can see it in my eyes.

I know that Vietnam was only part of my break-down—it may not have been half of it. Vietnam was just a piece of the whole tapestry of things, but it was an important piece because it was connected in so many ways to so many other things. It had been an incredible journey and it was in no way complete. Giving in to it somehow was important.

I still feel the incompleteness of the experience. It's not fully resolved for me. I get glimpses every once in a while of ways of completing myself but it's such an enormous battle. I'm luckier than most Nam vets because I've made a real journey. I've gone through the ten-year cycle. I've studied and relived and cried over my memories. I've worked through them and learned to live with them. I'm proud of that.

But it's not over for me. I can still get too wound up about it. I'm reasonably calm and organized about it all, but I've spent a lot of time getting that way. There are times which come at me unexpectedly out of the dark when I just absolutely fly off the handle about something and know it's because of Nam. It is that anger that's triggered. When I encounter something really stupid, it's Nam that makes me angry. Then I leave, because I know if I stay, someone is going to provoke me to violence. The reservoir would be tapped and I would be in big trouble. If it got tapped, I would be put away and all the lawyers in the world couldn't keep me out of a ward.

I keep thinking I'm past that now. I'm on top of that. I'm in control and there's no reason for the anger anymore. I'm over being mad. But I'm not. I'm not. Anger is part of me now. I'm going to go through my whole life dealing with my anger. It's going to come back at me time and time again in one form or another. Maybe by the time I shuffle through this coil, I'll be able to deal with it.

I get into this survivor head sometimes, and I'll say to people, "But you don't understand. You don't understand what you're doing to other people when you fuck up like that. You don't understand that this stupidity of yours, this self-conscious and deliberate stupidity, this distortion of the truth, this deliberate dishonesty of yours, hurts. I'm not even going to bother to talk to you about how it hurts you. I know you're not ready for that. But let me count the ways that you are hurting somebody else. Let me try to make you understand that when you behave that way you jeopardize other people's lives, Asshole. I don't care if we both have M-16s in our hands and it's on the front, or if we both have checkbooks in our hands and it's back home. It's the same God damn thing.'' It's a miracle we all survive from day to day, the world is so filled with assholes. I do asshole things too, but I don't do them deliberately anymore.

I get so angry when I realize that people are doing bad things with awareness. That's the ruthless side of me. The assholes of the world do need to be ruthlessly weeded out. Because they endanger other people's very lives.

I wouldn't feel any of this with this much passion if it hadn't been for Vietnam. I would probably be just as crass as the rest of them, because I was sure as hell geared for it. I probably would have had my nervous breakdown at the age of forty-four, from which I would never recover. I know that I am saner because of my experience than I ever have been in my life or than I would be if my life had gone the way it was tracked to go.

I also discovered for myself in Vietnam that people are capable of much more than we think they are. I get really annoyed when people can do better and they don't because it's not important enough. I figure there's no reason not to deal with all of it as though it were important. It seems to me that it is.

* * *

I still dream about it. My wife hears me screaming in the middle of the night. I swear to God, it's so real sometimes. I feel like I'm in my dream and can't wake up. This has got to be a dream. But, God Almighty, it's here again. I'm back in Vietnam. I'm on my third tour. I only got two more months to go. Then, I'm getting shot at again, getting hit again. My rifle won't work and then I don't have a rifle. I'm standing by myself and I don't have nothing and these fucking gooks are coming at me. I wake up and my stomach will be real funny-feeling. I get headaches and things.

*　*　*

Basically, I enjoyed Vietnam. It was the most vivid part of my life. I enjoyed the anarchy of it. You know, self-law. No one ever bothered you. You know what it's like to walk down the road with twelve guys armed to the teeth and anybody who shoots at you is in trouble? You're living every minute. You're with the guys who really look after you. You can trust them. I missed that a lot when I got back to the States. You really appreciate that now when you're getting fucked over all the time dealing with society.

When I came back to America, I'll tell you a little secret, I was doing a lot of stick-ups. Because I wanted that *thing*. Stuff didn't bother me, like what happens if you get shot. Fuck that. I been shot. Being in trouble doesn't bother you. Big fucking deal. How bad can it be?

The guys I was working with were vets, too, really insane. There's a lot of sick crews out there, shotgun teams doing this stuff, and they're all former Marines like me. They were doing it because they couldn't get a jump when they came back to civilian life. They couldn't find a way back into society so they just stayed outside. It wasn't the money with me. I was doing things for a handshake. I wanted the adrenaline pump.

It was like being in Nam again. I had a chance to get shot at and I had a chance to shoot at other people. That was the only thing I knew. I wasn't afraid to die. Plus if I was to die at twenty-three, I figured I was still ahead of the game because I should not have made it past nineteen in Vietnam. So I was playing Russian Roulette with life here in America, racing toward the death wheel without even knowing it.

You know how people say at certain times they can

see themselves doing something, like your brain steps out and looks back at the rest of you? That's happened to me four or five times in my life and it was always because I was doing something I wasn't supposed to do. Doing stick-ups was like being in Nam going on patrol. I had a reason for doing what I was doing, some sense of priorities. It gave me direction and a sense of being. And I was sharing something with two or three other guys.

We'd set up drug deals in which there was no drugs. Buyers show up, we play cop and take the money. Once we did it and the guys we snatched turned out to be real cops, on the force. But we were out in the street in front of God and everyone. Women are standing there holding their children, people are looking out their windows. So I run up to the cops and say "Anti-crime." Me and my partners start cuffing them. A squad car pulls up and I send them down the street after a Cadillac with out-of-state plates. I don't know where I got the brains at the time, but everything started coming naturally. I was pretty shocked that I was so sharp. It was exciting and I didn't give a fuck and it sort of reminded me of Nam.

I was carrying a gun for a long time. I didn't like the whole idea of being stripped of a weapon, especially in New York. It was very unkosher, as far as I was concerned. I lost more blood in Brooklyn than I did in Vietnam. I've been stabbed three times, shot at twice. I said to myself, "Man, you made it through two years in Vietnam and all the shit that was going on over there. You don't want to die in no stupid gutter."

Matter of fact, I went away for carrying a piece, possession of a weapon. They made me do two years. I should have gone some nice easy place and done some easy time, I should have been playing golf with the white-collar guys from Watergate. But coming out of orientation they put all the Vietnam vets in the worst possible situations in the prison system.

They know that *you* know what danger is really all about. They know that I know a guard with a shotgun can shove it up his ass after 70 meters. It just ain't going to do no good. They know that you'll take a chance because you have already. It's nothing new to you to run at someone who has a gun or to run away from one —just zig-zag, what the fuck? But it turns out that Vietnam vets make the best prisoners—although I caused them a lot of trouble. I made the motherfuckers earn their money to keep me, man.

But what hurt was going before the fucking parole board. I figured they'd say, "Well, the guy's a Vietnam veteran. He did the right thing for his country, he's got his honorable discharge. We'll let him go." I thought I should have got play. But these motherfuckers tell me, "You got off too easy," and they stick me with more time. Plus they tell me I'm emotionally disturbed, but not once did anybody try to set me up with a psychiatrist. "Well, being as you did the right thing for your country, we got to fuck you again, kid."

They wanted a song and a dance. Let him dance. I walked in and didn't say a fucking thing to them. I was too proud for that kind of shit. When I saw two broads on the board, I knew I was dead. Women have no notion of what is evil and what isn't evil.

I don't do any of that shit no more because I've really calmed down now. When you first come back there ain't a thing you can't do. If you want to be a millionaire, you can. But as the years go by you get caught up in what all the other people are worrying about. Test papers, having a big car and having a color television. Then you become just another dopey-mopey, doop-de-boop civilian. You can't do nothing and your head's up your ass.

When I first entered this society again, I felt superior to everybody. I did for five or six years until I had to go up for two. Now I'm wandering around aimlessly, wondering why am I existing. There's no purpose for me. I'm not married, I don't even have a girl. I don't get a kick out of nothing no more. That's why things are dangerous for me. When you don't get a kick out of anything no more, what's the next step? I'm on the end and I'm very easy to push off.

The real meaning of life is to eat and get by. The main

thing the VA wanted to push on me when I got back was
to go to school. I can't eat books. I ain't got no formal
education anyway.

I can't get a job. Before I went over, if you wanted a
job, you went and talked to the boss. If he liked you,
you got the job. When I come back they got something
called filling out forms. It took me an hour to fill them
out. I got an eighth grade education. I never had a job
besides the Marines, anyway.

The attitude people had to you was you were an asshole for going to Nam in the first place, so fuck you.
They would go out of their way to have nothing to do
with you. You're not housebroken. They can't control
you.

The only people who were happy to see me come back
were my friends from Brooklyn. I was with the street
people. I got my parade when I came back.

The first guy that turned himself in when they gave
amnesty to draft dodgers was a personal friend of mine.
He came up to me and said, "Hey, it's good to see you
man. You're still alive. I wasn't fucking going, because
I knew they'd kill me." Ain't nothing wrong with that.
But don't tell me I was wrong for doing what I did.

Every once in a while, especially in jail, I get to thinking about being free, and Vietnam comes to me very
vivid in spots. I remember kids that went out with the
squad and I say, "I wonder what happened to him?"
Then I go through certain fire fights in my mind and
figure out that guy got hit and died in Vietnam. It was
all so chaotic I didn't even remember the guy was dead
for ten years. *Boom-boom-boom, bang-bang-bang*, call
in the casualty reports. Wait for the shit to hit the fan
again. And it would. It was like a crazy game. They put
you at the starting line and the name of the game was to
make it. Everybody was out for themselves and nobody
gave a fuck. "Okay, man, here you are for thirteen
months and you can do anything you want to as long as
you stay alive. But remember, nobody gives a shit if you
live or die."

The real atrocity in Nam was not the fighting. The

real atrocity to me was the American people not backing up their troops.

What I really missed being back in the States was the stand-up American boy. I'm sure that down South they're still American. They were raised to love the flag and drink up and you ain't taking weapons away from them. That's bullshit. The South's not like the industrial cities, the money cities. But apple pie and Chevrolets is gone. When I look around and see what robots the American people are, it really scares the shit out of me. I would love to see a foreign army come to this country and blow some people away just to straighten them out. That's how bad I feel about certain things—like how a lot of guys were done wrong. Just let the people get a taste of it, man.

I like this Iran thing and the stuff in Afghanistan. It's great to see Americans get pissed off. When I first heard the building was snatched, I thought, "Big deal. They do that kind of thing all the time and nobody gives a fuck." Suddenly, people were wearing "Fuck the Khomeini" T-shirts. I said, "Hey, America's got a little spark under it. How about that?" It felt good.

I asked a couple of guys I know that were pissed off about Iran if they would join the service and go and fight if the government decided to do something about setting things straight. They said no, they wouldn't. I don't understand that. How can your blood boil and you're not willing to do anything about it? So there's something wrong with America. It's all these young people today, their mothers are our sisters and they saw what happened in Nam. So they ain't sending their kids. I wouldn't send mine either, especially if the government isn't going to back the kids.

*   *   *

I used to be a cop. And when I would be in a shoot-out, it was a fire fight for me. I'm in the Nam. People said to me, "Man, you're brutal. What's wrong? What's with you, man? What's happening? You're not here to destroy people. Relax yourself." But the thing had my mind going that I was in the Nam. Just for that minute, my mind snapped and I'm in the Nam. Whenever I hear gunfire and see flashes, I'm back there. Even now after all these years. I'm talking about eleven years.

My wife couldn't understand. I tripped off on her. I just got turned off with my wife. I didn't have no feeling, no nothing. I started going down into depression. My child died. I think she was affected by Agent Orange. I remember them spraying it, the mist as they came across the field.

I hadn't had feeling. I was drinking a lot. I was arresting people and I was beating people up. I was in my own private Nam. I was in glory again. I created my own Nam, right here in the streets. Until they realized, "Hey, there's something wrong with this guy. He's sick." I had my power back again. My wife couldn't understand that. She couldn't sense that the Nam messed me up.

I would sometimes sit in a room by myself. I didn't want to bother with nobody. Just be in a room by myself. Don't want to be in this so-called World. I'd be sitting there thinking about Nam. Telling myself, many's the time, "Why didn't I die in the Nam, like they told me? I don't belong here in this World. I belong in that Nam that was happening."

Before I got there, I was scared and I was thinking I shouldn't go into that world. Once I got in Nam, there was no turning back. Your mind clicks and it's hard for it to click back. Maybe that's the difference between being sane and insane. I couldn't adjust back now unless they created a Nam, the same thing, with the shooting and the incoming. Then I'd be happy as a punk in Boys Town. I could survive.

When they took us out of Vietnam, they should have put us on a rifle range. The first week they give you a thousand rounds. Next week they give you 500. Like dope. Cut us down real slow. They just sent me home and said, "Okay, you're normal again. Go to it."

The Deer Hunter was the first Vietnam movie that I have seen. I went with a young lady. I said, "Let's go to the flick. Let's go see this picture *The Deer Hunter*. It's about the Nam." I'm walking in there thinking that this is an ordinary picture, like *The Green Berets* with my man John Wayne that I saw on TV. That wasn't no Nam. I laughed about it. But *Deer Hunter* was a different story.

There's one part in there where two white guys are hanging on to the skids of a helicopter, scratching for dear life to get on it. One dude fell off because he was weak. The other dude said to hell with it, jumped off and ran off through the water after him. That was the Nam I knew. I put myself there. I was sick to my stomach. I got cold and sweated. I tried to fight it. It was like a drug addiction. The girl thought I was flipping out.

"I'm in Vietnam again," I said to myself. "I'm back in Vietnam." All of a sudden they are in a fire fight on the screen and if I had had a gun on me I would have started shooting. Can you imagine if I had really opened up on the crowd in a theater? The cops walk in and tell me, "Okay, we're taking you to jail." Can you imagine me telling them that I thought I was in Vietnam again?

I'm serious, I came apart. I crouched down behind the seat and crawled up the aisle of the theater and out into the light on my hands and knees. I didn't know that it was a movie anymore. I was back in the war and that was what I had to do. The judge would look at me and say, "No, I don't believe you was back in Vietnam. Lock him up."

I'm thirty-three years old, been out of the Nam since 1969. If I watch a movie like that and I have a weapon in my hands, I will react like I'm in the Nam. That's how much it affected me. I cannot control it. I try to. Maybe I should be in some kind of counseling with psychiatrists. To me I can function normally, get a police job. I've had other jobs. I got a college degree, but when a picture like that come in front of me, it made me feel that I'm in the Nam and I don't know why.

*   *   *

I don't know how we got on to it. I told this next-door neighbor of mine that I had been in Vietnam and he wanted to see my pictures. I only had a couple of beers, maybe two or three. We started looking at the album and I just flipped out. I started throwing shit everywhere. I beat my wife over the head with a full quart bottle of beer. I threw that guy out of the trailer.

They called the cops. They had two cops on each door of the trailer and I was lucky, because usually they would have just blown me away. I told them, "Keep your motherfucking ass out of here." I had a handful of butcher knives in each hand and I was threatening to cut them. I said, "You're not coming in here. No you ain't."

They had their weapons out but they didn't shoot. They called an ambulance and the driver was crazy enough to come in to where I was. He somehow made me come back to reality. "Look, man," he said, "if you don't fucking go with me, the cops are going to take you. And it won't be in one piece." He walked right into the trailer. He was a brave dude.

I said, "Shit, I'll go with you." I'd started coming down by then. They took me to the VA hospital and pumped my stomach. They thought I'd taken a whole bunch of pills. I told them I hadn't taken any drugs. I had a few nerve pills that I'd gotten from them, but I wasn't taking any then. I had them in my possession and they thought I had taken a whole bottle of them.

They went through the whole thing of putting the hose up my nose. They don't really pump your stomach. They just make you throw up. "All you're going to get is a chicken sandwich," I told them. Then I let them have it with the chicken sandwich. They didn't find a drop of drugs.

They put me up on the mental ward for a couple of days. But they found out I was as well as anybody else out on the street. I just had a lot of anxiety built up. I got out as soon as I could. The psychiatrist said, "There isn't anything wrong with you, man. You're just a little hyper and overanxious."

"Yeah, I know that." I just flipped out when I saw those pictures in that book. My head just went away. I don't know what happened. I just lost it for a while.

* * *

I don't know what this is but I can't hold my hand steady. Earlier this week I noticed it. Somebody shook my hand and I noticed that my left hand was trembling. I don't know what the fuck it is. I was with a friend the other night and he says, "You better get to a doctor, you're ready to check out. Your head is shaking." Like, I'm doing a Katharine Hepburn. What the fuck is going on here? I never had it before.

I'm afraid to go to a doctor and find out what it is. I don't think I want to know. Just let me die in my sleep. If you lucked out in Vietnam, you got killed.

* * *

I went to a memorial rally for the GIs who died in the Vietnam war. I had never protested, I never joined anything. I was just trying to find out what had happened to myself. At the rally, there were all kinds of politicians and movement people. But as I was walking through the crowd, everybody was just getting stoned. They were picking each other up. A few people up front were concerned, but the rest of them were just getting off on this get-together. They were selling all kinds of shit and making money. I lost it. I couldn't understand. They didn't give a fuck about the guys who died in Vietnam.

I wasn't prowar, I wanted to end it. I knew the body counts were bullshit. I was just fucked up over the war. I wanted a real end with some justification for all the men who had died. It just kept continuing. "Fuck," I thought, "they should have pulled us out in '65. If they're not going to fight it, why didn't they get us the fuck out in '65?"

I didn't know what happened until one Sunday morning. I woke up and went downstairs and bought *The New York Times*. I opened it up and there were the *Pentagon Papers*. I read as much as I could on that Sunday afternoon. I became violently ill. I actually threw up and got a blinding headache. I was rolling around on the floor of my apartment. I couldn't fight the pain, I couldn't succumb to it—it just blew me the fuck away.

Containing Communism was only worth 5 percent of the war. Generate capital for corporations was 41 percent. "I pledge allegiance to the flag" just died. I was pledging allegiance to Dow and Monsanto and all the large corporations.

That shattered my whole image of the United States, of freedom and democracy, of the world we live in, all the ideals I had gone to Vietnam with. The sacrifice was a lie. The war was a fraud. I had recently reexamined what had been said about my being a murderer. Now, I thought I just might be. I was of total insignificance, except to be used. It was more than depression. I didn't want to be a part of this planet, this sickness.

I took thirty Seconal tablets and a bottle of aspirin and a whole bunch of other shit. Then I called everybody I knew and told them goodbye. It was my last plea for somebody to help me, to say that I was worth it. A couple of vets came over and got my ass. If it wasn't for them, I wouldn't be here today. I woke up the next day and I was angry because I was alive. I was pissed at them, because they had saved me.

Trying to figure out where it got turned around for me is impossible, because it's not turned around. I deal with severe depression all the time. With the physical pain. I just know who the enemy is now. I know where and how it's going to change for me.

The war's not over for us. That's why it won't be over until somebody takes their rightful responsibility. The federal government and the chemical companies.

*   *   *

I had no expectations of being a hero when I came back. I *did* expect to get a job. I thought the government would take care of us. But we were Kennedy's children and when we got back, Kennedy wasn't around, so we got fucked. Things might have been different with him. I probably would have been working for the phone company. A fat little Italian boy, and I'd have hated myself. So I'm glad it didn't happen.

*   *   *

I was strong-willed and pretty strong in the head. I went along with the program, I went along with the people criticizing me and I almost believed that the war was bad. The people didn't bother me for some reason. Because I was just as big a hypocrite as they were and just as insincere. I told myself, "Play it cool, play the role, don't let it get to you." It was like self-hypnosis, or self-brainwashing. But when I went home by myself, I cried. I was looking for the pat on the back. I got, "Shame, shame, shame." Even the guys I came back with, we used to talk in whispers when we talked about the war. I blocked it out.

But the older I get, the more it keeps coming back. Particularly now at age thirty-five. Now I read military things more and go over what I did. I am very proud of what I did. I have no qualms. I didn't get fucked up like a lot of guys did that went.

I got into a lot of fights. I wanted to commit suicide almost every week, but that was because everything I did seemed pedestrian, no matter what the fuck I did or tried to do—I tried going to college, sales, insurance, all these Charlie-Straight-Arrow fucking jobs. I was bored to fucking death. To this day it's still hard for me to find my place. Now I'm a civilian. I'm not in the military anymore. That elation of going out and killing and having somebody try to kill you, the comradery I had with men was something I've never found since then. You look for that.

The only friends I really have are vets. They're my closest friends because at least I know they'll be in my foxhole and won't fall asleep on me. For me to look at most men, they look like fucking virgins to me. They didn't go through those turmoils and deprivations. Something happens to you there.

I'm a good bartender, but I hate it. Being the peacemaker that I am, no matter who comes in there, I see everybody who deserves a punch in the face. Somebody tries to hit on somebody else's girl friend, suddenly I'm back in combat again. The only difference is I don't

have my weapons with me anymore. I could beat somebody up, but then the cops come down. So who needs
it? I tend bar for the money. I'm a hypocrite. I have a
Master's degree in hypocrisy. In order to survive, you
have to.

* * *

I was shot to shit. I had forty-five holes in me and I
felt guilty. I'd walk down the ward trying to find
somebody with both arms and legs. When you see a
paraplegic who has no feeling in his body anymore, you
feel sorry he's like that. But you don't show empathy
for him. "You got fucked, but *there*'s a guy who's a
blinker—the quadriplegic—and he got worse than
you." Nobody cut any slack for anybody else in the
hospital. Inside you can. You see a triple amputee, you
felt bad, but you didn't let them know it. You could get
tremendous hang-ups for not being fucked up enough.

One day I went to sit on the bed with a guy I shared a
room with named Pete. He used to kick off for an SEC
college at football games, a huge Adonis of a guy. He
had tremendous legs, except one leg was missing. It was
blown off above the knee. He used to take me home
with him every once in a while. We'd go drinking beer in
the local bars.

I walked into the room one day and I had on a pair of
Bermuda shorts. At that time, I still had the holes in me,
but they were long red welts, beet red and the holes
weren't altogether closed. The stitches were removed,
but they hadn't all closed. My legs were horrendously
ugly, but he had no leg.

"I'm not taking you home with me," he says.

"Why?"

"Because you got ugly fucking legs. Look at my nice
new leg, no marks on that," and he pats his prosthesis.

Another buddy of mine, Mark Cole, had been a
Special Forces officer that lost an eye and an ear and an
arm and a leg. He'd get drunk in a bar and start banging
at the glasses and throwing things. You'd be sitting
there drinking your beer and you'd feel guilty because
you still had everything. Yet the presidential aspirants

were all talking about how we shouldn't be defoliating the trees in Vietnam. Fuck defoliating the trees, how about defoliating us?

* * *

At first I didn't know what it was. In '74 I got sick. I went to doctor after doctor and they sent me to specialists. Nobody could tell me what was wrong with me. I lost thirty pounds in a year and a half. I was skin and bones. I was going to work with a fever of 102 degrees every day. In one year I had $17,000 in hospital bills and I ran out of money.

I had a terrible pain right in my liver and I just couldn't take it anymore. So I went to the VA. They admitted me and kept me for about five months. They took out my spleen, my gall bladder and my appendix. They were inflamed, they said. That was the problem, they said. After the operation I felt better psychologically for a little while, but I didn't get no better. I'm still fucked up.

I blame it on being sprayed eight or nine times with Agent Orange in Nam. Nobody has ever seen this kind of disease before with every organ in my body eaten up. I say to myself, "What the hell am I? Why should I be the only one in America with this fucking disease? Where did I get it? Who did I catch it from? Somebody else must have it, if I got it, right? I don't dream up my own diseases, you know."

So I blame it on my constant exposure to the herbicide. I got my claim in, but the VA is fighting me all the way. They realize they got a can of worms. If they pay one guy, then they'll find out that every Vietnam vet doesn't feel so good.

There's no cure. It's really a lousy condition.

* * *

Coming back to America, I was shocked, not by the fact that no one cared, but that no one even talked about it. I was shocked because I didn't know we lost the war. We weren't losing while I was there.

*   *   *

I feel better when I talk about Vietnam and get it out of me every once in a while. You can't keep it inside you. If it's in you it stays in you. It'll stay with me for my whole life. But I got to be cool. You get to feeling, "God damn, I got to say something to somebody about this."

At first I didn't talk about it, but after I got loosened up a little bit, I decided there ain't no use in hiding it. If I'm hiding, people might think something *is* wrong. Or something wasn't all that right. There are things that you're afraid to talk about because you don't know what's going to happen if you say anything about it. Like going kicking ol' pregnant women in the stomach and blowing babies away when their mama-san is rocking them to sleep, singing and all that, blowing away papa-san because he was dying and helping him a little bit by blowing his fucking head off with a .45—didn't give a shit. Just walked away. You go nuts. That's what it does to you. I'm not ashamed to say it. I've done it before. I wasn't too proud of myself after a while, but I've done it. It was just the thing after you get over there. You fuckers want me to kill somebody, I'll kill somebody. I'll kill anything I can. Chickens, dogs, anything. I done it.

It's a shame it was so crazy though, because I met a lot of decent people over there. To me they were decent people. They kept me alive and I kept them alive.

*   *   *

There were so many people that I encountered in Vietnam that most of the world would call mediocre who weren't ordinary in any way that I could think of. Then they got relegated to pariah when they got back. That's a great injustice.

*   *   *

The hardest thing to come to grips with was the fact that making it through Vietnam—surviving—is probably the only worthwhile part of the experience. It wasn't going over there and saving the world from Communism or defending the country. The matter of survival was the only thing you could get any gratification from.

* * *

I had been romantically involved with a girl before I left. We had just stopped writing to each other while I was gone. I came back and spent a day with her and got intensely involved in a love affair.

It was the best thing that ever happened to me. I was afraid when I came back of being this really cold dude. I had become a monster, a person that could watch all this horror and not cry or not lose his mind. I was afraid of myself. Getting involved with this woman did more for me than ten years with a shrink could have done. I was a person again. If I could be in love with this girl, I couldn't be a monster. I mean, she was *nice*.

* * *

The town I live in has settled quite a few of the boat people and the refugees. We have a local newspaper and they do a lot of articles that run, "This is the latest boat people family that we've rescued from the jaws of death."

It's kind of hard for me sometimes. There are several Vietnamese children that live a few houses away. They know I'm a Vietnam veteran. At first they were sort of afraid of me. I don't know why. Maybe it's because I'm in a wheelchair. For some children, if they're not old enough to be openly inquisitive, the idea that you're in a wheelchair is frightening.

I used to talk to them in Vietnamese. They'd be very shy, very reluctant to answer. They didn't know what was coming off. Is this guy going to shoot me or what? What's he up to? Does he think I'm one of the enemy? A lot of GIs were booby-trapped by children throwing hand grenades at them. Who was the enemy? Anybody was fair game if you were in a contested area.

But I don't hold any grudges against the Vietnamese. The kids love me now. They know I'm a real sucker. The little girl came over selling Girl Scout cookies and I bought about ten dollars worth. They've got me pegged. Halloween they came by and I had candy. A lot of my neighbors just shut their lights off and pretended they weren't around. But I love children. They came by and I was happy to see them. I feel good about that.

I'm sure a lot of other Vietnam veterans probably hate the sight or the mention of the Vietnamese. It's Pavlovian conditioning. I still experience it. If you see someone who happens to look Vietnamese and he's closer to you than you want him to be, or he or she is unexpectedly in your territory, if someone encroaches on your personal perimeter, you react. Hey, what are you doing here? Get the hell away from me.

I saw the Vietnamese people. I worked with them and shared a common experience with Vietnamese soldiers as well as Americans. I found them to be just like us, only a different color and a different culture. They love their children and their wives. They weren't the insensitive, inscrutable people that Orientals are made out to be. They were just as saddened by someone being killed as anyone of us. The only thing I feel bad about is that we didn't allow all of them the opportunity to get out of Vietnam if they really wanted to before we let it fall. It was inevitable.

*   *   *

Looking back at Vietnam and then where I am today, maybe I *am* crazy, but I've got it under control. Nam has been beneficial in coping with life. I look around at my problems and I say, "Damn, this is nothing compared to the hell and shit I had to go through in Vietnam." While I was there I said, "Man, when I get home, I'm going to be sleeping between clean sheets, eating with silverware. Look what I've been through. There's nothing at home that's going to bother me. It shouldn't upset me in any way after going through a year of this hell." That attitude has come along with me all this time.

* * *

I find myself trusting people on more of an instinct basis. I can turn on a certain degree of trust.

It's a general faith in people. People are generally reasonable and they generally come through for you. I've seen the worse asshole do it right at the right time and that sort of builds up your faith.

* * *

One of the ways that Vietnam changed my life the most is precisely the territory of compassion, kindness and caring—deeply human concern. I saw in Vietnam among men—male people—more capacity for understanding and sensitivity and love than I had ever before encountered in my life.

I have seen it since. I'm a lot older now and there are other ways of coming to that place in your life, one way or another, especially if you were close to a situation where people suffered physically or mentally. On the one hand, I was engaged in the one activity which is the ultimate macho experience. Within that I found myself and others capable of a tenderness which society only assumes of women.

Then you come back to the Land of the Big PX and it's business as usual. Men are being male in traditional ways, stepping on each other's toes on the way up the ladder, not with genuine ruthlessness, but with sloppy masculinity.

That's one of the most difficult adjustments: to re-enter the world which you were conditioned to live in since childhood, but you've gone through an experience which taught you a level of existence that you could not have even imagined of yourself. You've found in yourself a capacity for compassion that you did not even believe existed. You've been hurt more deeply than you thought you could be hurt. You have given, in some cases, more than you ever thought you could give, to yourself even, let alone somebody else.

Then back home you look around at a bunch of people who don't even want to listen to you. People confront you who are not willing to deal with the same amount of necessary ruthlessness or compassion on a daily basis.

*   *   *

I miss the sounds of the nights in Vietnam, with the choppers landing and the outgoing—not the incoming—fire. Although, even the incoming was exciting. The sounds are particularly vivid. The force after a large gun fires or a round lands, the feel of the gas from it on your face. Thinking about Vietnam once in a while, in a crazy kind of way, I wish that just for an hour I could be there. And then be transported back. Maybe just to be there so I'd wish I was back here again.

GLOSSARY

–A–

gunner—an assistant gunner.

AIT—advanced infantry training.

AK-47—Soviet military assault rifle supplied to the North Vietnamese Army and the Viet Cong, also called AKs.

APC—armored personnel carrier.

–B–

beans and motherfuckers—C-ration delicacy composed of lima beans and ham.

beehive rounds—an explosive artillery shell which delivered thousands of small projectiles, "like nails with fins," instead of shrapnel.

bends and motherfuckers—the squat-thrust exercise.

Big Boys—artillery.

boot—a soldier just out of boot camp, inexperienced, untested.

brown bar—a lieutenant. Sometimes called a butter bar denoting the single brass bar of the rank. In the field, officers wore camouflage rank which was often brown or black instead of brass.

busting caps—firing a weapon; a reference probably derived
  from the paper percussion caps used in toy guns.

–C–

capping—shooting at.
Caribou—small transport plane for moving men and
  materiel.
C4—a plastique explosive carried by military personnel in
  Vietnam, which would burn like Sterno when lit.
cherry—slang used to denote youth, inexperience and vir-
  ginity.
Chu Hoi—"I surrender"; not a literal translation.
Cobra—an Army helicopter.

–D–

diddy-bopping—carelessly walking.
doo-mommie—an English approximation of the Vietnamese
  words *du ma*, meaning literally, fuck mother.
double veteran—having sex with a woman and then killing her
  made one a double veteran.

–E–

EM club—enlisted men's club.

–F–

finger charge—explosive booby-trapping device which takes
  its name from its size and shape's being approximately that
  of a man's finger.
fleshette—a mine without great explosive power containing
  small pieces of shrapnel intended to wound and kill.
FNG—fucking new guy.
frag—a fragmentation grenade.
fugazi—fucked up or screwed up.

–G–

G3—division level tactical advisor, a staff officer.
GR Point—Graves Registration Point; that place on a mil-

tary base where the identification, embalming and processing of dead soldiers takes place as part of the operations of
the quartermaster.

grunt—infantryman.

–H–

H&I—harassment and interdiction, commonly called H&I
fire. Artillery bombardments used to deny the enemy terrain which they might find beneficial to their campaign.
The targets for H&I were general rather than specific, confirmed military targets.

hard-stripe sergeant—rank indicated by chevron insignia,
equivalent to E5 or E6, but denoting some limited authority
as well. Others of the same rank without the stripes were
little more than PFCs.

hooch—combination tent/shacks used to house military personnel in base camps; also used to refer to the thatch and
bamboo homes of the rural Vietnamese.

hoochgirl—young Vietnamese woman employed by American
military as maid and laundress.

–J–

jungle boots—footwear that looks like a combination of combat boot and canvas sneaker used by the U.S. military in
tropical climates, where leather rots because of the damp-
ness. The canvas structure also speeds drying after crossing
streams, rice paddies, etc.

jungle utilities—lightweight, tropical fatigues.

–K–

K-bar—a military knife.

klick—kilometer.

–L–

Lurps—members of Long Range Reconnaissance Patrols.

LZ—landing zone; usually a small clearing secured tempo-
rarily for the landing of resupply helicopters. Some become
more permanent and eventually become base camps.

–M–

M-16—the standard U.S. infantryman's weapon. A light-weight semiautomatic rifle manufactured by Colt Firearms.
M-60—a machine gun.
M-79—a grenade launcher.
mama-san—pidgin used by American servicemen for any older Vietnamese woman.
Mike-Mike—a military term for millimeter (mm).
Montagnard—indigenous hill-dwelling people of Indochina.
MOS—Military occupational specialty.

–N–

No. 10—the worst.
NVA—North Vietnamese regular army.

–O–

One-Oh-Five, One-Oh-Six, etc.—artillery pieces.

–P–

papa-san—pidgin used by U.S. servicemen for any older Vietnamese man.
pogue—derogatory term for military personnel employed in rear echelon support capacities.
point-man—the first man in line as a squad or platoon of men walk along a trail or through the jungle.
pseudomonas—a genus of bacteria causing various suppurative infections in humans. Its presence gives pus a blue-green color.

–R–

rack—bed or cot.
RPG—a type of rocket used by the Viet Cong and NVA.

–S–

S2—staff officer for intelligence at battalion or brigade level.
sapper—a soldier who would try to infiltrate a base or camp to destroy lives or property.

Sgt. Rock—a combat-scarred World War II comic book character.

shaped charge—an explosive charge, the energy of which is focused in one direction.

short-timer's stick—when a soldier had approximately two months remaining of his tour in Vietnam, he might take a long stick and notch it for each of his remaining days in-country. As each day passed he would cut the stick off another notch until on his rotation day he was left with only a small stub.

six-by—a large flat-bed truck usually with wooden slat sides enclosing the bed and sometimes a canvas top covering it, used for carrying men or anything else that would fit on it.

slick—slang for helicopter.

Spooky—a large propeller-driven aircraft with a Minigun mounted in the door, capable of firing 6,000 rounds per minute; also used to refer to gunship helicopters equipped with Miniguns. Also known as Puff the Magic Dragon.

Strak—adhering to the letter of military rules and regulations.

–T–

TC—tactical commander.

TOC—tactical operations center.

Top—a top sergeant.

Thermit—a mixture of powdered aluminum and metal oxide which produces great heat for use in welding and incendiary bombs.

tracer—a bullet or shell chemically treated to leave a trail of smoke or fire.

–U–

unbloused—pants not tucked into boot tops.

–V–

ville—short for village indicating any location from a small town of several hundred inhabitants to a few thatched huts in a clearing.